HOW PARIS BECAME PARIS

*The Age of Comfort: When Paris Discovered Casual—and the
Modern Home Began*

*The Essence of Style: How the French Invented High Fashion,
Fine Food, Chic Cafés, Style, Sophistication, and Glamour*

*The Reinvention of Obscenity: Sex, Lies, and Tabloids
in Early Modern France*

*Ancients Against Moderns: Culture Wars and the Making
of a Fin de Siècle*

*Tender Geographies: Women and the Origins
of the Novel in France*

Fictions of Sappho, 1546–1937

HOW PARIS BECAME PARIS

The Invention of the Modern City

JOAN DEJEAN

BLOOMSBURY

NEW YORK · LONDON · NEW DELHI · SYDNEY

Published by Bloomsbury USA, New York

All papers used by Bloomsbury USA are natural, recyclable products made from wood grown in well-managed forests. The manufacturing processes conform to the environmental regulations of the country of origin.

LIBRARY OF CONGRESS CATALOGING-IN-PUBLICATION DATA

DeJean, Joan E.
How Paris became Paris : the invention of the modern city / Joan DeJean. — First U.S. edition.
pages cm
Includes bibliographical references and index.
ISBN 978-1-60819-591-6 (alk. paper hardcover)
1. Paris (France)—History—17th century.   2. Paris (France)—Description and travel.   3. Paris (France)—Social life and customs—17th century.   4. Paris (France)—Guidebooks—History—17th century.   5. City planning—France—Paris—History—17th century.   I. Title.
DC729.D39 2014
944'.361033—dc23
2013031527

First U.S. Edition 2014

3   5   7   9   10   8   6   4

Typeset by Westchester Book Group
Printed and bound in the U.S.A. by Thomson-Shore Inc., Dexter, Michigan

In memory of
Fannie DeJean Genin (1924–2012),
who never made it to Paris but would have loved it.

CONTENTS

A NOTE TO THE READER

This project began with paintings: the numerous views that depict the new monuments of seventeenth-century Paris. I chose black-and-white details from these early views of the city to illustrate all chapters. Some of the most important of these canvases are also reproduced in color. These images provide a vivid introduction to Paris as it appeared in the seventeenth century to those who watched its invention unfold—and to Paris as they wanted it to be seen by the world outside.

References for all quotations as well as references to relevant secondary sources can be found at the end.

"Capital of the Universe"

W HAT MAKES A city great?
   Prior to the seventeenth century, the most celebrated European city was one famous for its past. Visitors made pilgrimages to Rome to tour its ancient monuments or its historic churches: they were seeking artistic inspiration and indulgences rather than novelty and excitement. Then, in the seventeenth century, a new model for urban space and urban life was invented, a blueprint for all great cities to come. The modern city as it came to be defined was designed to hold a visitor's attention with quite different splendors: contemporary residential architecture and unprecedented urban infrastructure rather than grand palaces and churches. And this remade the urban experience for both the city's inhabitants and its visitors alike. The modern city was oriented to the future rather than the past: speed and movement were its hallmarks.

And, as many Europeans quickly recognized, only one city was truly modern: Paris.

Near the end of the seventeenth century, a new kind of publication began to appear: pocket guidebooks and maps specifically designed for visitors who planned to explore a city on foot. These ancestors of today's guidebooks were created to introduce Europeans to Paris. It was a city that, their authors felt, had become such a revolutionary kind of place that it needed to be seen in this way to be understood. The genre began in 1684 with the first edition of Germain Brice's *Description nouvelle de ce qu'il y a de plus intéressant et de plus remarquable dans la ville de Paris*, soon translated into English as *A New Description of Paris*, destined to become the best-selling guide to any city until the 1750s.

Brice presented information street by street, neighborhood by neighborhood, so that, as he explained in his preface, "in one walk, people can see a number of beautiful things." His guidebook's organizational principle indicates that Brice—a native Parisian and longtime professional guide for foreign visitors—had taken stock of the fact that tourism had spread beyond the happy few who traveled in private vehicles from one monument to the next, paying little attention to the surrounding areas since the urban landscape itself was of no particular interest. By the 1680s a new infrastructure had made walking easy, and there were sights aplenty all along the way. The city itself was the monument.

With the 1698 edition, Brice's guidebook also included a handy new feature: a fold-out map to guide visitors during their walks. As soon as Paris' infrastructure began to evolve at a rapid pace, a golden age began for French cartography. And since the cityscape was in constant flux all during the seventeenth century, new maps were continually issued. Each mapmaker told the story of Paris in a different way, with topographic maps, bird's-eye views, portraits.

The first map aimed specifically at the growing numbers of foreigners in the city was published by Nicolas de Fer in 1692. A contemporary periodical described it as especially useful to "those who know nothing about the city," and de Fer's organization is still being followed in today's tourist maps. On its left side, the map lists the streets of Paris in alphabetical order, and on its right points of interest: churches and palaces, but also bridges and embankments. The map is laid out in squares, numbered 1 to 14 horizontally and A to L vertically, each measured in steps, "so that someone can see in a glance how many he'll have to take to get from one place to another." De Fer was offering in effect a combined map and guidebook for tourists on foot—and in 1694, he published a small-format map (nine by twelve inches) that was easily carried about in one's pocket. This detail from that 1694 map shows how convenient it would have been for exploring the new Champs-Élysées neighborhood, just then becoming part of the fabric of Paris. No one saw the potential of de Fer's innovations more clearly than Brice—hence his decision to reissue his own guide in 1698 with a fold-out map and a listing, in alphabetical order, of the streets of the city.

There had been earlier books about Paris: Father Jacques Du Breul's 1612 work on its antiquities, for example. But these volumes—like works such as Andrea Palladio's 1554 introductions to ancient Roman monuments and medieval pilgrimage churches—were destined for visitors who measured a city's greatness by its history, and they focus on civic and religious monuments.

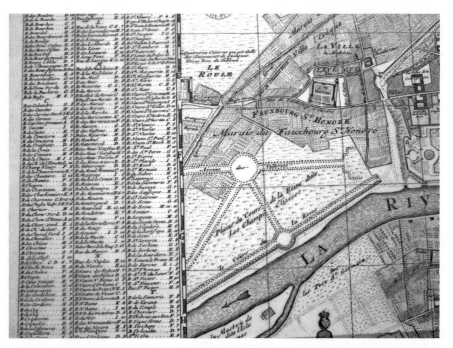

*In 1694, Nicolas de Fer designed the first pocket map of Paris to help visitors explore
the city on foot. This detail depicts the newly laid out Champs-Élysées.
The city's streets are listed along with numbers and letters that
made it possible to locate them quickly on the map.*

John Stow's 1598 *A Survey of London* and Thomas De Laune's 1681 *The Present
State of London* also have an antiquarian slant; they evoke modern-day London mainly as a center of commerce and the nation's financial hub. In contrast, guidebooks to Paris present a city bristling with creative energy, a
cultural magnet, an incubator of the kind of ideas that could revolutionize
urban life.

Recent research indicates that once a city acquires a reputation—as an exciting place or as one where nothing ever happens—that image tends to survive unchanged for long periods of time. The original guidebooks to Paris
help explain how one of the most powerful urban images of all time was put
into place.

Both Brice and de Fer had the same idea of why modern tourists might
choose to visit a city. In Brice's opinion, visitors no longer wanted detailed
historical information. Visitors now preferred a guidebook that included "an
account of the latest trends in modern residential architecture, rather than the
translation of [Latin] epitaphs in a cemetery." Thus, Brice, like de Fer, included

recent architectural achievements—both private homes and innovative public works such as avenues—that in the course of the seventeenth century had become central to the experience of Paris.

What attracts visitors to a city? A guidebook such as Brice's, a map such as de Fer's, and other novel publications that were introduced in the 1690s all offered new answers to that question. Take the example of Nicolas de Blégny's volumes from the early 1690s, the first-ever insider's guide to a city. In *Adresses de la ville de Paris* and *Le Livre commode*, *Addresses in the City of Paris* and *The Useful Book*, Blégny includes information never before considered noteworthy, such as where to find the best Brie cheese or the most buttery brioches, the names of tailors who outfitted court notables, the addresses of caterers for "your special events," and the right source for every kind of luxury merchandise.

All these publications indicate that a new model for the city had been put into place in the course of the seventeenth century. According to that model, a great city should be more than a collection of major buildings or a monumental capital. A city was worthy of a visit because it was great in the here and now, because of its contemporary architecture, because its economic life, its cultural activities, and the range of entertainments it offered made it vibrant. Visitors who wanted to contemplate ancient monuments still went to Rome, but those in search of the novel and the cutting edge—in the arts and architecture, in technology, in commerce, in fashion, and in cuisine—were traveling to Paris to discover a very different experience. And they were doing so in new ways: they walked its streets with Brice's guidebook in hand, as English physician Martin Lister did in 1698, and as Louis Liger was still advising readers of his guidebook to do in 1714. They spent less time in churches and more in cafés and public gardens, less time touring cemeteries and more visiting shops. They wanted to eat well and be well outfitted as much as to tour a famous cathedral.

Paris had not always been a magnet for visitors. During the second half of the sixteenth century, France had been ravaged by decades of war between Catholics and Protestants. By the century's end its capital had been reduced to a state succinctly summed up by the first great historian of the city's development, Michel Félibien: "In 1597, there was nothing splendid about Paris. It was in deplorable shape and lacked everything." In fact, at the turn of the seventeenth century, wolves roamed freely in the streets of the French capital.

Between 1597 and 1700, that urban disaster was rebuilt and transformed. For the first time, rulers asked professionals—from architects to engineers—to study the city's layout, and they followed the professionals' suggestions to plan the capital's development. Because of the revolutionary public works that resulted from these collaborations and the manner in which these public works were woven into their surroundings, Paris became known as technologically advanced, the European leader in city planning and modern architecture.

Breakthrough projects only become origins, the inspiration for those who live elsewhere and for subsequent generations, when someone draws them to the attention of a broad public. As soon as urban planning began to remake Paris, a second transformation began: for the first time ever, a city was instantly elevated to legendary status—almost before the mortar was dry on the public works being celebrated.

All through the seventeenth century, every time its cityscape was redesigned in an important way, Paris benefitted from what would now be called a rebranding campaign. In a continuous stream of publications and images, writers and artists publicized the city's transformation from urban ruin to urban wonder and advertised the city as a destination, the epitome of a sophisticated, cosmopolitan place. In the Paris represented by playwrights and novelists, by historians of the city and the authors of guidebooks, by painters and cartographers and engravers, both the city and its inhabitants had a special glow: it and they were more elegant and more seductive than anywhere or anyone else. A mythic idea destined to survive for centuries thus took root.

The numerous visions of Paris then created reflect simultaneously the reality of a city being transformed and the fantasies about urban life of those who celebrated it. Many also surely served to some extent as propaganda. The stories they tell may not always be as completely factual as they claim to be, but they provide something very rare: a city's sense of itself. The vast and varied literature of Paris then produced shows us how the city represented itself to itself. These books and images also helped produce a new kind of city. They made Parisians proud and thereby created a sense of community. They also taught people how to use revolutionary public works and services—how to mingle in public gardens, how to take advantage of street lighting and public transportation to negotiate an expanding urban footprint. All these works combined show us the original vision of Paris as the key capital of modernity.

Paris' many admirers turned to hyperbole to give a sense of the excitement it now inspired: "a city that has no equal," "a microcosm of the world," "a world unto itself," "everyone's homeland." World traveler François Bernier declared that "all the most creative ideas originate in Paris." Playwright Pierre Carlet de Marivaux had a character categorically affirm: "Paris is the world. Next to it, all other cities seem mere suburbs." And one of the first true Europeans, the Marquis de Caraccioli, proclaimed it both "the capital of the universe" and "the metropolis of the universe."

What had been an urban wreck was now a legendary city.

Paris had become the country's capital and the official residence of the kings of France in 987, but its position was unstable for the following centuries. It was a theater of violence during first the Hundred Years' War (1337–1453) and then the Wars of Religion (1562–98). In 1415, after the French defeat at the battle of Agincourt, their monarchs abandoned the city. In 1436, Charles VII reclaimed it from the English, but throughout the sixteenth century the kings of the Valois dynasty mainly ruled from their châteaux in the Loire valley rather than the Louvre. In 1589, when Henri III was assassinated by a religious fanatic, the Valois dynasty ended. Henri IV, his successor and the first king of the Bourbon monarchy, twice failed to take Paris by force. He finally won over through diplomacy a capital exhausted and ruined by decades of war. The city he entered in 1594 was big—the largest west of Constantinople—but in no way a functioning capital. However, Henri IV was a fast worker.

By 1598, he had accomplished the first objective of his reign, peace, by promulgating the Edict of Nantes, which made religious tolerance official state policy, and by signing a treaty with the Spanish. He then reorganized the country's administration. During the Wars of Religion, provincial governments had enjoyed great autonomy. Henri IV began the process, continued by both Louis XIII and Louis XIV, by which Paris fully became the seat of the French government; administrative functions became increasingly centralized, and the French monarchy became increasingly absolute. But it was with his work as a builder that Henri IV changed Paris most profoundly.

Throughout a cityscape devastated by war, Henri IV started ambitious public works projects. In the little more than a decade before he was himself assassinated in 1610, he put Paris well on its way to becoming a place that could be billed as "the capital of the universe."

Indeed, the king conceived of his plans for Paris in just such grandiose terms. In March 1601, Paris' municipal government was informed that "His Majesty has declared his intention of making the city in which he plans to spend the rest of his life beautiful and splendid, of making [Paris] into a world unto itself and a miracle of the world." And he quickly put those intentions into action. A contemporary periodical, *Le Mercure françois* ("French Mercury"), informed its readers that "as soon as [Henri IV] became the master of Paris, you could see construction workers all over the city." Only six years later, the king wrote France's envoy to the Vatican, Cardinal de Joyeuse, with "news about my buildings." He listed the public works of which he was most proud and concluded: "You will hardly believe what a changed city you'll find."

A century later, the original historian of its municipal governance, Nicolas Delamare, confirmed the king's proud words: before Henri IV, it was as if "no one had done a thing to beautify the city." The list of accomplishments that both the king and his contemporary admirers proudly enumerated as the architectural highlights of his reign always began with the urban works referred to as "the two wonders of France": the Pont Neuf, a bridge that would revolutionize the way European cities related to their rivers, and the Place Royale, today's Place des Vosges, a square that would transform urban public space. Commentators stressed how "at the beginning of Henri IV's reign, Paris had wide stretches of barren terrain—fields, prairies, and swamps, uninhabited and devoid of construction." The king began making empty land into a novel kind of urban landscape, creating in the process "a city completely different from what it had been in 1590," as foreigners and Parisians who returned after even a few years away never failed to point out—"*une ville nouvelle*," a new city.

Paris became ever newer as the century progressed. Henri IV's son, Louis XIII, made far less grandiose plans. But he did see some of his father's most daunting projects through to completion—in particular, the idea of turning more "barren terrain" into one of the city's most elegant neighborhoods, one that still looks much as it did upon its completion in the early 1640s: today we know it as the Île Saint-Louis. And Louis XIII produced a son whose ambitions for his capital made him truly his grandfather's heir.

Two phrases from the pen of Louis XIV's chief minister, Jean-Baptiste Colbert, both from 1669, illustrate this. The first is a list of major construction projects that ends: "grandeur and magnificence everywhere." The second could be called the categorical imperative of Louis XIV's monarchy: "This is not a reign that does things on a small scale."

The total terrain built up during Henri IV's reign was in no way comparable to the massive development during the later decades of the seventeenth century. Left Bank, Right Bank, at the city's periphery as much as at its center, edifices (even one as iconic as the Louvre) were then rebuilt, and neighborhoods were redesigned—or invented. This 1677 engraving depicting the remodeling of the Louvre's façade gives a sense of the kind of major construction site then found all over the city. It would have been impossible to walk fifteen minutes in any direction without encountering reminders of the fact that Paris was a city in transition, shaking off its past in a hurry.

Representation des Machines qui ont servi a eslever les deux grandes pierres qui couvrent le fronton de la principale entrée du Louvre.

Major construction sites were found all over seventeenth-century Paris. Sébastien Leclerc's engraving shows the Louvre's remodeling in the 1670s.

And Louis XIV followed all these projects in the smallest detail. In May 1672, when Colbert wrote to ask if he was bothering the king with too many specifics, Louis XIV's reply was categoric: "I want to know everything about everything."

In London after the Great Fire of 1666, plans to modernize the devastated areas—including one by Christopher Wren that closely followed the Parisian urban model—were submitted to Charles II. But property owners concerned about their rights and taxes quickly began rebuilding. All thoughts of major change had to be abandoned. In Paris the combined efforts of a determined

Icon Machinarum quibus subleuati sunt ingentes duo Lapides tympano majoris portæ Luparæ incumbentes.

monarch and equally determined municipal authorities made it the first capital in modern history not to grow randomly from a village into an urban sprawl. Instead the new Paris became a vision of straight lines, right angles, and oblique radiating avenues—a vision that shaped many cities to come, first in Europe and later well beyond. In 1698, an English visitor remarked: "The streets [of Paris] are so incomparably fair and uniform that you would imagine yourself rather in some Italian Opera . . . than believe yourself to be in a reall Citie."

Of all the public works then realized, one of them represented the biggest thinking of all, as historian of city governance Delamare first pointed out in

1705: "Until now, every ruler with authority over Paris has improved its fortifications to protect it from invasion." Because of Louis XIV's military victories, Delamare explained, "the capital no longer had anything to fear, and its fortifications thus became useless." Louis XIV had them torn down and, in their place, had a magnificent, tree-lined walkway laid out all around the city's rim: it became the original boulevard.

The Sun King was thus the first ruler to respond to the changing nature of warfare and of national defense: from the seventeenth century on, each European country's line of defense shifted from individual cities to the nation's perimeters. Louis XIV replaced an architecture of paranoia with an architecture of openness; he thereby made Paris the first open city in modern European history. This was a crucial step in the transition from the walled city to the modern cityscape.

The transformation of bulwarks into a green promenade was also by far the biggest public works project ever undertaken in Paris—it was completed only by Louis XIV's successor and only in the 1760s—and one whose cost is not taken into account by critics who argue that Louis XIV lavished money solely on Versailles. Like many of the ideas that transformed Paris into a modern city, "the rampart," as Louis XIV originally named it, was financed jointly by the crown and the municipality.

Urban works are most often attributed solely to the monarch without whose approval they would not have gone forward and to the ministers who implemented royal design—Maximilien de Béthune, Duc de Sully, for Henri IV's reign; Armand Jean du Plessis, Cardinal-Duc de Richelieu, for that of Louis XIII; and first Jean-Baptiste Colbert and then François Michel Le Tellier, Marquis de Louvois, for Louis XIV's. The projects that most profoundly altered the city's course required, however, not only the cooperation of municipal leaders but also major funding from City Hall.

At the two moments in time when Paris' modernization moved forward most actively, the Prévôt des Marchands, provost or chief representative of the merchants of Paris—in effect, the head of the municipality—was both a decisive and highly effective leader and someone who enjoyed a close working relationship with the king. During their tenure as Prévôt des Marchands, François Miron (1604–9) and Claude Le Peletier (1668–76) were key partners for Henri IV and Louis XIV, respectively. From 1667 on, a third individual was essential to the transformation of Paris: Nicolas de La Reynie (1625–1709), appointed by Louis XIV to be the original lieutenant general of the Parisian police. La Reynie's wide-ranging duties—from street lighting to street cleaning, from crime-fighting to addressing traffic problems—were in fact much like those of a big city mayor today. And thus it was that the rapidly modernizing city acquired a more modern government.

In many cases, however, the vast construction sites that dotted the face of Paris were not publicly financed. Henri IV had inherited a financial system as devastated as his capital. He could never have accomplished so much so quickly had he not turned to private investors, and his two successors followed his example. Many of Paris' quintessential landmarks—the Place des Vosges, the Île Saint-Louis, the Place Vendôme, to name but one from each of the reigns—began as royal visions and benefitted from royal support but were carried out on a for-profit basis by financiers and real-estate developers.

At several moments during the seventeenth century, Paris was a boomtown: land speculation was both a sign and a cause of the boom. Developers bought up tracts of barren land, added infrastructure, and, in collaboration with architects who were themselves also speculators, built them up, always hoping to turn the property over for a huge profit. Some made fortunes, while others lost everything. A surprising number of those who did get rich through real-estate speculation were of quite modest birth; some had begun life, for example, as shop clerks. They used their new wealth to acquire the trappings of the good life formerly the exclusive preserve of the nobility: luxurious carriages, mansions as grand as and grander than those of the greatest aristocrats.

Their stories are symbolic of yet another facet of the new Paris: as a major center of finance and very ostentatious new wealth. These figures introduced Parisians to the idea that money could change the most fundamental social structures. The low-born real-estate moguls and masters of this universe ensconced in the finest residences on the Place des Vosges, the Île Saint-Louis, and the Place Vendôme were seen as evidence that, in a city driven by the winds of change, individuals were no longer locked into their past. They could start anew, reinvent themselves. In the modern city, you could pretend to be anyone or anything you liked, as long as you could afford to look the part.

Visionary urban works also altered the city's social fabric on an everyday basis. In 1600, Paris contained few spaces in which people from opposite ends of the economic spectrum interacted. But in the course of the seventeenth century, Paris' reinvention gave people places to go and sights to see. The experience of the city soon became far more physical and diverse when new attractions and a new ease of circulation encouraged Parisians to venture out of their homes and out of their neighborhoods, experiencing first-hand the city's size and its crowds. As they took in the ever-changing spectacle of the redesigned city, they might stand cheek-by-jowl and rub shoulders with people they would never previously have encountered.

Those who described Paris in the seventeenth century consistently evoked the experience of the jostling crowds that characterized a city "absolutely full of people." The first census dates from the end of the eighteenth century; prior to this, there are only estimates of its population. In 1600, there were roughly 220,000 Parisians; in 1650, approximately 450,000. Most now agree that, in 1700, Paris had about 550,000 inhabitants—slightly more than its only European rival, London, though behind the then most populous cities in the world: the cities we know today as Istanbul, Tokyo, and Beijing.

But the question of Paris' size at the end of the seventeenth century is more interesting than that. For the first time ever, numerous contemporary authorities offered estimates, all of which were based on scientific evidence: the findings of the most respected contemporary cartographer of Paris, Pierre Bullet; the statistics of an early genius in that field, Sébastien Le Prestre de Vauban; the data collected by Paris' first "mayor," La Reynie. The most serious contemporary assessments are without exception far higher than the figure now accepted: 710,000 (La Reynie), 720,000 (Vauban), between 800,000 and 900,000 (city historians relying on Bullet's figures.)

Thus Paris at the turn of the eighteenth century seemed to all its keenest observers far more populous than it apparently was in reality. This image of the city may have had its roots in the kind of multistory construction that, everyone agreed, was common in Paris but, as guidebook author Brice noted, "was very rarely seen in other cities where each person wanted his own home." Beginning in about 1650, architects, engineers, and urban historians pointed out how many residences of four, five, six, and even seven floors were found in Paris. They also stress, as Brice did, that "even the tiniest spaces in these seven-story buildings are all inhabited and are in such demand that rents are sky-high." Thus, Brice concluded, "those who had studied the question with care all agree that even though London was very spread-out, it was surely less populous than Paris."

This reasoning was also used to suggest that Paris held its own even beyond Europe. When the first ambassadors from Siam reached Paris in 1686, they concluded that "since the houses were six times higher than in their country, the population of Paris was certainly six times greater." Authoritative travel writer François Bernier decided that "since there were four Parises stacked one on top of the other," it must have a larger population than Delhi. (They were, it seems, about the same size.)

Many of the experts who pondered the problem of Paris' population pointed out that, while Paris continued to get larger, it was no longer growing from within. First Colbert in the 1670s and then La Reynie in the 1680s had statistics compiled on baptisms, marriages, and deaths in the city. These revealed that, year after year, the number of baptisms was almost identical to the number of deaths. Those who collected the numbers concluded that Paris continued to grow because its gravitational pull was attracting provincial French and, above all, foreigners. Provincials, they explained, came in search of economic opportunity. And foreigners? They came "out of curiosity" or "in search of pleasure."

There were many things to arouse the curiosity of foreign visitors; on this point, all those who commented on Paris' growth were in absolute agreement. There was, to begin with, something found only in great urban centers, great architecture. As the century unfolded, pathbreaking projects could be found in more and more areas of the city. Some of the new monuments, while certainly beautiful, were derivative, particularly in mid-century, when the skyline was transformed by the appearance of a number of Italianate domed structures—the Saint Louis–Saint Paul Church in the 1640s, the Collège des Quatre Nations (today the Institut de France) in the 1660s. Both before and after this, however, Paris became a center for types of construction that were both innovative and soon recognized as characteristically French.

Already in 1652, John Evelyn, an expert on contemporary architecture who had visited all the major European capitals, said that architecturally "none of them could equal Paris." Italy had the finest churches, but "for the streets . . . and common buildings, [Paris] infinitely excels any city elsewhere in Europe." Evelyn's remarks prove that an association between great cities and great contemporary architecture was beginning to be accepted. In addition, Evelyn pinpointed the shift from monumental and palatial to residential and public architecture that was to become increasingly central to the French capital. He added that the past forty years had been crucial to this development and advised travelers to keep an eye on the city's rapidly changing architectural scene.

Evelyn was right on the mark. During Louis XIV's reign, neighborhood after neighborhood was created: on the Right Bank, a vast one that began near the rue de Richelieu and culminated in the Place Vendôme; on the Left Bank, one even more vast that started near Saint-Germain-des-Prés and by his reign's end stretched to the Invalides. In every case, real-estate developers and great architects worked together from the start to guarantee the neighborhood's visual unity and to make each new area—beyond any single grand home in it—an architectural destination. In the century's final decades, they were aided and abetted by the French Royal Academy of Architecture, founded by Louis XIV in 1671. In 1674, for example, its members debated and set rules for such questions as the proper proportions for city squares and the correct height for the houses that surrounded them. As a result, by 1711 city historian Félibien followed his evaluation of the "desolation" that had characterized the city in 1597 by noting that "now all foreigners" thought Paris "the grandest and the most splendid city in Europe."

Foreigners were also attracted by the city's technological modernity. In the second half of the seventeenth century, the French suddenly outstripped the Dutch, until then the European leaders in city services and urban technologies. Between 1653 and 1667, Paris saw spectacular advances as the city acquired in quick succession three absolute firsts: a public mail delivery system, public transportation, and street lighting.

By 1667, it had become possible for Parisians and visitors to hop on a horse-drawn public coach at the line's terminus, the Place des Vosges, hand the fare to a uniformed attendant, and be taken to many locations across town—and, if they were traveling after dark, the entire trajectory would have been illuminated by thousands of lanterns that burned all through the night. Innovations such as these were seen as reason enough to visit. One early guide to the city, written in the 1690s by longtime resident Sicilian Giovanni Paolo Marana, advised foreigners that street lighting "alone is worth the trip, no matter how far away you live. Everyone must come and see something that neither the Greeks nor the Romans ever dreamed of."

Foreigners also came to live in Paris for the quality of life with which the city was increasingly synonymous. Theater and opera were not unique to Paris. Dance, however, was showcased there as nowhere else. In the 1660s and 1670s, Louis XIV made it central to the mandate of several academies; he also founded the first national ballet company. In 1700, Raoul Feuillet published *Choréographie* ("Choreography"), the earliest attempt at creating a system of dance notation. Paris thus became the original center for innovative modern dance. And with the concentration of artists and cultural institutions found there, Paris became the capital of an empire of culture, a culture that was widely exported to other nations.

But the most widely accessible new pleasure was one that has ever since been associated with Paris, that of simply walking its streets.

With the first modern streets, the first modern bridge, and the first modern city square, Paris became the prototype for the walking city, a place where people walked not merely to get around, but by choice and for pleasure.

By the end of the seventeenth century, Paris was full of pedestrians of all stripes—including Parisians who had rarely done much exploring on foot before, the city's aristocratic residents. One foreign observer, Joachim Christoph Nemeitz, noted that, except when it rained, aristocrats walked all the time, all over Paris. Foreigners were astounded to see not only that upper-class women were often out walking but also that most of them walked not in any protective gear but in the then most fashionable footwear: delicate mules. They were able to do so because in the course of the century the practice of paving the city's streets became increasingly common. The gleaming new paving stones were widely admired by visitors to Paris. They gave its streets a modern look, and they also changed the feel of the street in a radical way. They gave pedestrians an underfoot sensation both novel and modern.

In 1777, an acute observer of European life, the Marquis de Caraccioli, credited Parisians in the seventeenth century with having rewritten the history of urban walking. In 1600, he explained, "the upper classes in Europe had no knowledge of the pleasure of walking, perhaps because they were afraid of compromising their grandeur by putting themselves on the same footing as the common people." But by the end of the seventeenth century, "Parisian ways . . . had opened their eyes, and they dared step down from their carriages; they began to use their feet." And many accounts testify to the fact that the public works of seventeenth-century Paris taught urban dwellers other basic new ways of interacting with a city as well.

Nowhere was the city's new urban culture more evident than on modern Paris' first great monument, the Pont Neuf. As soon as the New Bridge was opened to the public in 1606, it began drawing record crowds. There, people first relished a sight considered ever since to be essential to the experience of Paris: the perspective over the Seine from a bridge.

In 1600, the Seine was Paris' commercial lifeline, used to bring heavy goods into the city. It was little appreciated for its beauty, for the simple reason that it was next to impossible to get a view out over its expanse. Most of the embankments were not yet developed; instead, houses were often built up right to the river's edge. All existing bridges were lined with houses, so there was no vista when you crossed over. Unlike other city bridges such as Florence's Ponte Vecchio or London Bridge, the Pont Neuf was built without houses, and in fact was built with little balconies, almost like boxes at the theater, that encouraged those crossing the Seine to step to the side, lean on the edge, and watch the river flow.

Every image of the New Bridge shows the balconies filled with river spectators, captivated by a panorama newly part of the experience of Paris (color insert). And from 1606 on, they had more and more to take in: many of the finest new constructions that were added to the cityscape were built along the Seine, making Paris the first European capital to use the river view to showcase modern architecture and the first capital to highlight the role that could be played by riverbanks in creating a beautiful, unified urban fabric.

Another novel experience that foreigners found irresistible also had its origin in Paris' new walking culture: now that upper-class Parisians were out and about in the city as nowhere else, on foot rather than in carriages, it was for the first time easy to appreciate every detail of their outfits. The people-watching scene that thus developed was considered unmatched in quality. Guidebook author Nemeitz tipped off his readers that Paris' public gardens offered a unique experience: they are "crowded with people of all ages, ranks, and of both sexes"; "great princes pass by so close to you that you can examine them attentively" and study carefully "all the best outfits and the latest fashions." Thirty-five years earlier, a historian of Paris had already observed that its gardens were full of foreigners because Parisians "dressed better than anyone else in Europe" and in the public gardens visitors "could learn about the latest styles." These seventeenth-century commentators thereby pinpointed an image central to the promotion of Paris as *the* destination city in Europe: its role as capital of high fashion.

Guidebooks for foreign visitors stressed another important reason to visit: not only could you observe the best-dressed people on the continent; you could have yourself made over in their image. The process was easy, one author explained, because "in Paris you find innumerable quantities of all luxury goods." As a result, "by the time you return home, you can be beautifully turned out."

France had long been a producer of luxury goods such as fine textiles. Until the reign of Louis XIV, however, French craftsmen had been overshadowed by their principal European rivals, the Italians. In the 1660s and '70s, Colbert set out to achieve absolute dominance for the French over the most profitable sectors of a highly lucrative industry by making sure that trade regulations and import duties favored the business community. Before the century's end, all over Europe the elite wanted only the goods crafted by French tailors and French cobblers, French jewelers and French perfumers.

French shops, too, were experiences unto themselves, the ancestors of today's upscale boutiques and so much finer than establishments elsewhere that one visitor called them "the quintessence of the shop." Objects for sale were laid out in elegant displays; customers were made comfortable while they shopped. The original shop windows, in which key objects were highlighted in glass niches to draw people in from the street, thoroughly entranced English physician Martin Lister when he arrived in Paris in 1698 with the new

English ambassador. He said they gave "an air of greatness" to the "very finely adorned" boutiques.

At night, merchants put so many lights in these windows that, as Nemeitz stressed in his guidebook, "they light up the street outside." The nighttime streets were also made brighter by the city's many "very magnificent cafés": another guidebook explained that these were "very brightly lit at night" and so full of large mirrors that their light reverberated out to "light up the streets" still more. The shop lights and the new streetlights combined to create a phenomenon that Nemeitz saw as the height of urban modernity: nighttime shopping. Many shops in Paris remained open until ten or eleven at night and, Nemeitz informed foreigners who would never have encountered this phenomenon before, "here you run into almost as many people on the street in the evening as during the day."

The highly visible imprint of luxury culture on the cityscape of Paris seemed excessive to some. One guidebook warned that "everything is expensive in Paris," and that "dazzled by the profusion of shops," you often "bought things you didn't really need." Lister cautioned that "luxury like a whirlpool draws people into its extravagance." Louis XIV himself "couldn't understand how it was that there were so many husbands crazy enough to let themselves be ruined because of their wives' outfits"; and the person who reported his remarks, the Duc de Saint-Simon, went the king one better: "He could have added—because of their own outfits as well." Such warnings, however, made not the slightest difference. Paris was ever more widely seen as the only place to go to learn what was fashionable and to shop for all the accessories that fashion required.

The experience of walking the streets made its presence felt in literature as soon as the city had begun to modernize. Shortly after the Pont Neuf and the Place Royale became part of the infrastructure, French comedies were for the first time set not in generic streets but in specific locations in Paris. Characters point out the brand-new monuments; their everyday behavior is shaped by innovative city services and urban works.

The first Parisian city writing calls attention in particular to the novel ways in which people could now negotiate Paris. Speed was shown to be a mark of the urban experience. Characters move fast, dashing through the streets in a hurry, evidently with things to do and places to be. In a 1643 comedy by Pierre Corneille, for example, in order to take in all the sights, a son so rushes his father around Paris at breakneck speed that the father complains that he is "out of breath and feeling ill."

Foreigners who lived in Paris confirmed the sense that, as it became a city of architecture and technology and of culture and luxury, Paris had also become a city of people on the move. In a guidebook designed for his fellow country-men, a German called Parisians "more animated and energetic" than other Europeans, "as fast-paced" as their city, while the Sicilian Marana described them as "night and day in a perpetual hurry."

The original Paris city guides recognized that modern visitors, like Pari-sians, were on a stepped-up timetable and wanted to use their days in Paris efficiently. Brice characterized each visit as a *course*, not just a simple walk but, as contemporary dictionaries defined it, "the movement of someone who's walking very quickly."

A correlation has recently been posited between the pace with which its in-habitants negotiate the streets of a city and that city's creative output. This suggests that those quick-paced Parisians and tourists were in step with the city on the go, listening to its streets and their creative pulse—that they were experiencing a sense of heightened expectations that came from living at what was widely seen as the center of the European cultural world.

Today, one individual is often seen as single-handedly responsible for the modernization of Paris' cityscape and the creation of its most iconic features: Baron Georges Eugène Haussmann. Those who now give Haussmann exclu-sive credit for having brought Paris into the modern age often add that Paris in the mid-nineteenth century still had the aspect of a medieval city.

The redesign that was carried out under Haussmann's direction in the mid-nineteenth century did replace some medieval streets with a network of bou-levards; following a plan based on straight lines and geometric precision, it remade a significant section of the city. It was, however, merely the second of two great periods of building that transformed medieval Paris into the city we know today. Those who give Haussmann sole responsibility for the modern face of Paris fail to recognize that the vision of urban modernity now associ-ated with his name had in fact become characteristically Parisian two centu-ries earlier. Haussmann was in large part following a template established by those who reinvented Paris in the seventeenth century.

When Haussmann began his work, the vast sections of the city that had been added between 1600 and 1700 were in no way medieval. In these parts of Paris, urban modernity already loomed large, in the form of the original grand boulevards, of broad and straight thoroughfares, of streets designed to open up the city and make travel through it easy. For example, when Hauss-mann razed all existing construction on the Île de la Cité, he largely spared the island next to it: the Île Saint-Louis featured grid planning and residential architecture dating from the seventeenth century but already fully up to nineteenth-century standards.

In similar fashion, the phenomena that developed on the new boulevards of nineteenth-century Paris and that are seen as inherently Parisian experiences—department stores and omnibuses, café culture and bright lights—all first became available to Parisians and visitors in the seventeenth century's final thirty years, as soon as the city's original ring of boulevards began to be traced. By then, the first decades of planned development in its history had changed the city more quickly than ever before. Paris had already become what Claude Monet referred to in 1859 as "*cet étourdisssant Paris*," "that dizzying" place, a "whirlwind" of seduction that, Monet added, "causes me to forget basic obligations."

In the course of a mere century, Paris was reinvented as a place impressive for its "grandeur," as Colbert had wanted, but also as a new kind of a "wonder of the world," famous for its streetlights and its boulevards, its shopwindows and its romance with the Seine—and its fast-paced pedestrian life. At the same time, something less tangible was also invented: "Paris" as one of those rare words to possess a true mystique and be imbued with a particular atmosphere and an aura of desirability.

In 1734, a Prussian aristocrat, Karl Ludwig von Pöllnitz, was the first to see what "Paris" had become. "There's never any need to describe Paris," Pöllnitz explained, because "most people know what sort of place it is, even if they have never been there."

A little more than a century later, this was still true for the literary heroine most famous for trusting in the intensity of dreams, Gustave Flaubert's Emma Bovary: "What was this Paris like? What a boundless name! She repeated it in a low voice, for the mere pleasure of it; it rang in her ears like a great cathedral bell; it shone before her eyes."

In 1900, Sigmund Freud evoked the spell Paris had cast over him long before he had ever had a glimpse of the city: "Paris had been for many long years the goal of my longings, and the blissful feelings with which I first set foot on its pavement seemed to me a guarantee that others of my desires would be fulfilled as well." The man who made the modern world conscious of the power of dreams presented "Paris" as the ultimate fantasy.

Paris has remained ever since a dream factory, a city that encouraged fantasies and one that somehow always seemed to live up to the expectations it had created.

As a result, Paris has been the most often represented and the most commercialized city of modern times. "We'll always have Paris" because Paris is all around us—in softly lit images of its bridges and its cafés, its boulevards and its cobblestones, its great buildings and their classic limestone façades. We encounter the romance of Paris in magazines and on TV and computer screens, being used to sell fine food and high fashion, and even romance itself—everything from engagement rings to honeymoons.

The magic of Paris, so carefully constructed in the seventeenth century, has never ceased to tantalize.

This is the story of the invention of Paris—both in stone and in fantasy—the story of when and how Paris became Paris.

CHAPTER ONE

The Bridge Where Paris Became Modern: The Pont Neuf

T HE INVENTION OF Paris began with a bridge.

Today, people simply flash an image of the Eiffel Tower to evoke Paris instantly. It's the monument that offers immediate proof that you are looking at the City of Light. In the seventeenth century, the Eiffel Tower's role was played by a bridge: the Pont Neuf. The New Bridge was Henri IV's initial idea for winning over the people of his freshly conquered capital city, and it managed that daunting task with brio. For the first time, the monument that defined a city was an innovative urban work rather than a cathedral or a palace. And Parisians rich and poor immediately adopted the Pont Neuf: they saw it as the symbol of their city and the most important place in town.

Artists quickly began to turn out images of this new kind of signature monument (color insert). Almost all of them are scenes of hustle and bustle, of hurly-burly, positively overflowing with people and activity. They portray urban life as diverse, gritty—fueled by sometimes uneasy excitement. One glance at any of them and you knew a great deal about the sort of place that Paris was becoming.

The New Bridge became the first celebrity monument in the history of the modern city because it was so strikingly different from earlier bridges. It was built not of wood, but of stone; it was fireproof and meant to endure—it is now in fact the oldest bridge in Paris. The Pont Neuf was the first bridge to cross the Seine in a single span. It was, moreover, most unusually long—160 *toises* or nearly 1,000 feet—and most unusually wide—12 *toises* or nearly 75 feet—far wider than any known city street.

The Pont Neuf was the first major city bridge built without houses lining both sides. Anyone crossing it could take in the sights from the bridge, and Parisians and visitors began a love affair with the river from a viewing platform seventy-five feet wide.

Along each side where earlier bridges had houses, the New Bridge featured instead spaces reserved for pedestrians; they were raised in order to exclude vehicles and horse traffic. We would call them "sidewalks"; they were something that had not been seen in the West since Roman roads and something that had never been seen in a Western city. Add to this the fact that the Pont Neuf was the first bridge whose entire surface was paved, as all the new streets of Paris soon would be, and it's easy to see why pedestrians saw themselves for the first time as kings of the river.

The bridge proved essential to the flow of traffic across Paris: before, just getting to the Louvre from the Left Bank had been a famously tortuous endeavor that, for all those not wealthy enough to have a boat waiting to ferry them across, required the use of two bridges and a long walk on each side. The New Bridge also played a crucial role in the process by which the Right Bank became fully part of the city: in 1600, its only major attraction was the Louvre, whereas by the end of the century, the Right Bank showcased important residential architecture and urban works, from the Place Royale to the Champs-Élysées. In addition, whenever a major event transpired in seventeenth-century Paris, it either took place on the Pont Neuf or was first talked about on the Pont Neuf. Nearly two centuries after its completion, author Louis Sébastien Mercier still considered the New Bridge "the heart of the city."

The Pont Neuf set higher standards for European bridges. The city's first pathbreaking public work also had a direct and profound impact on the daily life of Parisians. It introduced them to a new kind of street life, and it transformed their relation to the Seine. The Pont Neuf was never merely a bridge: it was the place where Paris first became Paris, as well as the place where the modern city's potential first became evident.

The construction of a new bridge over the Seine was initiated by Henri IV's predecessor, the last king of the Valois dynasty, Henri III, who laid the first stone in May 1578. Some early projects conceived of a very different bridge, most notably, with shops and houses lining each side. In 1587, construction was just becoming visible above the water line when life in Paris was upended by religious violence. With the city in chaos, work on the bridge ceased for more than a decade.

In April 1598, Henri IV signed the Edict of Nantes: the Wars of Religion were officially over. A month earlier, the new king had already registered documents announcing his intention to complete the bridge. Henri III had offered no justification for the project; his successor, characteristically, laid out clear goals for it. He presented the bridge as a "convenience" for the inhabitants of Paris, especially for its business community. He also characterized it as a necessary modernization of the city's infrastructure: the city's most recent bridge, the Notre-Dame bridge, was by then badly outdated and far "too narrow," as the king remarked, to deal with traffic over the Seine, which Henri IV described as rapidly expanding because new kinds of vehicles were now sharing the bridge with those who crossed on horseback and on foot. (In fact, vehicles with heavy loads had already been prohibited from using all existing bridges.)

The bridge the king mentioned, the Pont Notre-Dame, had been completed in 1510, and in the manner of medieval bridges, its construction had been paid for by the houses and shops built on it. The dwelling-free Pont Neuf was financed in a previously untested manner: the king levied a tax on every cask of wine brought into Paris. Thus, as city historian Henri Sauval, writing in the 1660s, phrased it, "the rich and drunkards" paid for this urban work.

By June 1603 it was nearly ready—ready enough at least so that Henri IV, never a patient man, decided that it was high time to show off the new public work. Some had already tried to use it to cross the Seine; all had taken a tumble and ended up in the river. However, a contemporary quoted Henri IV as having explained that "none of them was a king." The monarch had planks laid across the piles to form what this contemporary described as a "still shaky" structure, and in true kingly fashion, became the first to cross the bridge successfully—even managing to return home to the Louvre in time for dinner.

One thing not mentioned in early documents concerning plans for the bridge was its name: it was in fact first called the Pont Neuf just five days before its first stone was laid in May 1578. Even years later, official documents still usually refer generically to "the bridge being built" or "a new bridge."

It was certainly that. The Pont Neuf was only the fifth bridge in Paris and the first in nearly a century. In contrast, London Bridge was the only bridge over the Thames in London until Westminster Bridge was completed in 1750. London Bridge was also a typical medieval bridge—dark because of the several stories of houses and shops on each side and narrow (twenty feet at its widest point, only twelve in spots). Paris' new bridge was an immediate signal that the French capital had put the age of religious conflict behind it and had entered a new era—most obviously, an era of technological modernity.

The Pont Neuf was a feat of engineering prowess, something all the more remarkable because it was the result of several successive projects, each of

*Georg Braun's 1572 map of Paris depicts the site at the tip of the
Île de la Cité where the Pont Neuf would soon be built.*

them conceived by different specialists. Architect Baptiste Androuet du Cerceau played the biggest role in its design and Guillaume Marchant in its construction, but no one man created the Pont Neuf.

No prior bridge had had to deal with anything like the load the New Bridge was intended to bear—most significantly, a kind of weight that in 1600 was just becoming a serious consideration: vehicular transport. Earlier cities had only had to contend with transport that was relatively small and light: carts and wagons. In the final decades of the sixteenth century, personal carriages were just beginning to be seen in cities such as London and Paris. Nevertheless, with great foresight, each of Henri IV's documents on the Pont Neuf adds new kinds of vehicles to the list of those to be accommodated. He was thus the first ruler to struggle with what would become a perennial concern for modern urban planning: the necessity of maintaining an infrastructure capable of handling an ever greater mass of vehicles.

Contemporary documents also reveal the challenges posed by the chosen site at the tip of Paris' largest island, the Île de la Cité. To begin with, there was the question of the two small islands found there—the Île du Patriarche or Patriarch's Island and the Île aux Juifs or Island of the Jews—that were far from negligible land masses, as this detail from a map published just prior to the bridge's construction shows. Official documents concerning the bridge's design explain that the "little island" was "eliminated," as was "the tip" of the big island, one side of which was also "sliced off and reshaped to help the river flow more freely."

But when all construction was finally completed in the summer of 1606, the king within months had even bigger plans. Early maps indicate that the area on either side of the bridge had developed in haphazard fashion. Henri IV realized that the bridge would serve Paris effectively only when properly integrated into the city at large. He thus planned first a broad new thoroughfare, the rue Dauphine, to lead directly from the bridge into the adjacent Left Bank neighborhood. As this early eighteenth-century map shows, the rue Dauphine provided a preview of the wide and straight modern Parisian streets that would soon become the order of the day. Next to be built was a city square, the Place Dauphine, with an unusual triangular shape that gave an air of

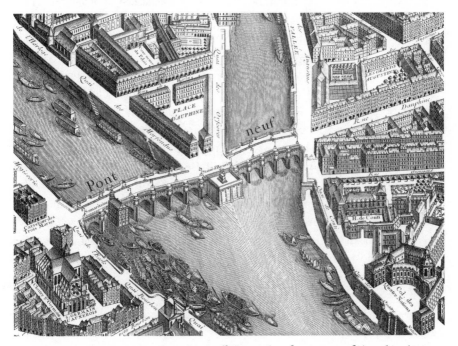

The 1734 Bretez-Turgot map shows off the results of a century of city planning: the kind of bridge and streets unknown in Paris before the seventeenth century.

modernity to the tip of the island visible from the new bridge. In barely a decade, Henri IV's thinking had moved well beyond the issue of overcrowded
bridges. By the end of his life, he had become the first French monarch whose
plans were informed by a broad vision for the city.

This eighteenth-century map also depicts another of the project's technological components: the Samaritaine (named for the Samarian woman in the
Biblical story) shown on the bridge's left end, a massive pumphouse designed
to provide water for the Louvre and the adjacent Tuileries gardens by raising
water from the Seine to the level of a reservoir positioned near the Louvre.
The Samaritaine's giant clocks (one facing in each direction) indicated the
hour, the day, and the month: by day, they were among the principal means of
telling time in Paris in the decades before pocket watches became common.
After dark, Parisians relied on the Samaritaine's chimes, which rang every fifteen minutes. (The Samaritaine was demolished in 1813.)

The map shows still another of the project's innovations: the statue of Henri
IV positioned in the middle of the bridge, the first public statue in the history
of Paris. When he commissioned a magnificent equestrian statue in bronze
from Italian artists, the king surely saw it as a tribute to his role in reinvigorat-
ing the city. But by 1614, when the royal effigy was at last in place, Henri IV
had been dead for four years and the Bourbon monarchy was once again in a
fragile state, not least of all because his son, the adolescent Louis XIII, and his
mother the queen regent were in open conflict.

The imposing effigy may have reminded the people of Paris of the century's
opening decade when, thanks to Henri IV's vision, their city was rushing
headlong into a new age. Parisians immediately turned the novel kind of monument into the most popular meeting place in the city. They created expressions such as "let's meet by the Bronze King," or "I'll wait for you beneath the
Bronze Horse." We know details such as these, and we know about the strain
of civic pride that the statue awakened, because the Bronze King was celebrated extensively in print: already in 1614, small, inexpensive books designed
to appeal to a wide audience began to advertise the fact that Paris, which now
had an equestrian statue like the great cities of antiquity, was taking over their
role as "the most famous city under the heavens."

The enthusiasm with which Parisians welcomed the bridge helps explain
why it became one of those rare public works that actually shape urban life.
On the New Bridge, Parisians rich and poor came out of their houses and
began to enjoy themselves in public again after decades of religious violence.
The Pont Neuf became the first truly communal entertainment space in the city:
since access cost nothing, it was open to all. The greatest nobles disported

themselves in ways amazingly unorthodox for a setting where anyone could see them. In February 1610, the sixteen-year-old Duc de Vendôme (Henri IV's illegitimate son) was seen running around on the bridge engaged in a "heated battle with snowballs."

And on the other end of the social spectrum, it was at the base of the Pont Neuf that public bathing in the Seine became popular, giving the least fortunate Parisians the chance to cool off from the summer heat. Soon after the bridge was opened, bathers and sunbathers began to congregate just below the bridge, in full view of all those crossing the Seine. The activity became more organized when bathing boats started to dock there, separate ones for women and for men.

François Colletet's periodical *Le Journal* ("The Daily"), reports on how much use those boats got during the heat wave of 1676. During the long hot summer of 1716, the police were obliged to step in first when nude men broke into the ladies' changing rooms and then when nude sunbathers were spotted, "on the riverbank by the Pont Neuf, where they were lying and walking about completely naked." An order was issued "to forbid men from staying out on the sand by the Pont Neuf in the nude." By then, however, men had been treating the riverbank nearest the bridge as a nudist beach for many decades, as this detail from a mid-seventeenth-century painting indicates.

Since everyone from princes to paupers crossed paths on the bridge, Parisians thus got their first real taste of an experience that touched the inhabitants

In the seventeenth century, men frequented the riverbank just below the Pont Neuf to sunbathe and swim in the nude.

On the Pont Neuf aristocrats mingled with their fellow Parisians on foot: this noblewoman has a page to carry her train so that she can move about easily.

of other European capitals only decades later: close physical contact with strangers, in particular with individuals completely outside their social sphere.

The numerous seventeenth-century canvases that represent the scene on the bridge showcase this radical social mixing. In this detail from a painting from the 1660s, for example, a pair of aristocrats is seen moving comfortably in the same space with bourgeois (the woman just behind them, the man on horseback) and even lowly street peddlers. (The man shown bending over is selling apples, but the woman's basket might contain the chestnuts, famous all over Europe, that were a specialty of bridge venders.) And just behind those strolling aristocrats are visible what are literally huddled masses: paupers who have taken refuge beneath the equestrian statue. In addition, the aristocrats are taking in the scene in the same manner as less privileged Parisians, on foot. The Pont Neuf was a great social leveler.

None of this was lost on contemporary commentators, who understood that the bustle and the diversity of the original urban crowd could be both a tourist attraction and a source of civic pride. In 1652, Parisian writer Claude Louis Berthod explained to friends in the provinces that he wasn't going to bore

*The Pont Neuf was a great social leveler. Men and women, individuals
from all ranks—even the paupers who gathered near the statue of
Henri IV—were in close contact on an everyday basis.*

them with still another account of the grand monuments of Paris. Instead, he
was going to tell them about the real Paris, "a place full not of marvels but of
chaos and commotion." He began his account with the Pont Neuf and its role
as a social equalizer. In his 1684 guidebook to the city, Brice observed that
visitors were perpetually surprised by "how busy and crowded" the bridge

was and the fact that on it "one encountered people from every rank and dressed in every possible way." He concluded that "all this gives a great and magnificent idea of Paris."

One feature certainly guaranteed that visitors would leave with a "magnificent idea" of the city of Paris: those sidewalks. The sidewalks on the Pont Neuf were the first the modern world had seen; they introduced Europeans to the idea of separating foot and vehicular traffic. Authors of guidebooks, aware that their readers would have had no previous experience with the phenomenon, explained, as Claude de Varennes did in 1639, that they were "absolutely reserved for pedestrians." Nemeitz's 1719 introduction to Paris still refers to the idea as a "new convenience" and one unfamiliar to foreigners. (It was only in 1781 that the first sidewalks in an actual Parisian street were added on the rue de l'Odéon, following the example of London's 1762 Westminster Paving Act.)

For decades, no one could agree on what this convenience should be called. *Banquette*, used to refer to a protective ledge in fortifications from which soldiers could fire, was the preferred term, but some said *levées*, embankments or levees, while still others preferred *allées*, walkways. The word used today, *trottoir*, originated only in 1704.

And no one knew what to call those who used these *banquettes*. In official municipal documents, the people who walked there were called *gens de pied*, literally "people on foot," a military term for foot soldiers. By the 1690s, French dictionaries included a new term, *piéton*, a pedestrian. Early references to *piétons* all involved complaints about badly paved streets and speeding carriages. From the start, the quintessential city walker was fighting for space in an overcrowded cityscape.

Indeed, the Pont Neuf was built just when the use of vehicles of all kinds to get around in Paris was about to skyrocket. And because of the New Bridge's size and its central location, a great many conveyances used it to cross the river. In no time at all, it thus became the poster child for what was quickly perceived to be one of the modern city's greatest ills: the traffic jam.

An image from about 1700 is the original depiction of a traffic jam: it has a double title, "The Pont Neuf" and "l'embarras de Paris." In the course of the seventeenth century and particularly in its final decades, that word, *embarras*, which until then had meant "embarrassment" or "confusion," acquired a new meaning: "The encounter in a street of several things that block each other's way." A new kind of urban "confusion" had taken shape.

Foreign visitors to Paris in the seventeenth century never failed to point out "the ruckus," "the state of perpetual hubbub" that characterized the city. Those who described themselves as "having traveled widely all over Europe" claimed that, in this, Paris had no equal. (One world traveler did say that Paris had a rival for the world's most congested city: Beijing.) They repeated that the growing number of carriages that clogged the city's streets not only made so much noise that it was impossible to hear a vehicle approaching but also went so fast that "pedestrians live in constant fear of being crushed." As one street-wise individual put it: "In Paris, you need eyes on all sides of your head." And visitors reported that one place was the most bustling spot of all, "day and night in perpetual motion": the Pont Neuf.

These visitors were not imagining things: in the second half of the seventeenth century, carriages were taking over. The first carriage had been spotted in Paris in about 1550. (Historian Sauval claimed that it had belonged not to the king or a great aristocrat but to the wife of a wealthy apothecary.) Carriages long remained as scarce as hen's teeth: at the time the Pont Neuf was built, it was said that there were not ten of them in the entire city—and that the king himself owned but a single one. But in the 1700 edition of his guidebook, Brice claimed that the total had grown to twenty thousand. Many new streets had been added during that half-century; many older streets had been made wider and longer; the city's overall surface had increased. None of this, however, was sufficient to counteract the significant spike in vehicular transport.

It is of course paradoxical that the first thoroughfare in Paris expressly designed to prevent traffic issues came to stand for the overly congested city, but every depiction of the bridge reveals why. The raised walkway was not continued in the central section where the statue was erected. In order to cross the bridge, pedestrians thus had to walk down several steps, move through the

The Pont Neuf was the first bridge to reserve space for pedestrians, sidewalks that were elevated so that carriages could not use them.

So many people crowded onto the Pont Neuf that the bridge's traffic jams became notorious. Artist Nicolas Guérard was the first to depict this new reality of urban life.

middle portion, and walk up steps on the other side. (The elevations were removed in 1775.) That central section, 75 feet wide and with its spectacular view, was the kind of public space the city had never known. It seemed that everyone, and not only those who traveled on foot, wanted to enjoy it—and that opened the door to complete anarchy.

The bridge had been designed as a multi-lane thoroughfare, wide enough for four carriages to cross at the same moment. Carriages, however, also had to compete for room with sedan chairs, with horse-drawn carts, with riders

on horseback; and rules had never been established to indicate how the area should be divided among the different modes of transport. In the foreground of the original image of a traffic jam, we see a water carrier who, because of the buckets draped over his shoulders, takes up a lot of space. There's a shepherd with his dog and his flock of sheep; some of them have broken ranks in order to get around a sedan chair and have knocked over the water being carried home by a working-class housewife. A man tries to help a woman thrown to the ground in the melee. An aristocratic couple is taking it all in, as oblivious to the chickens underfoot as to the sheep hurtling by. It was rush hour on the Pont Neuf.

And no one could have predicted how many activities would soon be vying for space on the bridge.

To begin with, the Pont Neuf provided one of the original illustrations of the big city's ever-accelerating appetite for news and of the rapidity with which technologies were invented to satisfy that craving. Rumors quickly spread through the crowd, giving rise to an expression: *c'est connu comme le Pont Neuf*—"everybody knows that already." For the most part, however, news spread in far more organized ways.

The first French newspaper, Jean Richer's *Mercure françois* or "French Mercury," began publication in 1611, well after the bridge had opened. It discussed a full year's news at a time and appeared only several years after the events it described: the initial volume, for example, included coverage of 1604. Finally, as government censors required, it reported mostly foreign news, as did the second French news periodical, Théophraste Renaudot's *Gazette de France* ("Gazette of France"), which began publication in 1631. To know what was going on in their city, Parisians relied on the Pont Neuf.

Engraved images of crucial people and events in the news were posted on the bridge. They were also available for sale in the shops that many printers set up either on or near the bridge. The same technique was used for printed news. Placards and posters of varying sizes were displayed prominently on walls throughout Paris, but nowhere more so than on the Pont Neuf. Contemporary accounts describe people reading aloud the posted news for those unable to read. (It's very hard to determine exact literacy rates since many essential archives no longer survive, but we do know that literacy was significantly higher in Paris than in rural France. Evidence such as the posting of news on the Pont Neuf indicates that urban literacy was growing and that new techniques were being developed to take advantage of its spread and to encourage it.)

The existence of this informal newsroom on the bridge explains the way in which political sedition erupted in 1648, when violence returned to the streets of Paris for the first time since the 1590s. That August, civil war broke out after the arrest of a beloved member of the Parisian Parlement, Pierre Broussel. Broussel lived very near the bridge, as did the future author of one of the definitive accounts of the conflict, the Cardinal de Retz.

Retz was thus able to provide eyewitness testimony to the chain reaction set off "within fifteen minutes" of Broussel's arrest at his home. The proximity of the Pont Neuf guaranteed that many Parisians were immediately informed of his arrest; they quickly formed an angry horde. The Royal Guard was on the bridge even as this was happening. The soldiers beat a retreat, but with a screaming mob on their heels. In no time at all, the crowd had grown to between thirty thousand and forty thousand. Retz described the "sudden and violent conflagration that spread from the Pont Neuf through the entire city. Absolutely everyone took up arms." And later, when the opposition forces obtained Broussel's release, observers noted "the cries of joy" that erupted from "the middle of the Pont Neuf" and described "the entire city of Paris" gathered around the bridge. Those who opposed the monarchy were called *frondeurs du Pont Neuf*—Pont Neuf rebels.

From then on, the Pont Neuf was considered a breeding ground for civil disorder. Edicts were repeatedly issued, forbidding "people of every rank from assembling on the Pont Neuf"—but to no avail. Contemporary sources claimed that a post on the Pont Neuf one afternoon was sure to assemble a crowd overnight. In addition, political songs were so successfully deployed during the civil war that, by the time the war was over, a music industry had developed, with "Pont Neuf singers" specializing in songs referred to as "Pont Neuf songs," "Pont Neuf vaudevilles," "chronicles from the Pont Neuf," and eventually just simply as "Pont Neufs." Paris' most prolific seventeenth-century letter writer, the Marquise de Sévigné, said of such songs: "The Pont Neuf wrote them." One of the bridge's most ardent admirers, Jean-Baptiste Dupuy-Demportes—he announced in 1750 his plan to publish six volumes devoted to its history—claimed that every great moment in French history had been commemorated in a song written and performed there.

Those songs were just the tip of the iceberg. Until the first professional theaters opened their doors in the 1630s, the Pont Neuf was the center of the Parisian theatrical scene. Actors performed on makeshift stages such as the one depicted in this painting from the 1660s. People from every walk of life have gathered on all sides—even under the stage. Some spectators have just wandered by, but a group of aristocrats has come expressly to catch the act. They have had their carriage turned around and backed up; a lady leans on the door. They thus have front-row seats.

Contemporary accounts make it clear that many acts seen on the bridge resembled today's stand-up comedy. Some performers became so famous that collections of their work circulated widely, both in the form of cheap pamphlets intended for a popular audience and of relatively pricey volumes for wealthier readers.

Henri Le Grand, whose stage name was Turlupin, said himself that he "harangued" the crowd. He delivered lengthy rants with interminable sentences, often extreme vulgarity—and a dead-on sense of rhythm and comic timing.

Parisians came to the Pont Neuf to see comedy performed on makeshift stages. These aristocrats have turned their carriage into a private box.

Turlupin created true populist art, at times angry, at others lighthearted. In his most pointed political commentary, he called out the king directly. He railed against—what else?—the ills of the modern city. One uncannily prescient harangue, for example, issued a warning that would be echoed by progressive philosophers and economists until the eve of the Revolution of 1789: a crushing tax burden was driving French peasants to flee the countryside for what they perceived as "the opulence of Paris." Once there, however, they were unable to find honest work and instead of "making wine" as they had in their villages, they became "beggars and thieves."

The performers depicted in this painting may have been intended to evoke the most celebrated street players of all, the team of Tabarin and Mondor (the stage names of brothers Antoine and Philippe Girard). They first collaborated when Tabarin served as valet to Mondor, one of the quack doctors or con men known as "charlatans" or "operators" (they claimed to be surgeons) who stood on the bridge and sold ointments and potions for which they made huge claims. (One foreign visitor remarked: "They'll make the teeth you've lost grow back; they'll cure incurable diseases; they'll whiten your skin and get rid of your wrinkles.") The pair used short skits to sell their cure-alls, and when these became a draw, dressed as a doctor and Pierrot, they began selling their jokes along with their pomades.

Then there was a very touching figure whose huge natural talent still leaps off the page—something that rarely happens when one is reading transcriptions of improvisational material several centuries old: Philippot, a blind singer-poet from the Savoie region who called himself "the Orpheus of the Pont Neuf." His refrains share the witty wordplay and easy charm of Cole Porter's lyrics. There were also performers, such as Gros Guillaume, or Fat William, the stage name of Robert Guérin, and Gaultier Garguille (Hugues Guérin de Fléchelles), whose acts prefigure the in-your-face obscenity of today's rappers.

Open-air performances contributed to the traffic gridlock, though not nearly so much as another kind of urban spectacle that also drew crowds to the bridge: shopping. As soon as the New Bridge was completed, a street market began. You could find trinkets, fashion accessories, and the most fetching bouquets in the city, sold by the *bouquetières*, or "bouquet ladies of the Pont Neuf." Each merchant had a bare minimum of display space—a table, a trunk, a tent suspended over wares laid out on the ground. Most used portable stalls, pitched up on the central section and the sidewalks. Booksellers were the first to set up shop; there were soon at least fifty bookshops on the bridge. In 1619, still more began to open along the nearby quais. The little stands they folded up every evening and attached to the bridge's side parapet were the ancestors of the bookstalls on the banks of the Seine today. Because of the wide range of titles they displayed, contemporaries observed that the bridge gave Parisians access to the largest public library in the world.

Wealthy consumers being jostled about and distracted by everything from buskers to stray sheep must have seemed easy prey. Money was surely stolen and expensive small items such as pocket watches pinched in the midst of those crowds. These obvious kinds of robbery barely get a mention in the seventeenth-century press, however. Instead, the New Bridge quickly acquired a reputation for a quite specific type of crime, clothing theft, and that of one item in particular: men's cloaks.

Periodicals and guidebooks, memoirs and novels—all make an explicit association between the Pont Neuf and *manteau* or cloak theft. The stories make it clear that, if you walked onto the Pont Neuf wearing your finest garments, you were in real danger of losing them before you reached the other side.

Clothing theft is a crime comprehensible only at times when fine apparel had quite exceptional value, and this was certainly the case in seventeenth-century Paris. In April 1672, the Marquise de Sévigné, for example, was asked by her son-in-law to have "a very handsome *justaucorps*" (the equivalent of today's suit jacket) made for him in Paris. The son-in-law was a count, mind you, as well as the governor of one of France's largest provinces, and Sévigné herself, while certainly not a spendthrift, was after all a major aristocrat and well accustomed to the high-rolling ways of wealthy Parisians. She nevertheless fired off a positively frantic response: What was he thinking? Did he not realize how much this would cost? ("between 700 and 800 *livres*"). Had something happened to the "very handsome one" he already owned? Her message could not be clearer: you needed only one such item at a time, and you used it "until every bit of it was worn out."

Despite all this, it's clear that when Parisians got an expensive new outfit, they couldn't resist showing it off by going for a stroll just where they knew it would be seen by the biggest crowd: on "the big stage of the Pont Neuf." By all accounts, it appears that women, for once, ran fewer risks than men. When they were robbed—and many fewer incidents made the news—thieves mostly grabbed the "handkerchiefs," or scarves really, that women wore to cover the upper part of their necklines when out in public. These were costly, mind you—it was a bit like stealing an Hermès scarf today—but inexpensive next to the man's garment that thieves systematically pinched: the *manteau* that aristocrats, as a contemporary dictionary put it, "draped over their shoulders when out and about in the city." As this late seventeenth-century print demonstrates, *manteaux* required *many* yards of costly fabric. They were also often adorned with the kind of elaborate braid that would gleam when nobles swirled their cloaks about to dramatic effect. Sévigné panicked at the idea of a new *justaucorps*; a second *manteau* would have provoked a reaction even more extreme.

It was a simple matter to pull off a garment draped around the shoulders—hence the early names for clothing thieves: *tire-laines* and *tire-manteaux*, literally "wool-pullers" or "cloak-pullers." Then the Pont Neuf opened and Parisians felt the need for a new term to call attention to the clothing crime wave that broke out.

The word *filou*—which today refers generically to any crook or shady character—emerged in the early seventeenth century with a very precise meaning: someone who *vole les manteaux la nuit*, "steals men's cloaks at night." The Pont Neuf was known to be their playground. The expression "Pont Neuf *filou*" was commonly used; cloak thieves were also called *avant-coureurs du Pont Neuf*, "early warning signals of the Pont Neuf" (if you noticed your cloak was gone, the bridge couldn't be far); "officers of the Pont Neuf," because they were the law of that land; and even "courtiers of the Bronze Horse," since they held court and lay in wait for victims near the statue of Henri IV.

Henri Bonnart depicted a seventeenth-century nobleman proudly displaying his manteau, *the expensive cloak that thieves tried to slip from gentlemen's shoulders while they were distracted by the sights and sounds on the bridge.*

Already in January 1614, the Parisian Parlement recognized the new reality of city life and asked merchants to keep arms in their shops to help the officers of the law capture "those we now call *filous*," "cloak-pullers who work at night."

Foreigners quickly began to warn each other of their existence. English ecclesiastic and author Peter Heylyn described his own encounter with "*Filous* or night Rogues" in 1625, as well as that of another English visitor, "unmantled of a new Plush Cloak" by *filous* while crossing the Pont Neuf after dark. By the end of the seventeenth century, longtime Paris resident Nemeitz concluded the first volume of his guidebook with the chapter "About *Filous*." He warned those coming to Paris from smaller cities that *filous* were a problem particular to Paris: because it was "the biggest city of all, a world unto itself," a *filou* could escape by blending into the crowd. To keep their clothing safe, visitors were instructed to avoid one place above all: the Pont Neuf after dark.

Literature celebrated the exploits of this new urban criminal. Claude de L'Estoile's *Intrigue des filous* ("The Filous' Game") was a huge hit when it was staged in 1646 and was still being reedited in the 1680s. It takes place—where else?—on the bridge near Henri IV's Bronze Horse. It features a gang of *manteau* pinchers with names such as Le Balafré (Scarface; Henri IV was sometimes known as Le Balafré) and Le Borgne (The One-Eyed Man). They operate at night and rely on the Samaritaine's chimes to keep track of time and thereby avoid the militia who patrolled the bridge at regular intervals.

We meet Béronte, surely the first fence in literature (and a dishonest fence at that, since he's been restealing stolen cloaks passed on to him by the *filous*). We learn that the rich have for the most part stopped wearing their finest cloaks when they know they will be crossing the Pont Neuf at night—unless they have several bodyguards along to protect not their life but their cloak. We meet Ragonde, a used-clothing dealer who unloads ill-gotten goods; conveniently, many used-clothing shops were situated near the New Bridge, even though these dealers, for obvious reasons, were not allowed to set up shop on the bridge itself. Cloaks were so skillfully altered before resale that it was said to be pointless to visit used-clothing shops searching for your stolen *manteau*; an article in the contemporary press explained that "two new *justaucorps* could be fashioned from a single cloak." The crime was harshly punished—an infamous female clothing fence named Valentin was publicly executed in March 1665—but the rewards were so great and all those *manteaux* so tempting that fences went right on moving stolen ones.

The fear of *filous* is easy to understand. They came upon you in the dark, often dressed as artistocrats. (They had the right clothes after all.) There are even tales of real aristocrats who thought it a lark to go to the Pont Neuf to steal cloaks.

And they also operated in broad daylight. Nemeitz devoted a chapter to daytime dangers in the city; it featured the Pont Neuf. This detail from an early seventeenth-century painting shows a pair of Parisians leaning on the edge, lost in the glorious view out over the river. And this, Nemeitz warned, was an

The Pont Neuf, Paris' first bridge without houses, provided a vantage point from which the Seine and the city skyline could be appreciated, as these two early river tourists are doing.

invitation to the ever wily bridge thieves, who could clip your cloak in the wink of an eye.

The Pont Neuf was in fact expressly designed to encourage pedestrians to linger over the vista laid out before them—and this may have been the most remarkable of its innovations.

The bridge was still new when, in 1612, Paris historian Jacques Du Breul became the first to introduce visitors to its pathbreaking features: "All along each side there is an armrest a foot wide," he began, with at intervals along its length what were known as "viewing shelves" or "balconies"; the two men shown here are standing in one of those balconies. Du Breul explained that, by making what he called simply "looking at the river" possible, the bridge would make Parisians aware that their city was now a sight worthy of visual appreciation. And so it did.

All through the seventeenth century, Parisians and foreigners repeated that such a view, possible nowhere else in Europe, should be a source of civic pride. Authors of guidebooks agreed that no one should miss the spectacle of "the marriage of the river, superb monuments, and the trees and hills in the distance." Brice reported that "one of the greatest travelers in recent centuries" considered the panorama "among the three finest of all those he had seen on his long voyages," rivaled only by the ports of Constantinople and Goa. In the 1670s, François Bernier, perhaps the most influential travel writer in one

*Hedrick Mommers' view from the 1660s represents the most popular image
of seventeenth-century Paris. Numerous paintings portrayed the
Pont Neuf as a bustling street suspended over the Seine.*

of the great ages for travel writing, went Brice's anonymous voyager one better and pronounced the vista from the Pont Neuf "the most beautiful and the
most magnificent view in the entire world."

Bernier, moreover, established himself as an authority on majestic views: he
had been all over the globe, except for "a few isolated corners of China and
Japan." He was therefore well placed to tell Parisians that "you don't have to
leave Paris to find the most beautiful and the most magnificent vista in the
world; all you have to do is take a walk on the Pont Neuf."

Bernier pronounced the panorama "all the more remarkable because it was
almost entirely artificial, the work of human hands." Technology and urban
planning had thus created the notion of a cityscape, an urban landscape, a
magnificent scene made by man rather than nature. Paris had no longer just
an isolated monument or two worthy of contemplation—Notre-Dame Cathedral, the Louvre. When viewed from the bridge, the Seine became a beautiful
sight, and the complete urban footprint, the landscape of Paris, became a masterpiece, as the many seventeenth-century paintings of the Pont Neuf illustrate
vividly.

This canvas from the 1660s is typical of the genre. In the foreground, it depicts one of those newly Parisian scenes of public mixing and street life. And

in the background it shows how the bridge was teaching Parisians from across the social spectrum to appreciate "the most magnificent view in the entire world."

At a time when bridges were cruelly lacking in all major cities and when the bridges that did exist were no more than functional, the Pont Neuf reinvented the bridge. It was technologically advanced, a center for characteristically urban forms of entertainment, a social equalizer—and essential to the process by which Paris won its reputation as a city both beautiful and modern. When Peter the Great visited Paris in 1717 to learn the ground rules for building a great European city, the Pont Neuf was naturally high on his list of essential sights.

Small wonder that the Pont Neuf became the first major modern tourist destination and that it inspired a true souvenir industry. The wealthiest travelers returned home with a painting of the New Bridge to hang in their salon or picture gallery, views that could remind them of the qualities of the Parisian experience that were to be found nowhere else. And for less prosperous visitors who wanted a reminder of Paris there was the equivalent of a souvenir trinket.

In the seventeenth century, hand-painted and decorated fans were among the favorite accessories of stylish women all over Europe. In April 1672, the Marquise de Sévigné was so pleased with her new fan that she pronounced it "the prettiest thing I've ever seen." The pretty scene it depicted was a view of

This eighteenth-century souvenir fan is painted with a scene of street life on the Pont Neuf.

the monument that Sévigné, a lifelong Parisian, described as "her old friend": the Pont Neuf. A number of such Pont Neuf fans have survived; the earliest date from the time of Sévigné's letter. The one shown here was painted in the eighteenth century and depicts the range of experiences possible on the bridge, experiences by then widely considered quintessentially Parisian—everything from a traffic jam to shopping and people-watching. It could thus have stood for the city in a tourist's mind and served as a reminder of travel past and a promise of trips to come.

Proverbial phrases used by seventeenth-century Parisians prove that the city's inhabitants also saw the New Bridge as the essence of their Paris. The many expressions then invented included *crier sur le Pont Neuf* or *chanter sur le Pont Neuf* ("to tell the whole town about it") and "amuser le Pont Neuf" ("to entertain the entire city"). A particularly difficult task was the equivalent of *faire le Pont Neuf*, "to build the Pont Neuf." They announced *je me porte comme le Pont Neuf*: "I feel as solid as the Pont Neuf." And about a particularly sure thing they remarked *Le Pont Neuf dans mille ans s'appellera Pont Neuf*: "In a thousand years, the Pont Neuf will still be called the New Bridge."

Four hundred and counting . . .

In 1689, Louis XIV added the next major bridge over the Seine, the Pont Royal. The Royal Bridge was scarcely fifty feet wide and only four hundred and fifty feet long, not even half as long as the Pont Neuf. At the end of the seventeenth century, the public work with which Henri IV began the modernization of Paris thus remained what it still is today, the longest and the widest bridge in Paris.

CHAPTER TWO

"Light of the City of Light":
The Place des Vosges

I N THE 1550S, Philip II of Spain wanted to commemorate his reign with grandiose monuments more glorious than anything the world had ever seen. He chose architect Gaspar de Vega as his counselor in architectural and artistic matters. In 1556, the king's special envoy toured Northern Europe and France in search of models that could inspire Spanish architects. His report on his visit to Paris in May of that year was brief and categoric: he had spent but a single day there, in order to tour the Louvre, which he pronounced "an outdated construction." "This is little time for such a big city," Gaspar de Vega admitted, "but I didn't remark a single notable building, and the only interesting thing about the city is its size."

This was the capital Henri IV found in 1598: a city an expert had decreed a virtual architectural wasteland.

As the seventeenth century began, Paris was lacking any notable public space. The French word *place* (literally "place" or "space") then designated simply any open-air location free of construction. What were then called *places* were either nondescript public spots such as market places, completely undeveloped and without infrastructure, or merely areas where streets were wider and where there was thus a bit of room for people to congregate.

By the end of the seventeenth century, the word had another definition, one that proves that a new kind of *place* had come into existence. A *place* was now described as "open, public space, surrounded by buildings," intended for precise purposes: "to provide a spot for public gatherings," "to ornament the city," and "to facilitate commerce" within it.

To illustrate the word's recently acquired meaning, all contemporary dictionaries gave the same example: the Place Royale, the Royal Square. Their new definition of a *place* was in fact tailor-made to suit the Place Royale. That exemplary *place* still exists and is now known as the Place des Vosges, a name that dates from 1800. It was Paris' first notable modern architectural project, its initial planned public space, the original modern city square—and the second spot that helped Paris become Paris. In the course of the seventeenth century, the Place was redefined on several occasions. Each time this happened, the space revitalized the city; each time, developments that originated there subsequently proved essential to Paris' identity.

In October 1604, when the Pont Neuf was opened to the public, the initial phase in Henri IV's master plan for the transformation of Paris was essentially complete. In fact, during the final months of 1603, the king had begun laying the groundwork for another project. He desperately needed to jump-start the Parisian economy, badly weakened by decades of religious warfare. Luxurious (and astronomically expensive) silk was then a darling of European fashion. France was importing great quantities from the dominant European producer, Italy, and the costly foreign import was draining French coffers. Henri IV thus decided to launch a silk industry in the French capital. What began as an attempt to revitalize Paris' economy subsequently evolved in ways no one could have predicted: the project resulted in the creation of both a groundbreaking model for the city square and a major new neighborhood.

In August 1603, when Henri IV assembled leaders of the business community to discuss the idea of opening a manufactory dedicated to the production of the highest quality silk upholstery fabric, there was little precedent for establishing any type of industry in an urban setting. In 1590, Pope Sixtus V had considered using the Colosseum for a manufactory to revive Italian wool production, but the plan was never carried out.

To realize his design, Henri IV turned to six of the wealthiest tradesmen and city officials. This is the earliest example of a phenomenon characteristic of Paris' reinvention: grandiose royal visions largely financed by private investment.

The king offered those backers titles of nobility and tax-free business conditions for the silk manufactory. In January 1604, he provided land for the construction of workshops and housing for workers. In return, he asked only that they promise to keep the new silk manufactory operational until 1615.

This early eighteenth-century map of Paris shows what a prime spot Henri IV had chosen. The main entrance to the city was the Porte Saint-Antoine, the Saint-Antoine gate, situated just beyond the fortress intended to protect

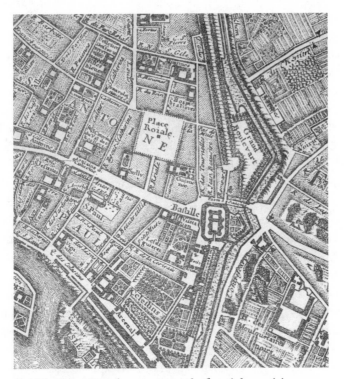

The Place Royale was among the first sights a visitor to seventeenth-century Paris encountered. It was situated near the city's principal entrance, the Saint-Antoine gate (just beyond the Bastille fortress), and easily accessible from its widest street, the rue Saint-Antoine.

the city, the Bastille. Visitors then proceeded along the broad expanse of Paris' widest street, the rue Saint-Antoine. The new square was both easily accessible from that artery and sheltered from its hubbub.

Initially, the project moved forward at a brisk pace. A March 1604 edict mentions the foreign workers who had arrived to teach French artisans silk weaving. Most commercial construction was finished before the end of the year, and by the summer of 1605 the manufactory was up and running, with an Italian, Sigismond Pestalossi, at its head and a mix of Milanese artisans and French apprentices living in twelve houses that had been built for them.

On March 29, 1605, Henri IV wrote his finance minister Sully about "that *place*" they had been discussing; this is the earliest mention of the larger context in which the silk workshop was to function, the moment when the commercial enterprise began to evolve into the first modern city square. The following July "that *place*" received its official designation—"which we wish henceforth to be named the Place Royale"—in a decree that defined three basic goals for the new square: to adorn Paris, to provide a setting for public ceremonies, and to give Parisians a recreational space. The last two of those goals were revolutionary. Previous French monarchs had developed plans designed to beautify the French capital, but Henri IV was the first to take seriously both the practical value of urban works and the role such projects could play in bettering the lives of the city's inhabitants.

The king decided to use the existing commercial buildings as one side of the square. The three remaining sides were to be composed of what he called "pavilions," nine to a side. Their ground floor was designated as commercial space (shops selling the new manufactory's wares) with a covered arcade that would protect visitors from the elements. Their upper floors were to provide residences. The land was given to investors in the silk works and other loyalists to the crown for a symbolic annual rental fee.

They were free to plan the interiors of their pavilions, but their façades had to be identical—"built according to our design." Thus the pavilions became a spectacular founding example of terraced housing, houses of uniform height and with uniform fronts that share a wall with neighboring units (color insert). In 1652, writer and city planner John Evelyn pronounced these "incomparably fair and uniform" houses a marvel of modern architecture. (In London, terraced housing was introduced by entrepreneur Nicholas Barbon only after the Great Fire of 1666.) The Place's pavilions had identical sloping slate roofs; their façades were composed of a mix of red brick and golden stone. The combination was not new to French architecture—it had already been used in a few sixteenth-century châteaux—but it was new in Paris, where it added a distinctly colorful footprint. The original owners also had to agree to "the same symmetry"—the same number of stories, of identical dimensions, the same kind of chimney in the same spot, the same number of windows and of uniform size. (There are in fact some variations, but they are small enough so that the impression of absolute harmony remains.)

Henri IV was so eager to see his latest project realized that he ordered it to be completed in a mere eighteen months. And to make sure that the workers kept hard at their task, he personally visited the construction site on a daily basis.

But despite the king's hands-on involvement, the Parisian silk industry was anything but a grand success. In April 1607, the king therefore abandoned his original goal and approved a significant modification: the workshops with which the entire project had begun were torn down and replaced with nine additional pavilions. Henri IV rewarded those who had gone about building most expeditiously. Pierre Fougeu, Sieur d'Escures, for example, had completed his pavilion on the east side in 1605: he received additional land on which he constructed a particularly fine residence, now number nine, the only one with a private garden tucked away behind its façade.

The Place's original population was economically and socially diverse. The first six owners included Pierre Sainctot, a prominent fabric merchant and leader of the business community, and Nicolas Camus (or Le Camus), whom contemporaries described as a poor boy who had arrived in Paris with twenty *livres* in his pocket. Camus began his career in the silk industry and went on to become a prominent financier. Near the end of his life, he made his children a present of more than nine million *livres*—and still had forty million in annual income. The biggest investor in the silkworks was Jean Moisset, who had literally clawed his way up from modest origins as a penniless provincial to become a pillar of high finance. Like Camus', Moisset's story is a very early example of a type of social ascension that became a familiar tale in seventeenth-century Paris but that before then was very rare indeed: the poor young man whose financial savvy makes him hugely wealthy.

By 1612 the group of residents had expanded to forty. Most newcomers were wealthy bourgeois such as Charles Marchant, the biggest real-estate developer of the day. They had, however, less wealthy neighbors, such as Claude Chastillon, royal engineer and cartographer, and even some average Parisians—master mason Jean Coin, for example, and master carpenters Barthélemy Drouin and Antoine Le Redde.

The new Place was designed as a radical departure from earlier models for city squares—the Classical forum or the Renaissance piazza—usually rectangular and designed to showcase an individual monument, a church, a town hall, or a central statue. The Place Royale was literally a square: seventy-two *toises* by seventy-two *toises*, or nearly four hundred and fifty feet square. And it had neither a political nor a religious mission. Despite its name, there was initially nothing royal about it: its center was in fact empty until 1639, when a statue of Louis XIII was added. The first modern square instead focused attention on great architecture that was designed for the inhabitants of a city rather than to celebrate its civic or religious authorities. It became an important origin of the French capital's lasting association with cutting-edge residential architecture.

The large open space also helped launch Paris' love affair with perspective. Before its completion, only the Pont Neuf had provided the kind of vantage point necessary for the proper appreciation of a monument—even

Notre-Dame Cathedral was closely hemmed in by constructions of various kinds. But by the end of the seventeenth century, all over the city various broad thoroughfares provided those exploring on foot with the distance necessary for contemplation of the buildings found there; boulevards and avenues made possible long-range views of the best-known monuments.

In the early seventeenth century, the French court had no regularly designated spot to stage festivities. The traditional site, the Hôtel des Tournelles, had been abandoned in 1559 by Queen Catherine de Médicis after her husband Henri II was killed in a joust organized on its grounds; she later ordered it to be demolished. The terrain functioned as a horse market until Henri IV decided to incorporate it into his silk manufactory.

To complete the project, he also acquired land from private investors. The king thus assembled a terrain large enough to fulfill the second function assigned the new Place in that 1605 decree: to serve the city as "the kind of *place* necessary on days of public rejoicing, when great crowds assemble." Built on a scale that until then had been reserved for royal palaces, the Place Royale was conceived as a palatial public space, open in some measure to all the city's inhabitants and designed for their enjoyment and their recreation.

On April 5, 6, and 7, 1612, the new space was officially opened to the public with one of the grandest public parties Paris had ever known. The occasion chosen was a momentous one: the celebration of the so-called "Spanish marriages," the engagements of Henri IV's two oldest children to two offspring of Philip III of Spain: the eleven-year-old future Louis XIII to the Infanta Ana, also eleven, and ten-year-old Elisabeth of France to the future Philip IV, then a boy of seven.

Previous royal celebrations had been commemorated in lavish books that appeared only long after the fact. In this case, numerous narratives went to press before April 1612 was out; commemorative engravings also immediately began to circulate.

The most widely distributed image of the event is this engraving by Claude Chastillon, who lived on the top floor of a pavilion on the east side (number ten today) and thus provided the definitive depiction of an iconic event: a bird's-eye view looking out over the square from his own window. The engraving was part of Chastillon's attempt to depict the monuments Henri IV was adding to the cityscape: he thereby became the first artist systematically to chronicle Paris and its urban culture.

Chastillon imagined a new way of recording public festivities: a single large sheet with an image in the center and text in the margins all around it. This format was designed to reach a far larger audience than earlier lavishly illus-

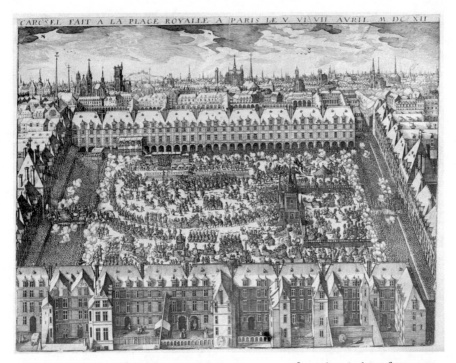

CARCEL FAIT A LA PLACE ROYALLE A PARIS LE V. VI.VII AVRIL M DC XII

The inauguration of the Place Royale in 1612 as seen from the window of engraver Claude Chastillon, one of the square's original residents. Chastillon highlighted the size of the crowd, which he estimated at roughly seventy thousand.

trated books—and to reach that audience far more quickly. His depiction also broke new ground by focusing on the spectators who turned out for the event as much as on the demonstration of royal power. This very early image of the people of Paris was designed to show above all that, motivated by the desire to be right in the middle of things, Parisians had positively crammed themselves into the new square.

Pinpointing the size of a large crowd is something that remains elusive even with modern surveillance equipment, so it's no surprise that estimates of the number who assembled for the festivities vary wildly, from 50,000 to 80,000. The Royal Square had been designed to accommodate over 60,000—a quarter of the roughly 225,000 people who then lived in Paris—and Chastillon depicts it containing a capacity crowd. One commentator explained that so many people had spent the night on the Place to be sure of getting a spot that, by dawn on April 5, it was already jammed; additional spectators filled every arcade. Another commentator added that spectators had even managed to find perches all over the roofs. Still another concluded: "It seemed as if the entire city of Paris was trying to find a spot near the square." One of the greatest diplomats of the age was an eyewitness: he remembered above all the "incredible" sound of the seemingly "infinite" crowd roaring as one. With this spectacular occasion, the square was inaugurated as the people's park, a space for all Parisians.

That overflow crowd witnessed a carefully scripted event, a cross between a parade and a play. In the center of the Place, a miniature re-creation of the pavilions around the square was named the Palace of Happiness, in a nod to the prosperity promised by the double marriage. A cast of thousands—about five thousand or so—paraded around it. There was a medieval princess atop a dragon that spat fire from its mouth; there were bands of slaves and savages, Indians and giants, pages and trumpet-blowers—with a half-dozen elephants and a rhinoceros thrown in for good measure.

And the costumes were as extravagant as the stage set. Those "savages," for example, were covered from head to toe with oak leaves made from green silk satin. The "Indians" wore plumed headdresses—also feather boas and even feather-covered ankle boots. The men of the French court sported outfits in gold lamé—and diamond bracelets.

Henri IV's widow, Marie de Médicis, understood that this event could become the kind of experience that Parisians had not often known in recent decades, one that gave them a sense of a shared identity that transcended religious differences. At the end of the second day, she therefore announced that the celebration would be continued in the city's streets so that "the Parisians who had not been able to find a place in the Place Royale could see all these wonderful things." Led by the royal family, a huge procession filed out of the square, down the rue Saint-Antoine, over the Notre-Dame bridge to the Left Bank, then proceeded along the embankment to the still very new Pont Neuf, where it crossed the Seine once again to reach the Louvre.

When night fell, Marie de Médicis asked "all those who lived in houses along the parade route" to light a lantern in each of their windows to illuminate the sights for the throngs who had quickly gathered up and down the route. More than six hours later and well after midnight, the last participants finally reached the Louvre. By then, it could truly have been said that virtually all Parisians had participated in the inauguration of the Place Royale.

The festivities were still being talked about decades later; Chastillon's image as well as printed accounts were republished as late as the 1660s. Their propaganda value was thus immense. In 1612, images and books combined trumpeted the news that all was well in a city that a decade earlier had still been emerging from destruction and civil war, a city that, less than two years earlier, had been in mourning after the assassination of Henri IV, the ruler who had planned the Royal Square. Paris was a city reborn, so far removed from the horrors of recent decades that it could serve as the glamorous setting for a grand celebration.

In the 1605 documents that established the Royal Square, Henri IV had assigned it a final function: to become a "proumenoir," "a space where the inhabitants of our city can walk; they are now tightly confined within their homes because of all the people who keep flooding into Paris in such numbers from all sides." He thus became the earliest monarch to address the need for a second and then unheard of type of public space: space intended for the everyday recreational use of the inhabitants of increasingly populated urban centers. With the Place Royale, Paris acquired the first purpose-built public recreational space in any European capital.

This seventeenth-century depiction of the Place Royale testifies to the way Parisians embraced it on a daily basis. Men and women, adults and children, nobles and bourgeois walk in the central square, under the arcades, and in the surrounding streets. Some are alone, others in pairs or in groups. Two boys chase each other. Some people lean on the fence; some sit on it, others on the

This engraving presents the Place Royale as a truly public recreational space, enjoyed by Parisians of all ages and from across the social spectrum.

ground nearby. Itinerant peddlers roam the streets; a few aristocrats on horse-back practice their martial arts. At a time when few homes had space set aside for social activity, the Place Royale was an immense outdoor living room where Parisians could enjoy their leisure time together. And they could do so, moreover, every day of the year. No early guide to the city of Paris failed to mention that because of the covered arcades "one can have the pleasure of walking no matter what the weather, protected from the sun as well as the rain."

Over time, however, the square ceased to function as a truly democratic space. Its initial transformation began in 1615, when the contracts that obliged the original investors to keep the silk works running expired. The manufac-tory had not proved financially viable, and Henri IV was no longer there to promote it; the original investors shut it down and forced the artisans who lived on the square to leave.

From then on, whenever residences passed out of the hands of the original owners, they were acquired by great noble families. The only home with a private garden, for example, remained in Pierre Fougeu's family until 1644, when his heirs sold the property to Honoré d'Albert, Duc de Chaulnes and Maréchal de France. By the 1640s, an aristocratic takeover of the Royal Square had been accomplished. In 1639, an equestrian statue of Louis XIII was placed in the middle of the square, as if to signal that the great urban room would henceforth be less democratic and more royal. (That statue was destroyed in 1792; the current monument dates from 1829.)

But a decade later, when civil war erupted in Paris all aristocratic pretension was forgotten for a time. The municipality commandeered the large and well-located space and used it to showcase its resistance to royal authority. In early 1649, both private militia and the cavalry fighting under the banner of the City of Paris paraded around the Place almost on a daily basis so that city of-ficials could prove to Parisians that they had the military might necessary for the city's defense. Soon the rebel army was camping out all over the Place Royale. Sights such as these seem to have convinced the increasingly ho-mogenous group of residents that it was time to take complete control over the square.

In the original design, there was no fence between the houses on the periph-ery and the recreational space at the center: the square truly belonged to the city. Louis XIV's cousin, the Duchesse de Montpensier, recorded in her memoirs how, soon after the civil war's end, residents had the central space completely remodeled. The canvas shown here, painted soon after that re-design, features the fence then added, the most visible sign that the Place

By the second half of the seventeenth century, the Royal Square was seen as a more exclusive recreational space, frequented above all by the upper-class residents of the adjacent area, then becoming known as the Marais.

would no longer be open to the city at large. Montpensier also described the striking new landscaping then undertaken. A lawn in a pattern she called "a grass carpet" (*parterre de gazon*) was planted; walkways between sections of "carpet" were covered with sand. The carpet was decorative, but it also divided the space into zones. As a result, as the painting shows, the square conceived as a wide-open recreational space had begun to function in a more sedate, decorous manner. Everyone in the square—and they are now all aristocrats—avoids the newly planted lawn and strolls only on the sand-covered walkways. One couple relaxes—no longer casually on the grass but on one of the benches that had been added at the end of each walkway when the square was redesigned. The central space was now as elegant as the architecture that surrounded it. (The trees that still rim the square were planted in the eighteenth century.)

This redesigned Place was used to prove to other nations that the civil war's battles had left no mark on Paris.

When an especially prominent dignitary arrived in France for a state visit, a ceremony known as an *entrée* or entrance was organized to give an ideal first impression of the French capital. All during Louis XIV's personal reign (1661–1715), every official visit followed the same scenario. The carefully scripted ritual was recorded for posterity by Nicolas de Sainctot, protocol officer in charge of such events. One of the first major visits of the post–civil war years took place in September 1656, when Queen Christina, who had recently abdicated the Swedish throne, rode into Paris on a white horse. She was immediately taken to what one account described as "the most beautiful spot, not only in Paris, but in any city in the world." There, a huge crowd was waiting: the most elegant women in Paris, "magnificently arrayed," "decorated" every window.

By the time of Christina's visit, the square conceived for all Parisians functioned instead as a private theater for aristocrats. In March 1659, a gazette described the "brilliant and novel party" that Pierre de Bellegarde, Marquis de Montbrun, threw there for his friends. In 1654, the Marquis had acquired number nineteen, the oversized corner lot that had originally belonged to real-estate mogul Marchant. He sold the property in February 1659; his party was thus a farewell to the Place. He had the square lit up by 2,300 lanterns and a brilliant display of fireworks. Many residents took it all in from number thirteen, owned by Jean Dyel, Sieur des Hameaux, Comte d'Auffrey, "as if they had been seated in an amphitheater."

*The first wrought-iron balcony on the square was added in
1644. Balconies were like viewing boxes from which
residents took in the activity below and showed
themselves off to those passing by.*

*Louis XIV frequently surveyed the state of his capital. In this view
from about 1655, his mother Anne d'Autriche is seated
behind him in the royal carriage.*

A new architectural element called attention to the control over the central
space now exercised by residents. In 1644, when the Duc de Chaulnes acquired the pavilion with the private garden, his home became the earliest to be
adorned with a wrought-iron balcony. This detail from the canvas painted
shortly after the Place's redesign depicts not only his balcony but the double
one that the Marquis de Montbrun had added to his corner home in 1654.
Those balconies gave the square's new aristocratic population a privileged
view over the domain laid out before them. In this case, they were also able to
watch as their king took pleasure in one of Paris' original great urban works:
the same painting portrays the young Louis XIV riding in a red carriage during one of his regular inspections tours, admiring the Royal Square and its
inhabitants.

By the late 1650s the diverse crowd that had initially frequented the square
was moving on to the far larger and more spectacularly laid out gardens and
walkways that were taking over the Place Royale's role as a center for public
leisure activities. The Place was becoming a protected spot watched over by
its inhabitants from their balconies and by the king himself. It then acquired
another mission, one to which public spaces often aspire but rarely achieve: it
became the center of a new neighborhood—a neighborhood created not by
royal or municipal decree but by the people who came to settle there.

The area immediately surrounding the Place had originally been reserved
for the craftsmen who ran the silk manufactory. The residences built for them

were torn down in 1615 when Henri IV's project came to an end. Then, as soon as the Royal Square became an aristocratic enclave, important Parisians unable to secure a spot on the Place itself began to build nearby. Shops providing the kinds of amenities that such residents required—from fine jewelry to fine pastry—were also established there.

By the 1630s, the area near the Place was being referred to as "the Marais," the marsh (some of the low-lying terrain had originally been swampy ground). The Marais became an official administrative district in about 1670; by then, it had been extensively chronicled by many of its original inhabitants. From their accounts, we learn above all that the Marais soon became the original example of an upscale Parisian neighborhood. From them, we also learn that a neighborhood like this fostered the development of various phenomena particular to urban centers, ranging from an artistic community to an unprecedented early manifestation of what would now be known as a youth culture.

Many of the Marais' early residents were writers: they highlighted the crucial role played in their daily lives by proximity to a beautiful spot. For satirical poet Théophile de Viau, for example, exile from Paris signified above all being deprived of "the sight of the Place Royale." When poet and novelist Paul Scarron—lifelong resident of the rue de Turenne right off the square—moved away, he penned a lengthy "good-bye to the Marais and the Place Royale," which he described as *d'une illustre ville le lustre*—the luster or light of a shining city.

Scarron also bid farewell to all those who would no longer be able to drop by "whenever they pleased," and his list is a veritable who's who of Parisian high society—duchesses, countesses, even a princess. Scarron's farewell suggests that, in the protected sphere of the Marais, friendship had become a social equalizer.

No resident gave a more complete picture of the Marais' early days than a woman born on February 5, 1626, in one of the residences that gave onto the Place Royale, the home of her grandfather, real-estate magnate Philippe de Coulanges. She grew up to become the Marquise de Sévigné, among the most influential women in France. A Parisian all her life, Sévigné always lived in close proximity to the square. The home in which she spent the longest period, now the Musée Carnavalet, the museum of Paris' history, is only minutes away. Sévigné was also a prolific letter writer; some fourteen hundred of her missives survive.

The kind of life possible in the Marais was crucial for Sévigné, who prided herself on always being the first to give her correspondents in the provinces the latest news from Paris. She knew that, in a neighborhood filled with people of influence, newsgathering was easy. She questioned the friends she met for coffee every morning. And whenever she heard a rumor, to confirm it she had only to "trot about a bit," walk a few steps from her home to check with a well-informed neighbor. When a cousin planned to move only a short distance away, she was incredulous: "How could anyone leave a neighborhood such as this?"

The center of literary Paris in the seventeenth century was often featured in literature. The tradition began in 1633, when two plays named *La Place royale* were performed with a re-creation of the Royal Square as a set design. Pierre Corneille's version was staged at a brand-new theater right off the Place, the Marais Company. More than any of his contemporaries, Corneille, then only twenty-six, suggested that the Marais had the potential to change Paris in still another way: in this privileged setting, a youth culture could take shape.

European literature had never seen anything like the plays the young dramatist created during the early decades of the Marais' existence: a new kind of comedy so decidedly urban that its young protagonists meet and fall in and out of love against the backdrop of identifiable city landmarks, the very monuments that were transforming Paris. *La Place royale* showcases a group of young people, wellborn and unattached, who live on or near the square. Phylis and her brother Doraste are the next-door neighbors of Angélique; their friend Alidor resides nearby. The young people spend all their time together, alone and unsupervised; their parents make only rare appearances.

In the safe haven of the Marais, they develop beliefs as unconventional as the architecture of the Place around which their lives revolve. Phylis proclaims that she has "more than 2,000 suitors" and pronounces fidelity a meaningless virtue. She prefers to play the field. Alidor is terrified of commitment; he announces early on that "many people have unhappy marriages." The play thus ends not as comedies should, with a marriage, but with Alidor, alone in the middle of the Place Royale, declaring that, now that he has managed to avoid marriage with Angélique, he "can begin to live" because he'll "be living for [him]self alone."

From then on, plays that would today be called romantic comedies—Antoine d'Ouville's *La Dame suivante* and Noël Le Breton, Sieur de Hauteroche's *La Dame invisible*, for example—continued to promote the idea that in the Marais young people lived as nowhere else, that the Place Royale was a setting that favored romantic encounters and young love. By making sure that the Marais was seen as much more than the sum total of its streets and its buildings, these seventeenth-century playwrights helped create the image of Paris as a city un-like all others—and that of the Marais as the most Parisian of neighborhoods.

As a result, by the late seventeenth century, a dictionary identified the Marais as "the fun part of town," a view reinforced by guidebooks. In 1670, François Savinien d'Alquié informed vistors that, once there, "it [would] be impossible to leave." And in 1715, Louis Liger's *Le Voyageur fidèle* ("The Faithful Voyager"), subtitled "A Guide for Foreigners that Explains Places of Interest in the City, and also How to Find Everything You Want There," proved just how easily a newcomer could fall under the Marais' spell.

Liger identified himself as a first-time German visitor to the French capital. His guidebook taught foreign travelers about the manner in which the original new-style tourists were visiting Paris. Liger started his first day with a visit to Notre-Dame Cathedral. In no time at all, however, he left the church and headed for the biggest nearby street, the rue Saint-Antoine, where he settled into a café for some refreshments. There he was only steps away from the Place Royale. Liger thus ended his first day in Paris in the Marais.

From then on, Liger devoted less time to traditional monuments and more to experiencing the upscale city living for which Paris had become known. As he explained to his readers, the best way to do this was to spend time in the Marais.

Day after day, Liger returned there, in order to explore the neighborhood, as he put it, "*à fond*"—"in depth." He always toured on foot—and he de-scribes his visits with a mapmaker's precision: when he's on his way to dinner in the Vieille rue du Temple, for instance, on his right he notes first the rue des Francs-Bourgeois and then the rue de la Perle. A visitor today armed with Liger's guide could follow along with him virtually step-by-step.

Liger quickly managed to become part of the youth culture chronicled in that long line of seventeenth-century comedies. He found friends in the Marais; they hosted him at late-night suppers and showed him their favorite spots for an evening out. He found love in the Marais (and he lost it there as well). In his view, it was simply "the best place in the world."

Of all the architecture new to Paris in the seventeenth century, the Place Royale was the most obviously influential—to begin with, in Paris itself. Under Louis XIV, the term *place royale* came to designate any square with a statue of a monarch at its center. The Sun King added two new royal squares to Paris— the Place des Victoires in 1686 and today's Place Vendôme (originally the Place Louis-le-Grand) in the 1690s—and many more were planned for cities all over France.

Historians and travel writers further contributed to its fame. Historians such as Jean Doubdan and Sébastien Le Nain de Tillemont explained the great monuments of the ancient world for their readers by pointing out comparable features on the Royal Square. And in the late 1650s, after spending time in all the major urban centers of the continent, the son of a wealthy Parisian merchant, Henri Sauval, began a history of Paris that compared it to its European rivals. About the Place Royale, his pronouncement was categorical: "It is the biggest and most beautiful *place* in the world"; "neither the Greeks nor the Romans ever had anything like it."

By the time Sauval made his pronouncement, it was already clear that rulers all over Europe felt the same way. With the Place Royale, Paris had acquired its earliest notable modern architectural monument, a monument that, like the Pont Neuf, was neither a cathedral nor a palace.

The Place Royale quickly became just what Gaspar de Vega had been searching for in 1556: a new departure for urban architecture. In London, its design was imitated in the 1630s: the result was the city's original fashionable square, Covent Garden. When Peter the Great arrived in Paris in May 1717 in search of ideas for the model city he was building on the Neva, his first day began at eight A.M. at the Place Royale. And in 1617, a mere five years after the Spanish court had witnessed the Place Royale's inauguration ceremony in celebration of his children's engagements, Philip III began work on the monumental city square that Spanish monarchs had long been dreaming of for Madrid. Today it is called the Plaza Mayor, and its debt to its Parisian model is evident.

CHAPTER THREE

"Enchanted Island": The Île Saint-Louis

I N   T H E   1630S, the Marais introduced Parisians to a novel urban experience—life in an upscale enclave, a privileged space that afforded residents both easy access to the city's amenities and the sense of living in their own private haven. The lesson was not lost on the wealthiest Parisians of the day.

Soon after, another major new neighborhood was added in the heart of the city, so quickly that some said it seemed to have happened overnight. When it was done, one commentator quipped that it had taken less time to create the loveliest area in Paris than it had to destroy major parts of the city during the Wars of Religion.

The planners of the second neighborhood that developed in the 1630s took advantage of lessons learned from both the Pont Neuf and the Place Royale. They chose a site in the middle of the Seine, thus giving residents highly desirable access to the river views and the urban panorama that the New Bridge had first made essential to the Parisian experience. By building on virgin territory, they were able to showcase residential architecture on a scale not possible in an area with preexisting construction such as the Marais. This second neighborhood thus provided a rare occasion to try out innovative ideas in urban planning and residential architecture. And the experiment paid off: the area, a complete neighborhood planned and built from scratch, played a key role in the transformation of Paris into the most beautiful city in the world.

It all began with a marvel of technology that surpassed even the Pont Neuf's construction. Henri IV initiated an undertaking without precedent and one not attempted again for nearly three centuries, the construction of a largely

man-made island in a major urban river. Today, Parisians and visitors know
the king's new island and the neighborhood developed on it as the "Île Saint-
Louis."

The Île Saint-Louis that visitors see today is a rare, almost perfectly pre-
served parcel of the urban past, an enclave that—nearly four centuries after
its creation—remains so close to its original incarnation that it could almost
have spent those centuries in a time capsule. Its streets are still laid out as they
were at the start; most of the residences are original, and they retain their
original appearance.

Today, two islands are central to the romance of Paris' river: the Île de la
Cité, with the spires of Notre-Dame and the Sainte-Chapelle, and the Île
Saint-Louis. But from Roman times to the early seventeenth century, today's
Île Saint-Louis was not one landmark island but two among a number of un-
prepossessing and uninhabited islets in the Seine. The larger of the two islets,
Île Notre-Dame, owed its name to the fact that it was under the cathedral's

*The 1609 Vassalieu map shows the site chosen for the creation
of a new island in the Seine and the two uninhabited islets
destined to become part of it.*

jurisdiction. The name of the other—Île aux Vaches, or Cow Island—was more evocative of the modest role the two specks had played in the life of the city until then. Small flocks of sheep sometimes grazed there; hay was stocked on them; they found occasional use as a dueling ground or for small-scale boat building. This 1609 map of Paris depicts the two islets as absolutely devoid of construction.

The islets were also isolated, with no connection between them or to the mainland. Thus no large-scale activity could have taken place on them; sheep to be grazed, for example, had to be ferried over by boat. Then along came Christophe Marie, engineer extraordinaire and among the developers who found his calling as a result of the Bourbon monarchs' expansive vision for Paris.

In March 1608, Marie caught Henri IV's attention with a bold move. He offered to build, at no cost to the crown, something the king had long wanted: a wooden bridge across the Seine strong enough to support new kinds of loads—from modern cannon to larger and heavier carriages. In exchange, Marie asked for the right to collect a toll from those who used the bridge. Marie's resulting Pont de Neuilly was such a success that he was named "general contractor for all bridges necessary in this kingdom."

In late 1609, Marie proposed yet another bridge, also for free, and this time in the material of the future: stone. The Place Royale was then still under construction; the bridge that Marie proposed was intended both to help connect the new square to the other bank of the Seine and to facilitate the flow of traffic through the city at large. His second bridge still stands and still bears the name of its developer: the Pont Marie.

This bridge became the springboard for one of Henri IV's most ambitious projects for Paris. The king bought those two undeveloped islets and gave them to Marie, to whom he assigned a far more ambitious undertaking. He was to create an unprecedented kind of island, a modern island that would be a model of urban planning and add a highly desirable neighborhood to the city's historic center.

The project was delayed for years, first of all by Henri IV's assassination in May 1610. (His carriage was stalled in traffic in one of Paris' notoriously narrow streets, giving his assassin a chance to get close enough to stab him.) Marie finally signed a contract to develop the island on April 19, 1614. Then in 1615, the cathedral chapter of Notre-Dame suddenly tried to assert its rights to the islets. Next, the municipality began long negotiations concerning the specifics of the island's construction. For years, it continued to send out teams of inspectors to consider questions such as the number and size of deep foundation piles and piers necessary, as well as their ideal placement. The effects of the construction on the Seine and commercial navigation were also weighed. To help finance what was becoming an ever more vast and complex undertaking, Marie took on two wealthy associates: François Le Regrattier and Lugles Poulletier.

Two maps, published only months after Marie signed the contract to create an island, testify to the excitement generated by the project among those who were recording the process of Paris' rebirth. The first, by Mathieu Mérian, portrays a provisional cityscape. The two islands are still separate and still barren brush; the projected bridges are sketched in, a sign of the transformation to come.

Jean Messager referred to his rendition of the future island as both "a map" and "a portrait." Rather than a portrait of a real place, however, Messager imagined the map of what he termed "*l'île passagere*," a provisional island. Messager's view could well have been a projection that the developers could have shown to prospective buyers. Messager laid out streets still a mere gleam in the developers' eyes, giving them his own names; he depicted embankments and bridges not yet built. Messager encouraged a vision of an ideal island to come: perfect boats sail around it; swimmers frolic in nearby waters.

But Messager's vision was not pure invention; anyone who looked back at his "portrait" a decade after he had completed it would have realized that he had surely had access to long-range plans for the development, for his depiction of the island about to be constructed is uncannily close to the island as it came to be.

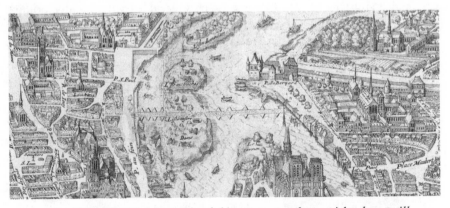

When Mathieu Mérian completed this 1614 map, the new island was still in the planning stages. Mérian used the rough outline of future bridges to represent the projected development.

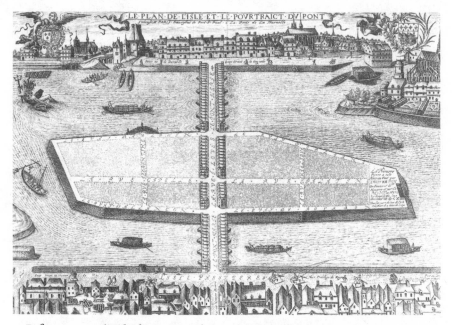

Before construction had even started, in 1614 Jean Messager imagined the map of what he called a "provisional island" as a placeholder for the real thing.

In order to bring that about, the two islets were joined together as part of a more impressive land mass, officially known for the first century of its existence as the Île Notre-Dame. The new assemblage was then given clean contours and shored up with stone embankments. Next, piles and piers were driven deep into the river to stabilize the now sizeable island. Finally, bridges were added to link it to the mainland, the Pont Marie to the Right Bank and the Pont de la Tournelle to the Left. And such a complicated urban works project naturally took time.

It was, for example, only in 1623 that work was undertaken to regularize the ragged, irregular ends of the two islets that are still visible in early maps. Only then did the island finally acquire the distinctive shape first depicted by Messager in 1614. The artificial island thus produced featured perfect points and a characteristic slant on each end—a design, Marie explained, that "facilitated both the flow of the river and the navigation of its current."

Once he had an island, Marie turned his attention to its infrastructure. At the center of a still medieval urban layout he introduced a tiny but perfect example of grid planning. This 1728 map of the island's definitive design shows how, in contrast to the largely random cityscape that surrounded it on all sides, the Île Notre-Dame's streets intersected each other at right angles. Marie also gave Paris a preview of the wider thoroughfares soon to become common elsewhere in the city: the rue des Deux Ponts (originally the rue Marie) and the rue Saint-Louis (first called the Grande Rue) were a handsome four *toises* or about twenty-five feet wide. (Prior to the seventeenth century, Paris had almost no streets more than fifteen feet wide.) In his landmark 1684 Paris guidebook Brice, still in wonder at the island's streets, said that they "seemed to have been traced with geometrical instruments, in absolutely precise lines right up to the river's banks."

After streets came amenities. In the original 1614 contract, Marie had promised to construct those he considered most essential: a public fountain, a bathhouse, and an athletic facility, a *jeu de paume* or court for a precursor to modern handball. In new documents drawn up in 1623, he also included shops for the merchants he hoped to attract at the start—a butcher, a fishmonger, a *rôtisseur* from whom residents could buy grilled meats, as well as *bateaux à*

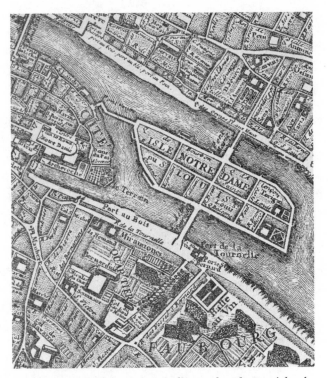

Abbé Delagrive's 1728 map indicates that the new island
was in the process of receiving its definitive name, the
Île Saint-Louis.

lessive, laundry boats that docked along the embankments so that residents could drop off their clothes to be washed.

Despite an innovative design and careful planning, there was no stampede of homeowners eager to live in those broad new streets. The earliest settlers were working-class Parisians, tradesmen and craftsmen. In 1618, master mason Charles Contesse and Jean Gilles, a tailor, acquired two of the first plots, both of them quite small. They were joined the following year by, among others, locksmith Étienne Boussingault and Claude Chevrereu, a roofer. Only in 1620 did a more elite clientele first show interest in the development. That year, Pierre de Vertron, an adviser to Louis XIII, started construction on a home on the island's principal thoroughfare.

But while the streets at the center were gradually filled, the largest and the most visible plots, those around the island's rim, remained empty; the wealthiest investors kept their distance from a development still very much a work in progress, one that lacked, most notably, a bridge to connect it to the mainland. And without major sales, the developers were running out of money.

On September 16, 1623, Henri IV's son decided that Marie and his associates could never complete the project by the deadline specified in their contract. Louis XIII therefore turned the islets over to Jean de La Grange, another close adviser. La Grange took on as his associates other members of Louis XIII's inner circle, all of them involved in the world of high finance, all of them far wealthier than the original developers. Among the new backers was Philippe de Coulanges, Place Royale resident, soon to become the grandfather of the Marquise de Sévigné.

The new consortium knew full well, however, that only one man had the expertise required to implement a project as ambitious as this. Therefore, after having forced Marie out, they soon brought him back on salary to carry out the work according to his plans.

It was thus under Marie's supervision that the bridge that bears his name, the Pont Marie, was at last completed in the early 1630s. And in August 1633, the investors finally had their first major sale, the biggest and the most prominently situated of the island's roughly 130 parcels of land. Soon after, the development was transformed into the third wonder of modern Paris with a rapidity that seemed magical to those who witnessed the process.

The individual who acquired the island's largest lot, Claude Le Ragois, was the client of their dreams. A member of a modest provincial family, he had quickly become a pillar of Paris' financial community, known as the Sieur de Bretonvilliers. (His contemporaries murmured darkly that "no one could

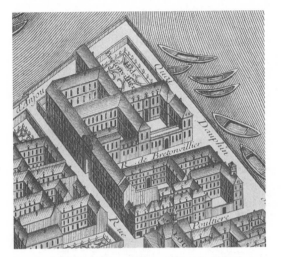

*The Bretez-Turgot map shows the Hôtel
Bretonvilliers, the grandest home on the island
(completed 1640), with its private walled garden.*

have made so much money so quickly by honest means.") He had a fortune,
and he wanted to build a grand status-symbol home.

Bretonvilliers used his vast wealth (estimated by his contemporaries at
many, many millions) to give the island its original architectural monument,
designed by the great Jean Androuet du Cerceau. It included rooms decorated
by the most renowned painter of the day, Simon Vouet, and a fabulous garden
situated right at one of the island's newly resculpted tips. Its construction,
which lasted from 1637 to 1640, inaugurated the brief period in the course of
which the Île Notre-Dame assumed its modern identity as a fabled spot, home
to many of the most legendary private residences in Paris. Within six years,
all the remaining lots were snapped up and magnificent residences very quickly
built.

During this same period, the monarchy had decided to increase France's
involvement in the Thirty Years' War in a dramatic fashion: the only way to
raise the sums necessary to do this expeditiously was to turn to the wealthiest
members of the Parisian financial community, who made short-term loans at
exorbitant rates. When the government paid the interest due, some of the richest men in Paris followed Bretonvilliers' example and funneled their profits
into real estate on the new island.

And thus Paris owes one of its most famously harmonious architectural en-
sembles to the fortunes of war.

This painting, the earliest attempt to record the Île Notre-Dame's rapid arrival on the cityscape, dates from the moment in the early 1640s when the island was freshly completed and was fully built up with 133 constructions, 120 of them private homes. Notre-Dame Cathedral stands to the left and, across the Seine and to the right, the Place Royale is visible in the background. The anonymous artist features the Île Notre-Dame, depicted as central to the beauty of Paris and its river. All the light in the canvas seems focused on the island.

At the same moment, playwrights were also attempting to record the shock of the new that Parisians felt at this marvelous apparition.

Two comedies from 1643 featured protagonists freshly returned to Paris after nearly a decade away. The hero of Pierre Corneille's *Le Menteur* (*The Liar*) celebrates his homecoming after years away at law school with a walk along the banks of the Seine: he is stunned to see that what was "only barren land" when he left has now become "une île enchantée," an enchanted island. Antoine d'Ouville imagined a gentleman from Southern France who had not visited its capital in a decade. He finds that "in just those ten years, a hundred palaces have been built on what was before a desert island; it is now a city unto itself."

The new "city unto itself" became known above all for the kind of radically innovative architecture possible only in an area developed from scratch.

This painting from the early 1640s is the first image of the new island. Notre-Dame Cathedral is visible to the left, the Bretonvilliers residence is at the island's right tip, and in the background are the new Église Saint-Paul, the Place Royale, and the Bastille.

Still in the 1640s, the average parcel of land in Paris had extremely narrow frontage and greater depth and was suitable only for the type of home that had been traditional in European cities for centuries. In established areas, there was no place for the development of more modern urban residences—with new kinds of rooms, improved traffic flow, and better lighting.

On the island the developers drew up more ample lots, just as they had laid out unusually broad streets. The plots were at least twice as wide as the standard Parisian parcel and in many cases were three times as wide. The island thus became the first neighborhood in Paris composed entirely of lots with the dimensions that could accommodate more generously proportioned homes and different kinds of floor plans. On the island, the city street took on a strikingly new look because of the development of a style of residential architecture that soon became known as characteristically French.

The island's architectural profile was also harmonious, since much of it was the product of one man's genius. Louis Le Vau, then at the beginning of one of the most brilliant careers in the history of French architecture, would design almost all the island's finest residences. Beginning in 1640, on the lot next to Bretonvilliers' land, Le Vau supervised the construction of a residence for Jean-Baptiste Lambert, Seigneur de Sucy et de Thorigny, still another trusted royal adviser. Lambert's legendary wealth was very new indeed, amassed in the late 1630s through war loans to the crown. Gédéon Tallemant des Réaux—known for sardonically dead-on biographies of his rich and famous contemporaries—said of Lambert that he "literally worked himself to death raking in money that he didn't live to enjoy." Lambert died in 1644, the very year that the construction of his grandiose new home was completed.

After his death, his brother Nicolas—he was even more exorbitantly wealthy; Tallemant des Réaux called *him* "the rich Lambert"—had the mansion's interiors decorated by the likes of the future chief artist in residence at Versailles, Charles Le Brun. Today, the Lambert residence still reigns over the Île Saint-Louis, perhaps the most spectacular private home in Paris. (It has remained the property of international finance leaders: until recently, Baron Guy de Rothschild, now the brother of the former emir of Qatar.)

Working for these clients with unlimited budgets, Le Vau developed on the island an architecture well ahead of its time, an interior architecture so innovative that its effects would be felt for centuries to come. He invented radically new layouts. He introduced rooms with novel shapes—oval rooms in particular. He replaced the multifunctional, generic rooms that dominated earlier homes with previously unheard-of spaces, each dedicated to one particular activity, including the earliest dining rooms and bathrooms in Paris—and perhaps in Europe. Elsewhere in Paris it was only decades later that architecture began to catch up with what was already happening on the new island in the 1640s.

The fact that most of the residences on the island's periphery were designed over a short period of time and by the same architect created a stylistically unified ensemble. That sense of harmony begins with the impression of whiteness highlighted by the artist who first depicted the island. It was on the Île Notre-Dame that the transformation of Paris from a capital in wood to a capital in stone and mortar truly began.

Prior to this moment, in Paris stone had been largely reserved for royal palaces such as the Louvre and the Conciergerie, and wood was the habitual building material for private homes. In the late sixteenth century, municipal authorities first attempted to ban wood construction as a fire hazard. Wood, however, remained dominant because it was the traditional building material and a far less expensive choice. At times, homeowners simply had their façades plastered over to cover up the wood underneath. The grand residence that the Duc de Sully built on the then broadest thoroughfare in Paris, the rue Saint-Antoine, in 1625–30 was a forerunner of things to come. However, like the small number of earlier residences built in stone (Hôtel de Sens, Hôtel de Carnavalet), Sully's grand home stood alone, an isolated example rather than part of an ensemble.

It was because of architects such as Le Vau and their fabulously wealthy clients that stone construction at last became both familiar and characteristically Parisian. The residences on the new island constituted the kind of architectural ensemble that no one could fail to notice. The vastly increased presence of white, bright stone in individual homes, as well as their more expansive and sophisticated designs, were among the most visible indications that Paris was leaving its medieval identity behind.

The use of stone entailed a revolution in building techniques. The island's all-white look was achieved through two very different types of stone construction. The first and far less expensive method was based on *moellon* or rubble masonry, using undressed or rough stones whose imperfections were then covered over with plaster or whitewash. The second, far more costly and found in all the grand residences at the water's edge, involved the use of *pierre de taille*, ashlar or dressed stone—that is, stone that has been cut and finished with square edges and smooth faces. *Pierre de taille* construction, still seen as characteristic of Parisian residential architecture, first became prominent because of the new island.

White stone construction transformed the face of Paris, and foreign visitors quickly took note of the city's dramatically different appearance. Already in 1644, immediately upon the island's completion, John Evelyn contrasted the architecture of Paris with that of London and concluded that "there is no comparison between the buildings and the materials; this being entirely of Stone and infinitely sumptuous." In 1664, a wealthy young Italian tourist, Sebastiano Locatelli, proclaimed the island a must-see spot because of "the stylistic harmony" of its architecture. On his 1698 visit, Martin Lister observed that at the beginning of the century, houses had been built in other materials, "but that is wholly left off now." Still at the turn of the eighteenth century, a noted English visitor, the widely traveled Lady Mary Wortley Montagu, believed that "Paris has the advantage of London in . . . the houses being all built of stone," and another wealthy Italian voyager, Nicolò Madrisio, marveled at "the whiteness" of Paris' cityscape.

The new island provided a lineup of spectacular homes, great architecture best appreciated from afar, that drew Parisians to the riverbanks to admire this "city unto itself," the Paris of modern architecture. And a pamphlet from 1649 described those who gathered by the riverside to watch the reflection of "those vagabond houses that roll like the waves, this new Paris that is a matchless and a priceless sight." For the first time, the possibility of viewing Paris reflected in the Seine could be promoted as a reason to visit the city.

And the island's wealthiest residents enjoyed a show all their own.

This early eighteenth-century map of Paris features at the far tip of the island its two largest homes, those of Bretonvilliers (on the right) and Lambert. The river is so deep at that particular point and the current flows upstream so rapidly that the maneuver of sinking piles proved especially tricky, which surely explains why, as an official report duly noted, the developers had still not completed the embankments on this end by 1636. Bretonvilliers thus paid dearly for his chosen location. In his guidebook, Brice added to the mansion's cachet by evaluating the cost of the infrastructure necessary to build on this particularly tricky site at eight hundred thousand *livres*, roughly the amount spent a few decades later for the construction of a huge and magnificent stone bridge across the Seine, the Pont Royal.

In exchange, however, Bretonvilliers got something beyond price. The richest man in the city had cornered the market on the form of urban spectacle to which the Pont Neuf had introduced Parisians: the magic of water views.

Beginning in the early seventeenth century, anyone who walked onto the Pont Neuf could have the pleasure of watching the river flow. Only someone in the last construction upstream, however, could enjoy a perfect, unobstructed panorama over the Seine. The island's two most famous homes therefore

The Bretez-Turgot map shows the island fully built-up with
133 constructions: the two largest, the mansions of Bretonvil-
liers and Lambert, completely fill one end.

included window-lined second-floor galleries that ran the buildings' full
length and functioned as screening rooms with controlled access to what was
widely considered "the best view in the world" and "a view that has to be seen
to be believed." A contemporary reported that Bretonvilliers' vista was so extraordinary that visitors tended to ignore all the treasures on display in his
home and "to pay attention only to the view."

Bretonvilliers' gallery was a majestic seventeen *toises*, or well over a hundred feet long, and featured six immense windows more than twelve feet high. It
culminated in the most private viewing box of all, a large balcony, modeled on
those on the Pont Neuf but with a far more sophisticated design. It was enclosed; it included a seventh huge window; and it jutted out like a ship's prow,
right over the spot where the Seine split into two branches. In June 1665, just
two days after Bernini arrived in Paris to design a new façade for the Louvre,
Colbert himself served as his tour guide to the sights most likely to impress
one of the most famous artists and architects in the world: the Sainte-Chapelle,

Notre-Dame, "and from there to the island"—the Île Notre-Dame, that is. They headed straight for Bretonvilliers' mansion, "to see its beautiful setting."

In 1874, Bretonvilliers' grand residence became a casualty of Haussmann's redesign: it was destroyed to make way for a bridge, which bears Sully's name, and a boulevard, named for Henri IV.

The Bretonvilliers and Lambert mansions offered the first clear proof that the modern city was a place where magnificence was no longer only, and often not even principally, the preserve of the king and great nobles. In the new Paris, the residences worthy of comparison to royal palaces were almost always built by a new breed of prince, the lords of finance. Bretonvilliers' and Lambert's residences were so grand, in fact, that they changed the French language.

Until the late seventeenth century, the French word for "palace," *palais*, designated exclusively "the king's home." In 1606, lexicographer Jean Nicot explained that in Italian and Spanish, the word could be used to refer to "any sumptuous home" but that "French doesn't allow this usage." By 1694, however, the definition in the original edition of the French Academy's dictionary begins in the traditional manner, "the royal residence," but then goes on to add "people now call magnificent homes palaces." Indeed, writers from Corneille to Brice had already compared those two grand homes on the island's tip to royal palaces.

All those who lived on the island's periphery wanted to share in this new urban dream. In the decade after the two palaces of finance were completed, wrought-iron balconies began to appear in front of the windows of many residences. Soon, the embankment that today is known as the Quai de Béthune and that in the seventeenth century was officially called the Quai Dauphin was referred to by Parisians as the Quai des Balcons, the Balcony Quay or Balcony Embankment. (The map on page 74 shows the name change taking place.)

"Balcony Quay" was not the only name that became attached to the Île Notre-Dame by popular demand. There was also the matter of the name of the island itself. Paris historian Sauval remarked that "it is often referred to simply as '*the* Island,'" as though, he added, "it were the only island in the world."

The municipality made the Île Notre-Dame an independent administrative unit in 1637, but despite this official recognition, that name, "Île Notre-Dame," never caught on. It appeared on maps, yet Parisians continued to speak simply of "the island" for roughly the first century of its existence.

In 1713, in legal documents discussing the possible sale of Bretonvilliers' mansion, the island was still referred to as the "Île Notre-Dame." But in the decade that followed it got a new name. In September 1728, the comedy *L'École des bourgeois* was staged for the king: in it, a character spoke of the houses on the "Île Saint-Louis." And the 1728 map drawn up by Abbé Jean Delagrive (page 67) confirmed that the name shift was becoming official: the island is identified as "Île Notre-Dame, or Saint-Louis."

The new name stuck. Soon, when Parisians wanted to evoke the marvel that had suddenly appeared in their river, they spoke no longer of "the island," but, as we still do, of the "Île Saint-Louis."

Today, countless tourist guidebooks and websites repeat that Paris is the most beautiful city in the world, in large part because of the structured handsomeness and uniformity of its residential buildings. Credit for the city's architectural distinction is always given to Baron Haussmann. And yet, two hundred and fifty years before Haussmann decreed the demolition of the grandest of its mansions, an artificial island in the Seine had convinced the greatest architects and architectural authorities of the day—from Bernini to Eveyln—that it held the key to the future of Parisian architecture and of notable urban architecture in general. Residential architecture uniform in design and gleaming in what was already seen as Paris' characteristic white stone, buildings laid out on generous parcels of land and facing wider and straighter streets—before the end of the seventeenth century, ideas first realized on the Île Notre-Dame in the 1640s would spread widely through Paris.

By 1645, three visionary urban works—the Pont Neuf, the Place Royale, and the Île Notre-Dame—had become the foundation for Paris' new image, as a city remarkable not only for its size but for its exciting and innovative constructions. The city at large, however, was as yet untouched by large-scale transformation. And this process was suspended for nearly a decade when civil war broke out in 1649.

CHAPTER FOUR

City of Revolution: The Fronde

W HEN LOUIS XIV'S reign began in 1643, the four-year-old future Sun King inherited from the first two Bourbon monarchs a capital city that had been transformed in many ways during nearly a half-century of peace. Paris' first modern bridge and first modern square were changing the way Parisians related to urban space; its gleaming, enchanted island was almost finished.

Then, in 1648, urban development came to an abrupt halt. The streets of Paris had often been the scene of bloodshed before, most recently during the sixteenth-century Wars of Religion. In the mid-seventeenth century, however, Paris' reinvention was temporarily blindsided by a different kind of war, a revolutionary struggle unprecedented in French history, fought not on religious grounds but over such economic and political issues as where the burden of higher taxes should fall.

By the time the conflict ended some five years later, the winds of change had blown through Paris, and Parisians had witnessed a preview of the uprisings of the future. High-ranking aristocrats and government officials had been insulted, dragged from their carriages, shot at, and stoned by simple merchants and workers. Much of the city had become a war zone—with shuttered shops, streets blocked off behind barricades, competing checkpoints, militia parading in its public squares, and frequent skirmishes among opposing forces. There was debate about whether to "demolish the Bastille." Parisians quickly became "hardened to the sight of the dead and wounded lying in the streets," as Louis XIV's first cousin the Duchesse de Montpensier later wrote.

And yet the civil war ultimately proved in numerous ways to be a constructive

rather than a destructive force. It made Paris still more public. In order to follow the latest developments, to strategize and learn of casualties, Parisians,
both men and women and from all walks of life, paced the Pont Neuf more
relentlessly than ever before. Aristocrats walked the city's streets on a daily
basis and at all times of day. They even began to eat and drink in public for the
first time, at the original political café, chez Renard in the Tuileries gardens,
where those who favored the insurrection met to exchange news of the war. A
strong new Parisian identity—identities really, since members of different
camps experienced the city at war differently—were thus forged among those
who remained in the French capital during those years. All those identities
were closely bound up with the city of Paris itself.

At key moments during the uprising, a critical mass of the city's inhabitants
shared a political cause, and the populace, the people of Paris, thus came to be
seen as a political force to be reckoned with. When a great aristocrat who opposed the monarchy, the Duchesse de Longueville, gave birth to a son in
January 1649, she named him Paris. One of her contemporaries reported that
"people are saying that the entire city will serve as his godparents." The war
also created a new respect for the might that came with the capital's growing
size. As a lady-in-waiting to the queen put it: "Since Paris is more like a world
unto itself than a mere city, an uprising in Paris quickly turns into an uncon-
trollable deluge." The city thus began to be viewed as a natural breeding
ground for political insurrection.

Events unfolded with a rapidity that even those a stone's throw from where
they were happening had trouble grasping. People found it hard to know what
the latest problem area was, where the center of events was located. Parisians
were constantly on the move, dashing through the streets, charging over the
bridges, and experiencing the city at a heightened pace, in newly intense ways.

This intense need to keep informed rapidly and at all times created a new
association: between a modern urban center and breaking news. The civil war
was not the first armed conflict since the introduction of media ranging from
newspapers to mass-produced images. It was, however, the first French war
during which both camps were media-savvy and actively exploited every
means at their disposal in order to create true propaganda machines. Never
before in France had so much been printed so quickly. Images, for example,
were no longer used after the fact to keep the memory of war's horrors alive,
as had largely been the case in the sixteenth century, but were deployed while
the iron was hot, to help shape public opinion.

Printers put out the news faster than ever before, and they found more readers than ever before for all they printed. Both the desire for instantaneous

news coverage and the media machines put into place to satisfy it put Paris on an accelerated timetable.

Contemporary readers quickly realized the significance of this media explosion and thus began to preserve the material distributed in the streets in collections, many of which still survive intact. (The pope was a collector, as was the much reviled chief adviser to the court, Cardinal Mazarin.) In addition, Parisians from all walks of life and representing every point on the political spectrum—from a great princess who fought against her cousin the king to a powerful magistrate to a Parisian about whom little is known other than that he remained in the city throughout the war and gathered news obsessively—composed detailed accounts of the conflict's events and their effect on the city and its inhabitants. No prior armed conflict left behind anything like the mass of printed material that survives from this insurrection. Four times more political pamphlets were published during the civil war years than during the five bloodiest years of the Wars of Religion (1589–93).

Once unrest had begun in Paris, it spread to the French provinces. The French insurrection also had international implications. It began just as the Second English Civil War was unfolding. During those years when King Charles I was a prisoner of the diverse factions struggling for political dominance, the queen of England—Henriette-Marie, the French-born daughter of Henri IV and Marie de Médicis—took refuge in Paris. It was there that she learned of her husband's arrest in December 1648, there that word of his execution on January 30, 1649, finally reached her on February 19. And the simultaneity of these two civil wars was not lost on contemporary observers. As that same lady-in-waiting remarked: "All kings seem to be under a bad star." Many Europeans were afraid that the revolutionary spirit could prove contagious, that an age of revolution might begin.

At its most critical junctures, however, the war was an inherently Parisian phenomenon, both made possible and shaped in essential ways by the size and the character of the new kind of city Paris was then becoming. Every memoir and the overwhelming majority of the propaganda material is literally mapped out on the city of Paris. Their authors rarely mention events without specifying the exact spot where they took place. They rarely talk about going out in the city without describing the specific route they took. They were thus helping both to expand awareness of the geography of Paris and to create an image of the city as a nucleus for political activity.

At no time was the civil war more inherently Parisian than during its opening year, the time when Parisian public opinion was most united, the moment when Paris was most clearly the uprising's main character.

It all began, as major modern political conflicts often have, with a question of taxes. In 1648, the devastating Thirty Years' War was coming to an end, and it had left France nearly bankrupt. When the crown decided to raise taxes, there were protests from all sides. Recent harvests had been bad and famine was widespread. The Parisian Parlement was up in arms because of the suffering of the French people—and also because the crown was attempting to increase a hereditary tax levied against its members. The national mood continued to darken: on July 30, when the queen regent Anne of Austria went to Parlement to make a speech granting some concessions on taxes, a member of her entourage noticed that, as the procession moved through the streets, "people did not cry out 'long live the king' as they usually did."

On August 20, 1648, the Prince de Condé led the French army to victory against the Spanish in the battle of Lens, the last major action of the Thirty Years' War. A Te Deum mass to celebrate this triumph was held in Paris on August 26, with the nine-year-old Louis XIV in attendance. As usual, troops lined the procession route from the Louvre to Notre-Dame Cathedral. Once the king was safely back in the palace, however, three battalions remained on or near the Pont Neuf in preparation for the arrest of one of Parlement's most respected members, Pierre Broussel, an individual particularly beloved by the people of Paris. The arrest had been planned by the queen regent as a public "humiliation" for the Parlement.

Broussel's arrest was the spark that set off the powder keg that Paris had become. Literally overnight, the city was transformed: as one observer put it, "the home of all earthly delights" suddenly turned into an armed camp. Parisians used a combination of chains and an estimated thirteen hundred barricades made up of carts, barrels, and other large containers filled with everything from dirt and rubble to manure to close off the city center. Those barricades were erected in haste, but an important magistrate and adviser to the Parlement, Olivier Le Fèvre d'Ormesson, pronounced them "more solid than those built by professional soldiers."

This engraving, among the earliest surviving images of the war, depicts the Saint-Antoine gate shut off behind barricades. It's a rather crude image, hastily produced in an effort to get the message out quickly that, behind those barricades, Paris was serene and well protected, as indeed it probably was. An estimated 50,000 to 100,000 Parisians (in a city with a population of between 450,000 and 500,000) had taken up arms to defend their city against the royal forces.

Whether or not the conflict that began that August day was a true revolution—and the question is still debated by historians—it had revolu-

Frondeur propaganda portrayed the opposition forces as well organized and able to defend themselves against royal soldiers. This 1648 image shows the barricades they erected to control the Saint-Antoine gate.

tionary consequences. The demonstration of force from the tens of thousands of armed Parisians soon obliged Anne of Austria to order Broussel's release. When he returned to Paris, a huge crowd led him to celebrate in the traditional royal manner, with a mass at Notre-Dame. Only then did the chains come down and shops reopen.

In the months that followed, Parisians remained jumpy. Rumors flew about the revenge the queen regent would seek, and those chains and barricades went up again on several occasions. All through this initial period, however, Parisians continued to be of one mind and to speak with one voice—so much so that when contemporaries described the forces united in opposition to the crown, they said simply "the city" or "Paris." Le Fèvre d'Ormesson "marveled" at how "in their uprising the city's inhabitants were able to maintain order at all times," at how "with neither a preelected leader or an administrative counsel, all over Paris, everyone shared the same goal." Indeed, the only problems of "organization and order" reported came from the Île Saint-Louis: the newest neighborhood on the map had thus not yet fully coalesced.

As far as change was concerned, the bottom line was always clear: Cardinal Mazarin, the king's Italian-born chief minister who was widely accused of financial corruption, had to go. "The entire city," Parisian doctor Guy Patin remarked, "is solidly united in opposition to Mazarin." The Duchesse de

Montpensier claimed that she "never heard anyone admit to being against the king." In the streets, however, she reported cries of: "Long live the king!—but no more Mazarin!"

This solidarity transformed the political landscape and created true oppositional politics, a nascent form of public opinion. It is in this context that Fronde, the name given the insurrection by its leaders, makes sense: the word *fronde* referred to a catapult children used to sling stones. Those opposed to the crown's policies quickly invented a verb to describe their activities: *fronder*, to fight against, to defend an opposing opinion. They spoke of *un vent de Fronde*, "the winds of change," and described themselves as *frondeurs*, individuals fighting for change.

In the early hours of January 6, 1649—ironically, this was the Epiphany, the day of the kings or the Magi—the queen regent finally took that long expected revenge. Under cover of darkness, Anne of Austria spirited her son out of Paris and set up court at a royal château at Saint-Germain-en-Laye. Even a member of her entourage, Françoise de Motteville, clearly disapproved of using Parisians' "fear of losing the king" to punish them.

Then, with the king safely out of the city, the queen regent showed just how far she was prepared to go: she cut Paris off from the world. What soon became known as either "the siege of Paris" or "the blockade" began on January 9. The queen regent ordered nearby villages to stop sending provisions, bread in particular, into the city.

Her actions only intensified Parisian solidarity. Thirty-six of the greatest princes and aristocrats signed a pact with the Parlement against Mazarin. (A palace insider said that they were "disgusted" by the attempt to "murder" the people of Paris.) They gathered troops to defend the city and displayed their militia in public places, most prominently in the Place Royale. One leader, the Duc de Noirmoutier, took his militia on a bold mission: they battled the enemy fiercely for a day—and returned in triumph with five hundred carts of flour. On January 12, the Bastille was attacked; when its governor surrendered, the Parlement named Broussel to replace him. Thus, as one observer pointed out, barely four and a half months after "the city" took up arms to keep Broussel from being imprisoned there, he was running the Bastille.

Such heady moments, however, were soon in short supply in the city under siege. A minor government official who lived through the blockade kept careful track of the two factors that undoubtedly contributed most to the general suffering: the scarcity of staples and the harsh weather that winter. Thus, we know that, in January, there were terrible snows. When they melted, the Seine was at its highest level since 1576, and people navigated the streets of the

Marais by boat. By January 23, there was almost no bread for sale, and the price of what little was available had tripled. By February, the price of meat was sky high—but fish was more expensive still, so the Archbishop of Paris gave permission to eat meat during Lent. The crown was offering thirty *sols* (then the price of a pound of meat and a pound of bread) per day to anyone willing to infiltrate the crowds and warn Parisians "that the Parlement was betraying them."

Even aristocrats knew hardship. In one of her earliest surviving letters, from March 1649, the Marquise de Sévigné wondered whether all Parisians "would soon starve to death." When the queen regent and her son had slipped out of Paris, among those left behind was her lady-in-waiting, Motteville, a penniless widow whose circumstances were decidedly straitened when the court was away. Her memoirs reveal the special kind of hell Paris became for those close to the royal family. Mobs threatened to "pillage" their homes; they "didn't dare show their faces in public without fearing for their lives." More affluent nobles hired armed guards, a protection Motteville could not afford. Thus, several days after the royal family had fled the city, in the company of her sister, she tried to rejoin the court. Her account of their attempt to reach the nearest way out of the city, the Saint-Honoré gate, shows how quickly and completely one of Paris' best neighborhoods had become alien territory for its most privileged residents.

The sisters were on the elegant rue Saint-Honoré near the Louvre when a crowd noticed them. They rushed toward some royal soldiers for protection, but the soldiers turned away; royal troops had begun defecting to the *frondeur* camp.

From that moment on, their escape attempt turned into a mad dash down the rue Saint-Honoré, past some of the most expensive real estate in the city. They ran to the nearby residence of the Duc de Vendôme, an aristocrat loyal to the queen regent, but armed guards slammed the door in their faces. Just then, the sisters realized that the mob "was tearing up all the street's paving stones in order to stone us to death." They ran ever faster to the Saint Roch church, where the mob followed them in. Even though mass was under way, Motteville was attacked by a woman who screamed that she "should be stoned and torn to pieces." The priest managed to save them and contacted other nobles in hiding, who helped them reach the Louvre, where the exiled Queen of England gave them shelter. Refugees living with a refugee, they set about stockpiling provisions.

When the siege began, the queen regent's advisers had assured her that "in eight to ten days at the most, they would manage to starve Paris into submission." The collective determination of its inhabitants was so fierce, however, that the city managed to hold out for three months. On March 30, a delegation of 186 nobles and members of Parlement announced that Anne of Austria had agreed to all their terms but the banishment of Mazarin, her most trusted adviser. The royal family finally returned to Paris the following month. The city to which they returned, however, was a far cry from the one they had left.

When commentators speak of twenty-first-century revolutionary movements, one word is constantly stressed: connectivity. During the siege of 1649, huge numbers of Parisians were able to think and act as one because of the original revolutionary connectivity. Information spread through the city quickly in a variety of formats, some of which had never been used before, and none of which had ever been used to the same extent and with the same rapidity.

Traditional ways of getting a message across still functioned: individuals got up on soapboxes—the one shown here looks suspiciously like the base for one of those recently erected equestrian statues of the Bourbon monarchs—and harangued a crowd. But this engraving from 1649 was an image designed to replace a traditional orator: a speaker could reach only one group at a time, whereas images could be seen in many places at once. When this image circulated during the siege, it bore a caption: "A *frondeur* encourages Parisians to revolt against Cardinal Mazarin's tyranny." The orator is armed and ready to

Using the royal palace the Louvre as a backdrop, this image shows a frondeur
addressing a socially diverse crowd of men and women.

LA MARCHE DE LOVIS XIIII, ROY DE FRANCE ET DE NAVARRE

Royalist propaganda depicted Paris as a city untouched by the violence of war. The young Louis XIV is shown returning home to the Louvre after the siege, riding over flawless cobblestones on the Pont Neuf.

defend his city: he's gesturing toward the Louvre, directly across the river. And a diverse crowd has gathered to hear him: lots of bourgeois, magistrates with their characteristic headgear, aristocrats such as the man in front wearing a plumed hat and one of those pricey cloaks. In the background, several women can be seen coming to join the throng.

Royalists turned out their own brand of visual propaganda. One engraving portrays a scene that allegedly took place "the minute the king returned to Paris at the end of the siege." The Seine is crowded with small craft, and happy boatmen are playing games for the entertainment of the boy king, who watches from the embankment. In this view of the young king's return, he is crossing the Pont Neuf, surrounded by loyal troops and a pristine capital, Paris at its best—the procession is passing over the cobblestoned surface of the city's finest bridge, the Pont Neuf, headed toward its most famous palace, the Louvre.

Engravings from both camps were on sale all over the city, and they were also on view in key spots for those who couldn't afford to buy them. A special column, literally a signpost, was set up on one end of the Pont Neuf. A leading

*During the siege of Paris, opposition forces posted placards like this
one all over the city—to give news and to stir up public opinion.*

frondeur, the future Cardinal de Retz, stressed how "intensely pity could be
awakened" by such well-placed images.

Printed placards put up in the most frequented spots could, in the words of
one Parisian, "blanket the city" overnight: one denouncing "the scoundrel
Mazarin" was posted brazenly at the entrance to Notre-Dame Cathedral. This
placard features a ship designed to remind Parisians of the one in the coat of

arms of the city of Paris. The text explains that the vessel, piloted by members of Parlement and great nobles, represents the French capital, which has "taken up arms" to save the kingdom of France. The placard appeared in the city's streets on January 8, 1649, two days after Anne of Austria had slipped out of Paris with the young king, and the day before the siege was to begin. It seems intended to encourage the city's residents to join these leaders in the effort to keep their city safe. It even sends a message that their actions will find favor with their ruler; the boy king hovers in the sky over the ship of the city, under the protection of a winged figure identified as "the guiding spirit of France."

Others placards were distributed door-to-door, hundreds of copies at a time, in the dead of night. Like images, they quickly reached a broad audience—even the partially or fully illiterate. Numerous accounts describe scenes of public reading, groups gathered around a poster, first reading its message aloud and then debating the opinions it expressed. In this vignette from a Pont Neuf painting, a man stands on the sidewalk reading to twenty or so intent listeners—men and women both.

Print was not only posted, it was also tossed directly into the streets. Small sheets of paper, called *billets* or "tickets" (they were about three to four inches by five) were printed and then strewn about, once again under cover of darkness, all over the city streets. They could thus be picked up and discreetly tucked away to be read later in private. *Billets* could stir up Parisians by warning them that some dire event (an arrest, an invasion) was imminent. They were also used, just like today's social media, to drum up a crowd quickly.

Print was even in the air of revolutionary Paris because of a new idea for

Pont Neuf paintings often depict individuals reading aloud. During the Fronde, such group readings helped the illiterate keep abreast of political news.

making political news entertaining that came into its own during the civil war: vaudevilles.

The word is a contraction that means roughly "what goes around the city," and that, these catchy tunes certainly did. There were vaudevilles prior to the civil war, but the political song had never before been an active genre. It was during the war that the vaudeville was first clearly defined as a popular song, easy to remember, that dealt with current events and was either satirical or seditious. It was during the war that Parisians rich and poor began a love affair with vaudevilles, singing or humming them in the streets. And from the start vaudevilles were identified in people's minds with the New Bridge: one of the earliest dictionary entries described them as "songs that are sung on the Pont Neuf."

The formula was a simple one: songwriters lifted the tune of a recent hit and wrote new lyrics that recounted current political events. Writers worked so quickly that they turned current events into song and had music and lyrics for sale within two days. Since the melody was already familiar, the tunes were easy to remember. And the contrast inherent in, say, a love song recast as a tirade against government corruption proved irresistible. One popular ballade, "Réveillez-vous, belle endormie" ("Wake up, beautiful dreamer"), resurfaced with new lyrics, a speech made to Parlement by a popular *frondeur*, the Duc de Beaufort: "Listen, people of France . . ." Individuals known as *coureurs* and *coureuses* ("runners," males and female) roamed the streets and were paid to sing the latest tunes, such as a song composed by "six female fishmongers" while the barricades were going up. So many vaudevilles were published during the siege alone that collections of the greatest hits began to be compiled.

And no print format did more to keep Parisians informed and to create a sense of community than the periodical press, what we now call simply *the* press: newspapers. In Paris under siege, a city covered with news, the French press became more of a mass medium than ever before.

Both in manuscript and in print, newspapers began appearing all over Europe during the first half of the seventeenth century. The news they published, however, was in most cases largely foreign: governments agreed to their distribution only if publishers limited their coverage of potentially inflammatory local news. In France, prior to the Fronde, Mazarin loyalist Théophraste Renaudot enjoyed a monopoly for his periodical, *La Gazette*, a weekly that presented the official version of current events. Thus, for instance, *La Gazette* dismissed the violence that exploded in Paris in the days after Broussel's arrest in a single paragraph, in which Broussel's name does not even appear: "The unrest had hardly begun when it settled down . . . It seemed to have taken place solely to create an occasion to have 'Long live the king' ring out for hours."

Then came the siege, and those who had censored the press left the city more or less to its own devices. Parlement repeatedly issued decrees warning printers that they had to ask permission to publish, but in such hectic times, formal procedure all but ceased to exist. A press more free than ever before sprang up almost as quickly as those barricades. Its focus was the here and now, delivered the sooner the better.

These newsmen chose a format slim enough to slip into a pocket—eight to about twenty-four pages, roughly six inches wide by eight and a half to nine inches long—and designed to be produced cheaply and quickly, even overnight. There was no binding; one quick stitch or a bit of glue held the pages together. Printers were probably sometimes setting the beginning while the end was still being written.

This new way of operating soon attracted many into the news business.

When the siege began, Renaudot followed the court to Saint-Germain-en-Laye and used a printing press Mazarin had set up there to produce royalist propaganda. Since *frondeurs* had their own border controls, however, very little of it reached Paris—although one noble was caught distributing anti-Parlement sheets in the dead of night on February 11. (They had been smuggled into Paris hidden inside sacks of flour.) Renaudot's sons, Isaac and Eusèbe, remained in the city and began to publish a pro-Parlement weekly, *Le Courrier français* ("The French Courier"), the first French periodical with a title featuring the ideas of running and speed. Henceforth, it suggested, the news would be breaking news.

The inaugural issue, devoted to the week of January 5 to 14, 1649, presented a minute-by-minute account of the royal family's flight from Paris; subsequent issues included such details of how the city was surviving the siege as the municipality's decision to order bakers to make one-, two-, and three-pound loaves to be distributed to the poor.

During the civil war years, more than thirty new periodicals began publication. Even if most did not last long, this was an information revolution. Not only did Parisians have for the first time a press centered on what was going on around them, but they could also compare varying points of view.

A second type of publication began with the civil war: political pamphlets that adopted the same convenient format as contemporary newspapers. Known as *mazarinades*, satires of Cardinal Mazarin, the vast majority promoted *frondeur* positions. In a city one Parisian described as "starving for news," the appetite for these pamphlets seems to have been insatiable. A thousand peddlers roamed the streets like modern newsboys, crying out the titles for sale that day: "Get your *France Is Badly Governed*; get your *Mazarin Arrested*."

It's said that at least six thousand of these pamplets were published during the war years, and that figure may well be quite low. A pamphlet printed at the siege's end claimed that thirty-five hundred had appeared during early 1649 alone. It's estimated that print runs ran to five thousand copies—and this at a period when five hundred to seven hundred fifty copies was considered a good print run. Popular pamphlets even went through multiple printings. One pamphlet, "Printers offer thanks to Cardinal Mazarin," published in the midst of the siege on March 4, 1649, explained that, unlike other Parisians in those hard times, printers had nothing to complain about: hatred for the minister was so fierce that "half the city is busy printing and selling pamphlets, while the other half is busy writing them. The presses never stop functioning, and printers now have the best job in Paris and are finally making the kind of money they deserve."

Some *mazarinades* resemble newspapers in that they recount a specific event. Some are mini political treatises that address such questions as why the people of France had a legal right to wage the war. Others are outpourings of moral outrage—in particular, over the misery of starving Parisians. All try to be absolutely to the minute; some even go newspapers one better and are dated with the precise time of day at which their typesetting was completed—"10 and ¾ in the morning." The best *mazarinades* are great reads, political commentary and spin combined. And they are all totally, resolutely in the here and now.

These pamphlets were another means of writing the city and also of creating a heightened consciousness of Paris' role in the conflict. In a significant number of *mazarinades*, Paris is the central character: coverage of a political uprising had never before been obsessively focused on the city in which it was unfolding.

In some pamphlets, the monuments of modern Paris come to life and get the chance to speak their minds concerning the state of their city. The statue of Henri IV on the Pont Neuf discusses his formerly wondrous capital with other monuments, for example with "his son"—that is, the statue of Louis XIII in the Place Royale. And in the dialogue whose title page is shown here Henri IV's statue commiserates with the Samaritaine, the tower at the end of the Pont Neuf, about the "miserable times" they are witnessing. The tower claims that its famous clock, normally so reliable, has "completely broken down," so that "time is out of joint." The Bronze King admits that he relies on the daily installment of *Le Courrier français* for a sense of "the present time."

In others, the city itself is given a voice and becomes a character in the unfolding drama of the civil war. In a *mazarinade* dated January 8, 1649, the "good

In this civil war pamphlet, the statue of Henri IV comes to life to lament the "sad times" that his capital is witnessing.

Lady, the city of Paris," takes "the wise Lord, the Parlement of Paris," to be her husband, and they vow to bring the state's finances under control. In another published near the siege's end, Paris explains that "all through the war, I was not Paris but hell." In these pamphlets, the city talked as never before.

During the war years, the emerging wonder of the modern world was indeed rapidly transformed into an urban nightmare. There are no precise figures on the siege's death toll, but by mid-May 1652, a moment when food was even more expensive than during the blocade, one newspaper claimed that one hundred thousand people, or more than one in five Parisians, were wandering the streets begging for food, "half-dead from hunger." Three months later, a pamphlet warned that "the cemeteries are too small to hold all the bodies, and wolves are starting to show up in Paris." Religious orders were overwhelmed by the magnitude of the crisis. Letters addressed by Parisian nuns and priests to chapters in the provinces tell of "thousands and thousands" starving at a time when municipal authorities could offer but "*le pain des pauvres*," "paupers' bread." A starving Parisian received a ration only every two to three days, and the piece was so tiny that one priest enclosed a sample in his letter to prove how dire the situation had become.

As the Fronde was ending, only three days after Louis XIV returned to Paris on October 21, 1652, a delegation of Parisians wrote their young king with a formal "request" for his help. They alleged that fifty thousand Parisians, or between nine and ten percent of the city's population, had died during the war's final six months alone.

In May 1652, one journalist wrote, "the kingdom is going up in flames, and it seems that this country is done for." Chains and barricades once again closed off streets: this time, however, merchants were no longer trying to bring about political change but to protect themselves from marauding bands. The unity of purpose that had joined Parisians across social lines was no more. July 4 witnessed the event later seen as the beginning of the end: a mob attacked and set fire to the Hôtel de Ville or City Hall, where a meeting to negotiate a new provisional government was under way. Important leaders of the Fronde and the Parlement were among the casualties; their militia killed many in the mob. Rumors immediately began to fly that one faction or another had turned average Parisians against the insurrection's original leaders.

After what became known as "the massacre at the Hôtel de Ville," more and more Parisians rejected the revolt and begged the king to return. It was then the custom to light a lantern in front windows on festive days. Upon the king's arrival on October 21, what Parisians dubbed "royal lanterns" hung in windows all over town.

When he again took up residence in Paris, Louis XIV was still only fourteen. The city to which he returned was heavily scarred by the war years but by no means down and out.

In 1652, when the Fronde was near its end, John Evelyn—English architecture expert, diarist, and husband of the daughter of the English ambassador in Paris—published *The State of France*, an unusual combination of travel account, tourist guide, and booster literature. Evelyn does not avoid the subject of the civil war. Instead, he stresses his belief that, as far as Paris is concerned, the setback will be only temporary. For Evelyn still "no city in the world equals [Paris]." He concluded his account of the French capital in 1652 by predicting that with but "a little time and Peace . . . [the city] must, without doubt, in a short time outgrow [its present size] and far exceed it." He also foretold many "incomparably fair" new buildings and streets to come.

Evelyn's book thus both confirms the reputation that Paris had begun to acquire before the war and suggests that the city's image had not been irrevocably tarnished by the conflict. Because of the news machine it had created, the war had in fact often served as an advertisement for Paris. The extraordinary outpouring of political commentary was avidly followed all over the continent. The Fronde publications gave war news, but they were also propaganda, reminding Parisians of the great city for which they were fighting and praising the city's delights. No image portrayed the events of the uprising without showing off the new public works of Paris as well.

A second publication that appeared just as the war was ending sounded a similarly optimistic note for the city. Its author, identified only as "Sir Berthod," was clearly a Parisian through and through. He reminded his fellow Parisians of the vibrancy of daily life in the city as they had known it, from its outdoor markets to the clothing for sale—including a wide assortment of stolen cloaks. Unlike the periodicals and pamphlets Parisians had been reading for the past four years, Berthod's work said nothing about the subject of war and the city. In fact, the Fronde is evoked precisely once in Berthod's pages: a used-clothing dealer offers for sale a garment left behind on one of its battlefields; to guarantee its authenticity, he points to "the bullet holes" in the middle. Berthod's message is clear: even before it was completely over, the Fronde was already just a souvenir.

Indeed, at the end of the siege of Paris, printers began to publish collections of the best-selling *maʒarinades*. Political pamphlets originally written to keep Parisians informed and to win them over to various causes began a second life, as a reminder of events past.

Louis XIV worked expeditiously to make the uprising seem old news. He banned from court the nobles who had taken a stand against his authority and from then on, he preferred never to evoke the civil war. The future Sun King found more subtle ways of proving that the past was not dead.

In the summer of 1660, Louis XIV was married to the Infanta of Spain; the wedding took place on the border shared by their two countries. When he returned with his bride to Paris, an elaborate entrance ceremony was staged. The event was widely publicized; it was even presented as the cover image of the official almanac for 1661, something that guaranteed that Parisians would not soon forget the public rite.

The king chose as the day on which Parisians would celebrate his marriage August 26, the very date on which, in 1648, another processional through the streets had led to the mass at Notre-Dame after which Broussel was arrested. As Guy Patin—well-known Parisian medical expert who corresponded with the greatest European men of science—wrote: "The members of Parlement will surely realize that, in their case, the ceremony is intended to be an act of expiation and punishment rather than a glorious cortege."

The Fronde may have been officially forgotten, but lessons learned during the civil war helped continue to transform Paris' image. The techniques developed to get out the war news—from posters to *billets*—continued to be used, above all in advertising. In March 1657, for example, more than twenty thousand

The almanac for 1661 featured this image of the royal court's triumphant return to Paris at the end of the Fronde.

billets were distributed to announce a bargain price on oysters; and similar campaigns later promoted the products of Paris' burgeoning luxury goods industry. The civil war had alerted Parisians to the advantages of connectivity: as a result, their city soon became known as a capital of advertising, a center of change that quickly and expertly heralded its innovations.

Paris had also begun to acquire a reputation as an intellectually defiant city, a cradle for revolutionary thinking and a capital where systems that challenged received ideas and established values readily developed. Beginning at the turn of the eighteenth century, the newly modernized city became the capital of perhaps the most provocative intellectual movement of modern times, the Enlightenment, a role it continued to play all during that century.

By 1772, when historian and journalist Jean-Baptiste Mailly devoted five volumes to the political history of the Fronde, he presented the Fronde as the precursor to the "troubled time" France was living in those years prior to the Revolution of 1789 and as "the war that almost launched the age of the greatest revolutions of all, those that transform the nature of government." Mailly's words must soon have seemed uncannily prescient during what is called the

Age of Revolution, the decades between 1789 and 1848 that witnessed the end of monarchies and long-established traditions in many nations. During those decades, Paris was the epicenter for the revolutions and revolutionary ideas that reshaped the European world, and the city itself was once again torn apart in the course of three successive revolutions.

The third of those revolutions, in 1848, overthrew Louis Philippe, the last king to rule France. Less than a decade later, the second planned redesign of Paris, that of Baron Haussmann, began. Key ideas guiding Haussmann's work had originated in the immediate aftermath of the first modern political insurrection Paris had known, the Fronde.

It is sometimes said that Louis XIV never forgot the way Parisians had opposed his monarchy and that, for this reason, he lavished all his attention on a new palace at Versailles, neglecting his rebellious capital city. But this theory overlooks an essential period in the history of Paris, the twelve to fifteen years that began in 1660. At that moment, working with an extraordinary team of ministers and civil servants, the Sun King initiated many bold projects— among them, projects that led to what have been ever since two of Paris' characteristic features, boulevards and bright lights. Less than a decade after the Fronde's end, the still young monarch began to modernize his capital—and no longer one monument at a time, as the first two Bourbon kings had done. He developed instead what was the termed "the grand design," a comprehensive plan for the city at large.

As a result, John Evelyn's 1652 prediction quickly came true: "incomparably fair" streets were laid out, and Paris became associated with urban planning as never before.

CHAPTER FIVE

The Open City: The Boulevards, Parks, and Streets of Paris

LOUIS XIV WAS never one to waste time or to think small. Already in 1667, he began the first of many wars to expand the territory of France, the War of Devolution, for control over the Spanish Netherlands. As a result of his conquests, Paris' position in his kingdom was soon redefined. In 1705, the first historian of Parisian urban planning, Nicolas Delamare, explained that, prior to this moment, Paris had been "nearly on the border," whereas after Louis XIV's victories, it was "at the center of the kingdom."

The king then initiated a nationalized system of protection for the country's new frontiers: Sébastien Le Prestre de Vauban, among the most brilliant military engineers of all time, virtually surrounded the country with a ring of fortified places so technically advanced that they were long considered impregnable. It was a hugely expensive endeavor: the country's defenses cost about four times as much as all civic architecture of Louis XIV's reign combined—in Paris, at Versailles, and at other royal palaces. This vast expense, however, allowed the king to make his capital into a new kind of city. He thereby became the first French monarch able to implement a vision for Paris in its entirety.

In 1669–70, the groundwork was laid for one of the most ambitious public works projects in Paris' history. It was a bold move, a key turning point in Paris' evolution and among the most innovative ideas in urban history. At a time when other European cities remained as they had been for centuries, fortified units enclosed within walls designed for their protection—and when some cities were adding new fortifications, as the Dutch city of Haarlem did in 1671—Louis XIV decided to redefine the city.

Rather than shore up the ragtag fortifications that surrounded his capital, as many were encouraging him to do, the king announced that France was in such a strong position militarily that Paris no longer needed to be enclosed within a system of defenses. He ordered all of its walls demolished; parts had been built by his father, while other sections dated from the reign of Charles V in the fourteenth century. This decision sounded the death knell for medieval Paris.

Under Louis XIV's rule, Paris was indeed safe from invasion. And the country's new and newly fortified borders helped protect it for some time: no foreign enemy set foot in Paris again until the Russian czar captured the city in 1814.

The period in Paris' history that began in 1670 lasted until 1784, when the Farmers General in charge of collecting taxes on imported goods persuaded Louis XVI to build a new wall designed to control traffic into the city. Those one hundred and fifteen years were the first time since Paris' founding by the Romans and the only time prior to 1920 when Paris was not a walled enclave, shut off from its surroundings, but instead a kind of city then unfamiliar to Europeans—an open city.

The king had the fortifications replaced with parallel rows of elms, what he later described as "a rampart of trees all around the city's rim." The green wall was soon given a mission: it was to serve as a *cours*, a gigantic walkway or space for communal walking—more than one hundred and twenty feet wide and extending, in the description of one of its architects, "in a straight line as far as the eye can see." Prior to this moment, no city had dedicated this kind of space to its inhabitants' leisure activities. The *cours* was by far the largest recreational space that had ever been conceived.

The still young king adopted lessons learned from the Pont Neuf and the Royal Square and gave Parisians from every part of the city the opportunity to enjoy their capital. In 1600, there was no public walking space in the city. Then, with its sidewalks, the Pont Neuf had introduced Parisians to a new way of experiencing a city on foot, and the Place Royale had given them their first recreational space. Louis XIV applied these concepts on a citywide scale. As a result, by 1700, Paris had become the original great walking city, a place where people walked not just to get around but for pleasure.

The rampart also opened Paris up to the countryside and its green vistas. When that Tax Wall went up in the 1780s, Parisians complained bitterly that they felt hemmed in by it, no longer free to contemplate the woods and fields beyond the cityscape.

The *cours* defined Paris under Louis XIV's watch as what its early historian Delamare called "*un lieu de délices*," "a place dedicated to pleasure," the kind of public city where people expected to find every entertainment associated with modern urban culture—from opera and dance to shopping and fine food—and where they expected to take pleasure in simply walking in the streets.

Louis XIV's vision for his capital was evident even before he arrived there with his new bride in August 1660. Nearly six months earlier, he began planning the first major festivities of his reign and of the post–civil war years, a celebration in which the Place Royale was to be featured. A huge crowd was expected: one journalist estimated that more than one hundred thousand visitors came to watch the king "take possession" of the city. The fledgling monarch decided that much needed to be done and done "instantly," as he put it in the edict he issued on March 15, in which he decreed that all the approach routes leading to the Royal Square be "completely opened up" and access thus "freed up." The king wanted to make sure both that those attending the festivities would have the best view possible onto the square as they arrived and that traffic would flow smoothly. That 1660 decree announced Louis XIV's signature style in urban planning: open Paris up; make its streets wider.

After Mazarin's death in 1661, Louis XIV had assumed greater responsibility. By 1665, he had found a new modus operandi with Jean-Baptiste Colbert in charge of royal finances; for the next two decades, they formed a brilliant team. Very early in their partnership, Colbert sent the king a letter laying out his philosophy of kingship and discussing the criteria on which rulers should be evaluated by posterity. He warned Louis XIV—who was just beginning his long infatuation with a new palace at Versailles—that Versailles would be seen as his private "pleasure palace," a mere frivolity. If he wished to go down in history as a great monarch, the king had to focus on one thing alone— "grandeur"—and on the two factors that were used to measure a reign's grandeur: "stunning" military victories and the kind of "superb public monuments" that could make Paris the new Rome.

Although the king did not stop work on Versailles—far from it—he did lavish attention on Paris. Nothing demonstrates this more than the biggest—in terms of scale, duration, and long-term impact—urban work of Louis XIV's long reign: the transformation of the city's fortifications into that tree-lined promenade.

Several factors explain why the project began to take shape in 1669. The previous year, Claude Le Peletier—a judge and adviser to the Parlement in whom the king had great confidence—had been appointed Prévôt des Marchands, provost or leader of the merchant community, de facto head of the municipality. That same year, François Blondel—among the most brilliant architects of the age, an engineer who undertook major military and civilian projects, future chief architect of the city of Paris and the first head of the French Royal Academy of Architecture—returned from the West Indies, where he had been sent by the king on an inspection tour of French possessions in the New World. As of 1669, Blondel was in charge of public works in Paris. Colbert's unflagging support and the synergy among the king, the municipal leader, and the professional expert drove the plan to turn bulwarks into a green walkway. Every parkway, every grand avenue in today's major cities, has its origin in that rampart of green for which they laid the groundwork in 1669.

All the participants clearly understood the project's significance. To say that they left behind an impressive paper trail in no way does justice to the number of decrees, mandates, statutes, and publications of all kinds that participants quickly began turning out. No urban works in the history of Paris had generated anything like this publication frenzy; few developments in the early history of the modern city can be studied in such detail.

Those working on the rampart all soon realized that it would only function successfully if it was integrated into a street grid, a network of easily negotiated thoroughfares. In the long run, the transformation of Paris' walls led therefore to a refashioning of virtually the entire urban design within those walls, to an integrated, systematic master plan for Paris' development. This was the capital's first large-scale planned reconstruction.

The city of which Louis XIV "took possession" in 1660 still had the layout of a medieval city: most of its streets were mere alleyways, narrow and dark. This detail from Braun's 1572 map shows how such premodern streets functioned: they helped people negotiate only their immediate neighborhood. Indeed, in the early seventeenth century, the French word *rue* or street designated simply "any passageway between houses or between walls." Late-seventeenth-century dictionaries make it plain that these were no longer considered streets: "in Paris, the old passageways have been opened up and broadened." Dictionaries further advised that "when walking in Paris, one should always take these big streets." In less than a century, the rebuilding of Paris had transformed the concept of a street.

In the late sixteenth century, when municipal authorities first evoked the possibility of creating broader streets, anything over fifteen feet wide was considered impossibly huge. By 1700, the French Royal Academy of Architecture had begun to establish norms: its members determined that a width of twenty-one feet was "an absolute minimum." Several years later, Delamare noted that "the average width of a Parisian street is now between thirty and thirty-two feet."

While Henri IV had added but a few streets and none that served the city at

*Georg Braun's 1572 map depicted the streets of sixteenth-century
Paris as mere alleyways serving only the immediate neighborhood
and not the city at large.*

large, his grandson assigned that basic unit of urban space a key role in the
transition from medieval to modern city. A series of similar and interrelated
projects initiated under royal command in the early 1670s prove that the king
and his planning team had a concept of a model street in mind, as well as a vision
of central Paris where traffic flowed easily. Each decree involved a particular
street, described by the authorities as "too narrow," "unevenly wide," "improp-
erly aligned." All over the city, street after street was opened up, evened out
("same width all along"), straightened ("a straight alignment"). Individual
streets were connected with others and new streets created to form axes that
guided traffic across the city "to make it possible for two vehicles to get by at
the same time" and thereby "to ease congestion." Work was carried out "for the
convenience of Parisians"—and of Paris' business community, given that
the new streets facilitated the passage of "vehicles transporting merchandise
and provisions."

Perhaps the most impressive fact about this large-scale transformation of a
cityscape was that it was accomplished without the wholesale destruction associated with Paris' second major redesign in the nineteenth century. The architects of seventeenth-century Paris were free to create. They had no need to
raze parts of a crowded and aging capital, as their nineteenth-century successors
would decide to do in the name of modernity and urban renewal: they were
instead able, for the most part, to use barren terrain for their new construction.
But even when existing construction did stand in the way of the implementation

of their ideas, they deliberated carefully and chose the least radical solution possible.

When their plans made it necessary to demolish existing public works, in an early instance of what is now called historic preservation, the city's architects studied them carefully to determine their architectural merit. Thus, in the case of the double Saint-Antoine gate, Blondel decided that one could be torn down but not the other, "because of the beauty of its bas-reliefs" by noted sixteenth-century sculptor Jean Goujon and of "the exceptional design" of one of its archways. The resulting blend of old and new was universally praised; an eighteenth-century historian of the city still considered it "the most successful of Paris' gates."

In addition, in the narrow streets that were candidates for widening, the city's inspectors were told to keep an eye out for any house that was "particularly old" and/or in unusually bad shape; the opportunity was then seized to have crumbling dwellings taken down. But when no such possibility existed, the houses lining these streets were moved and officials appointed to determine compensation for their owners. Occasionally, homeowners tried to fight displacement; they were never allowed to obstruct the transition to urban modernity.

By 1672, street widening, first promoted as a way to improve traffic flow, was being justified in a new way: "His Majesty wishes to ornament his city of Paris," "to make Paris the most beautiful city in France," and to make it possible "for Paris to outdo in every domain all the world's most celebrated cities." From then on, a combination of aesthetic and utilitarian concerns drove the capital's redesign.

Those combined concerns modified the streets of Paris in highly visible ways. Prior to the seventeenth century, there was very little paving in Paris. In the course of the seventeenth century, paving became common and paving stones acquired standard dimensions (seven to eight inches square, eight to ten inches thick), creating the cobblestones long considered characteristically Parisian.

From the start, those cobblestones were presented as essential to the city's beauty. Until the 1660s, the municipality had simply encouraged individual property owners to clean in front of their homes. But in November 1665 the inception of official street-cleaning was announced in the press: "4,000 men have begun to rid our superb city of dirt." The newsman, Adrien Perdou de Subligny, explained that the king had taken time off from his military campaigns to make sure Paris was running properly and had decided on this new measure. The following year another journalist declared that "our paving stones are now gleaming."

He added that on an inspection tour of the streets the king had personally "admired" their new gleam. And this tour was no isolated occurrence: through-out the years when the master plan was taking shape, journalists regularly recorded sightings of the king "walking all over the city" like an average Parisian—to be sure that Paris was becoming the kind of city in which "everyone . . . can walk about with great ease."

That goal could not have been attained without the most visible sign of the pedestrian's place in the modern city: the sidewalk. Despite the concept's great success when it was introduced on the Pont Neuf, it had not been quickly adopted for Paris' streets. The innovation, however, had not been forgotten.

Quai, the term still used to designate the embankments along the Seine, first appeared in 1636. The Île Saint-Louis project was then in full swing, and mu-nicipal authorities were discussing the Right Bank shore facing the new is-land, when they announced their intention of adding a paved river walk that would both be functional (particularly for loading and unloading merchan-dise that had reached Paris by boat) and give Parisians a space where they could "walk with great ease" while admiring their river—and, of course, the Île Saint-Louis. They named that space the "Quai des Célestins." In 1636, the riverbanks still remained completely undeveloped (see page 84). The new word, *quai*, indicated a fresh consciousness of their importance. Indeed, in the course of the seventeenth century every *quai* was built up and acquired a riverside walkway.

At first, these unprecedented spaces by the Seine reserved for pedestrians were called either *banquettes*, like the raised walkways on the Pont Neuf, or *marche-pieds* ("walkers"). In October 1704, the king ordered the Quai de La Grenouillère near the Louvre evened out and paved; the edict included a pro-vision for a *trottoir*—the first appearance of the term that soon became the definitive French word for sidewalk. When the construction of the Quai d'Orsay was mandated in August 1707, the plans specified a *trottoir* nine feet wide "in order to give people on foot a place to walk."

At the moment when Paris' redesign moved into high gear, a second bril-liant architect-engineer, Blondel student Pierre Bullet, was given a key role; he was soon named the city's chief architect. Bullet went on to a distinguished career building mansions in the elegant neighborhoods that developed later in the century near the completed rampart—including what is today the Ritz Paris hotel. In 1672, Bullet was going about the streets, literally house to house, to evaluate infrastructure. On the king's orders, along with Blondel, he also began work on a new map of Paris to help coordinate the increasingly ambitious plans being made for the city's future.

What is now known as the Bullet-Blondel map is a magnificent record of the layout of Paris at this key moment in its evolution. Contemporaries immediately praised it as by far the most accurate view available, and this accuracy is easily explained. As Bullet was taking stock of things on the ground, he grasped the difficulty of the mapmaker's task "in overcrowded city centers" where they were expected "to measure inaccessible straight lines." He therefore invented an innovative "geometrical instrument," which he termed a "*pantomètre*, an instrument that can measure anything."

The new map, however, was designed to depict much more than what Bullet was able to size up. Very early in their deliberations, all concerned realized both that they needed to be able to visualize the effects of all the changes—those already accomplished, those under way, and those still in the planning stage—on the cityscape and that they needed to be sure that the original intentions remained clear as the project moved forward.

Maps often mix fact and fantasy in various ways; mapmakers may represent, for example, certain features as larger than life in order to give them added importance. As their map's title explains, Bullet and Blondel created a more unusual blend of realities, the actual reality of what Paris already was and the virtual reality of what it would become: "A Map of Paris, That Shows All the Public Works Already Completed to Beautify the City and to Make It More Convenient—As Well As Those His Majesty Wishes to See Carried Out in the Future." That title is a clear indication that no destruction would be necessary to reinvent Paris: the city its inhabitants knew would live on with new urban fabric added around it or between existing constructions.

In this detail of their plan, depicting the Place Royale and its vicinity, the present and the future of the cityscape are both clearly mapped out. Dark solid lines indicate existing streets, many of them recent and serving to connect the square to the new promenade. To the right behind the Place and at the city's edge, the dark double lines stand for the trees on the rampart's first completed section. The lighter broken lines on the upper left represent the next section of the rampart, as well as new streets to connect it with the Marais—public works planned but not yet undertaken.

A copy of the map was prominently displayed in Paris' City Hall so that it could be easily consulted to determine if what Bullet termed the king's "*grand dessein*," his "grand design" or master plan for Paris, was being respected.

And the map's impact extended far beyond City Hall. So many people wanted to see the master plan for Paris that its second printing appeared only a month after the map was first published on August 8, 1676. It continued to be reprinted, and Bullet and Blondel continued to update it until just before Blondel's death in early 1686.

To guide the redesign of Paris, in 1676 Louis XIV commissioned a new map from architects Bullet and Blondel. The map hung in City Hall and was still being followed in 1715.

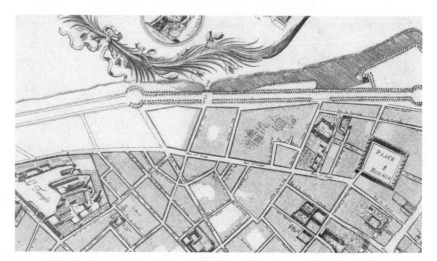

*Bullet and Blondel used dark solid lines to indicate existing streets and
lighter broken lines for streets planned but not yet completed.*

All those involved, from the king to his architects, described the map in
print, often and in detail. The various descriptions, although directed at different audiences, shared a common goal: to publicize the capital's remodeling. Every description proclaimed that a new era had dawned for Paris:
henceforth it would be known as a great city not simply because of its size but
because it was both an open city and an urban center whose "magnificent public
works surpassed those of all other cities in the world."

Their commentaries always singled out the rampart—which they described
as "a delightful beltway for the city" or "a public promenade space"—as essential to the "adornment" of Paris. The beltway became the centerpiece of
"the grand design."

The descriptions were all heavy on propaganda. Blondel characterized the
rampart as "the most significant public works project in the world." Bullet
categorically affirmed that "it would never be equaled." And Louis XIV's
team of scriptwriters outdid themselves. When the map was made public in
the summer of 1676, its images were accompanied by two extensive documents signed by the king. "The ancient Romans believed that only those who
had added new territory to the empire with their conquests should be allowed
to change Rome; . . . since the limits of France have now been extended beyond the Rhine, the Alps, and the Pyrenees, the king is legitimately able to
decree that his capital city should receive a new and a newly beautiful beltway,"
one began. The other concluded: "Because of the number and the beauty of its

public works, Paris will serve as proof both to foreigners today and to posterity of the greatness of our nation and of this reign."

Ample evidence indicates how seriously both the king and municipal authorities took what soon came to be known simply as "*the* map." In a royal statute dated November 4, 1684, the king notes with evident pleasure the amount of work already completed on the promenade. A decree from October 1704 shows that the Bullet-Blondel map still served as an absolute reference: the king chided city authorities because works depicted on it had not yet been undertaken. And in December 1715 an edict signed jointly by "Louis and the Duc d'Orléans, Regent" reminded a new set of municipal leaders that the 1704 decree had still not been fully carried out, despite the fact that "the late monarch had had the map of Paris drawn up so that we would have his wishes constantly present before our eyes." Three months after Louis XIV's death in September 1715, forty years after Bullet and Blondel had first published their work, his successors still saw "the map" as the official blueprint for Paris' future.

As the repeated reminders to respect the map indicate, even the Sun King was unable to change the face of a city as quickly as he would have liked. In principle, the plan to build a vast public recreational space was simple. The fortifications would be quickly reduced to dirt and rubble. The rubble would be used to fill in the moats, and the dirt that had reinforced the walls used for planting trees. But with any project of this magnitude, architects encounter obstacles along the way; this time, they were of majestic proportions. In the early 1680s, for instance, when architects reached roughly the halfway point of the Right Bank promenade, near today's Opéra Garnier, they informed the king of quite literal bumps in the road: "It will be necessary to flatten several mounds of earth."

The *buttes* or mounds they had in mind were sizeable, depicted in seventeenth-century paintings as small hills. The tallest of the lot were covered with houses; windmills lined their crests. They were in fact giant garbage or compost heaps. As long as Paris had remained a fortified city, many residents had dealt with trash by simply dumping it over the wall. Out of sight, out of mind, and for centuries the *buttes* kept growing. Then the walls came down, and Louis XIV pronounced them "an unpleasant sight for those who are taking pleasure from walking on the rampart" and immediately began passing decrees designed to cure Parisians of a well-engrained habit. Each neighborhood had to appoint inspectors who would report directly to those in charge of the rampart project. Inspectors were to make frequent rounds of the promenade to ensure that "its surroundings were absolutely free of rubbish"; anyone found guilty of dumping would be fined five hundred *livres* and their house and vehicle impounded—and this at a time when the chef in a great house earned three hundred *livres* a year.

There were other maintenance issues as well. Inspectors kept on the lookout for spots where the terrain wasn't level enough for easy walking, and in such cases, the original potholes were filled in. If they noticed bad smells, drainage systems were added. And then there were those recently planted elms. Tree inspectors zeroed in on two issues: carriages that cut curves too close and nicked their trunks and horses that grazed on their tender leaves. New decrees announced fines for "tree damage."

There was also the problem of access. The creation of several new streets heading from the Place Royale to the initial stretch of the rampart near the Saint-Antoine gate was announced in 1670–71 (see page 106). As the rampart was extended, streets were laid out along the way. In April 1672, the planning team was concerned about access from the upper Marais, near what is now Strasbourg-Saint-Denis. And by June 1700, the Place Louis-le-Grand, today's Place Vendôme, had been recently added to the cityscape and planning was under way to embed the new square in the street grid and thus "to facilitate access to the promenade for the inhabitants of this neighborhood." This early eighteenth-century map shows the rampart running just behind the new square and already fully accessible from it.

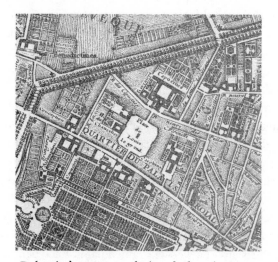

Delagrive's 1728 map depicts the last city square added during Louis XIV's reign, the Place Louis-le-Grand, today's Place Vendôme, equidistant from the then newest section of the boulevard and the Tuileries garden.

On occasion, architects realized that existing streets had to be eliminated to carry out the master plan. In October 1679, the municipality drew up a contract with a Parisian painter, Louis Dumesnil, "for the upkeep of the busts that we have begun positioning and will continue to place at the corner of every street that is closed off." The busts, as English visitor Martin Lister explained, were "Busto's or heads of the Grand Monarque"; every time Louis XIV eliminated a piece of Paris' past, he commemorated the change with his portrait, thereby creating a landscape of memory.

Many foreigners visited Paris during Louis XIV's reign. Perhaps the most exotic of all and certainly the visitors who caused the biggest flurry arrived in August 1686. Known as "the Siamese ambassadors," they were actually a delegation of important nobles and civil servants sent by the king of Siam, Phra Narai, as part of his plan to open his country to the West. Every move they made was chronicled in the press. Thus we know that when they visited City Hall, they were presented with a deluxe edition of "the map." And when they toured the rampart, they offered an astute assessment: "When this public work is completed, it will be worthy of Paris." In 1686, however, the end was not yet in sight.

It was only at the turn of the eighteenth century that work on the first half of the rampart, on the Seine's Right Bank, was at last nearing completion. Serious planning was under way for the parallel segment on the Left Bank, when the planners—and by then it was a completely different team—encountered the most significant difficulties yet, in the transitional zone where right and left banks meet up on what was at that time Paris' western edge. Today, this is among the most scenic areas in the city, with the Place de la Concorde on the Right Bank and the Invalides on the Left, each of them surrounded by a vast complex of public works. In 1700, however, development of this sizeable terrain was only just beginning.

When the city's architects turned to this crucial juncture, they found that the "grand design" simply could not be made to work: "the map" had to be extensively redrawn. In addition, rather than the wide streets chosen by their precursors to connect rampart and city center, the architects of 1700 preferred far more expansive thoroughfares, in particular two kinds of supersized streets that have ever since been emblematic of both Paris and French urban planning: the boulevard and the avenue.

In French, neither was a new word: around 1700, however, both were first used in a new way. *Boulevard* has its origins in the Dutch *bolwerc*, which became *bulwark* in English and in French *boulevart* or *boullevers*. This was a military term created to designate various types of fortifications, in particular a defensive rampart or bastion. In Paris, the city's walls had originally been reinforced at

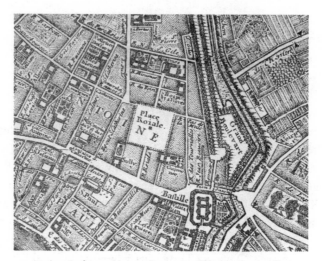

*Delagrive's 1728 map shows the "big boulevart" or
bastion near the Bastille fortress. The dark double lines
leading out from it represent the tree-lined walkway
known as "the boulevard."*

regular intervals with *boulevarts*: this detail from Abbé Delagrive's 1728 map
shows the "*grand boulevart*" near the Saint-Antoine gate and the Place Royale.
Once the rampart project was initiated, these bastions no longer had a function
to play. Soon, *boulevart* had become *boulevard*, a term first used to designate
the section of the rampart on the Right Bank, which became known as "the
boulevard."

Through most of the seventeenth century, *advenue* referred to any way or
passage by which one arrives, an access route. In the late seventeenth century,
the word acquired its modern spelling and a new definition: "a tree-lined walkway." The first avenues appeared in the area where the map had to be reconfig-
ured. It was there that the most mythic avenue of all, the Champs-Élysées,
was laid out.

In the late 1660s, when the Tuileries gardens were expanded by Louis XIV's
favorite landscape architect André Le Nôtre, various documents related to the
garden redesign refer to "the avenue of the Tuileries." By 1709, that avenue
had received its definitive name: "Champs-Élysées." This detail from Delagrive's map, among the first to refer to the avenue as "Champs-Élysées,"
depicts it as an essential link between the existing cityscape (the edge of the
Tuileries gardens is visible on the extreme right, the rue du Faubourg Saint-
Honoré just above) and the largely tree-covered expanse toward which Paris

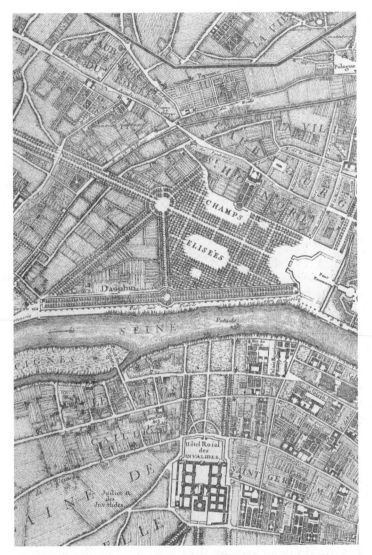

*Delagrive's 1728 map was the first to indicate the newly laid out
and planted Champs-Élysées neighborhood with its walkways
emanating from a central circle, "l'Étoile."*

was expanding. On Sundays and holidays, the Champs-Élysées and the surrounding area were used like a modern city park, where, as a guidebook to Paris
explained, working-class Parisians came to enjoy their day off surrounded by
trees and greenery.

The map also shows, just across the Seine, the Invalides with several equally

wide thoroughfares jutting out from it. These were called not avenues but boulevards: "*les boulevards neufs*," "the new boulevards"—to distinguish them
from "*the* boulevard" on the Right Bank. And ever since, "avenue" and "boulevard" have often been used as synonyms.

By 1707 as Brice's guidebook informed visitors, Louis XIV's green wall
"encircled half the city with an uninterrupted promenade space." You could
begin walking where the rampart started, at the river just beyond the Île
Saint-Louis, and continue past the Bastille, then get a view of the Place Royale
on your left. You could skirt the Marais, continue on behind the Place Vendôme,
all the way around to the Saint-Honoré gate, where you might head into the
Champs-Élysées. It was far from the full circle the Sun King first dreamed of
in 1670, but it was a very long and very fine walk all the same—and one that
still exists today.

By then, Parisians had a new phrase, *sur le boulevard*, "on the boulevard."
They used it much as we now say "on the boardwalk," to refer to a pleasant
place designated for strolling that was in various ways also an entertainment
zone. Parisians went "on the boulevard" to admire the beautiful new homes
being built within view of the green walkway and "to hear singers performing
the latest hits from the Paris Opera." They also went there to get "fresh air,"
as Louis Liger did on his first day in Paris in 1715, and they even went there
out of a developing belief: "that walking was good for one's health."

As all this indicates, the boulevard was no ordinary city thoroughfare. Parisians did use it just to get around in their city, but it also functioned as no mere
street ever had. It was an immense display space, a place where pedestrians
showed themselves off and where they took in visual spectacles of various
kinds. The original boulevard was an essential part of the first leisure industry
to develop in a European city.

All the activities that made the boulevard experience so popular also flour-
ished in the center of Paris in a series of increasingly grand and increasingly
public gardens. In those gardens, daily entertainment devoted to the leisure
activities of the city's inhabitants first began to develop.

Parisian gardens began on a modest scale, but before the century's end they
were famous all over Europe. In 1606, Queen Marie de Médicis had elm trees
planted in four parallel rows and thus initiated the Cours-la-Reine, the
Queen's Walkway. The Cours—on the Seine's Right Bank on terrain that
would become fully part of the urban landscape only in the eighteenth century—
was designed for promenading in what was in the early 1600s the latest status
symbol, the carriage. Its central drive was so wide that five carriages could fit
side-by-side; in the middle, there was a traffic circle to allow carriages to turn

around. Since deep ditches running along each side and an iron gate at each end closed the Cours off from the city, and since porters were stationed at those gates to control admission, it was only minimally a public garden. In the 1628 decree that founded it, Louis XIII declared it the exclusive preserve of the court, open to the public only when courtiers were not using it.

The entertainment provided by the Cours was decidedly upscale, the privilege of the happy few who could afford to own or to rent that costly luxury, a carriage. The activity of driving around in this still new form of transport—showing off one's own vehicle and admiring the features of those owned by others—became such an essential leisure activity that the Cours' central drive often turned into what two Dutch visitors in the 1640s described as "one giant *embarras* of carriages." Later in the century, when carriages had become more common, it was estimated that from seven hundred to a thousand at a time crowded into the Cours. It could take hours to extricate one's carriage from these bottlenecks. Other entertainments developed to distract people during traffic gridlock: venders walked from vehicle to vehicle selling fruits and sweets, and messengers hand-delivered billets doux. The Cours, a space open only to the elite and whose activities revolved around carriages, had created a carriage set, the original coterie defined by access to expensive vehicles.

The Cours-la-Reine also became the prototype for a kind of urban space and entertainment that soon became widely viewed as quintessentially Parisian: public display space. In April 1662, a gazette reported that Louis XIV had been spotted at six P.M. strolling in the central drive with "seven richly appointed royal coaches trailing after him"—the kind of scene, the reporter added, "only possible in Paris." In the Cours, contemporaries pointed out, "luxury abounds": "all the beautiful things in Paris are brought there in order to be shown off"—"*pour en faire montre.*" The Cours-la-Reine was the original Parisian showcase for everything bright, shiny, and new.

It was, however, just a warm-up for the moment in Louis XIV's reign when the greening of Paris became for the first time central to a ruler's vision for the city. During that extraordinary moment in the 1660s that produced the master plan, the monarch who so carefully took the measure of the Cours-la-Reine that April day in 1662 initiated still another grand public works project: the Tuileries gardens. Because of the Tuileries, the Cours-la-Reine, and the rampart combined, by the turn of the eighteenth century Paris was known, in journalist Charles Dufresny's words, as "*le pays des promenades,*" "the birthplace of the public walkway."

The Tuileries also had a modest start. In 1564, Henri II's widow, Queen Regent Catherine de Médicis, planted a small private garden hidden from the city behind a wall in front of the Tuileries Palace. This garden was expanded and integrated into the cityscape over the decades, but it really came into its own only once Louis XIV had given landscape architect extraordinaire André Le Nôtre free rein. Le Nôtre had the original garden torn up and replaced with the steps and the esplanade that still today connect the Tuileries and the Louvre.

This view of the garden complex after the redesign, "The Tuileries Garden As It Is Now," foregrounds the most evident difference between the new garden and the Cours-la-Reine. The Queen's Walkway was designed for the wealthy to enjoy while riding in their carriages. Despite the fact that the Tuileries' central walkway was clearly wide enough to accommodate them, as this image shows, carriages were strikingly absent. Instead, it was in the Tuileries that, as the Marquis de Caraccioli later remarked, Parisians began "to step down from their carriages and to use their feet." And once this happened, the Tuileries became the first truly public Parisian garden and the prototype for public gardens all over Europe. Caraccioli added that "it was a pleasure to see people of all ages and all walks of life taking advantage of these superb gardens." (Vauxhall Gardens, the Tuileries' London rival, originated in the mid-

The Perelle brothers' engraving of the Tuileries shows each area of the newly redesigned garden being used in a different manner: big groups gathered on the esplanade; couples strolled in the side walkways.

1660s as the quite modest New Spring Gardens; its potential only began to be realized after the property changed hands in 1729.)

This depiction shows that each section of the Tuileries functioned in a specific way. Socializing in larger groups centered on the esplanade and the central walkway, while couples and solitary walkers frequented the more intimate side alleyways. The setting, it seems, encouraged casual behavior: some sit on the grass, others by the reflecting pools. The scene also depicts the ease with which the sexes interacted in this new garden: men and women promenade together, as foreign visitors—taken aback by a phenomenon unheard of in their own countries, where women were so rarely seen out walking—never failed to point out. It's all very much the way the Tuileries still functions today, more than three and a half centuries later.

Early guidebooks all single out the Tuileries as a focal point for any visit. They make their readers aware of the numerous leisure activities that had developed in the largest and the most public garden in Paris.

Their authors explain to begin with that the garden worked differently at different times of the day. One guidebook advised visitors that "anyone seeking privacy for a tête-à-tête" should choose the afternoon when it was less crowded. At other moments, thousands were out walking—and this was particularly true when the thermometer rose. In April 1671, for example, when the Marquise de Sévigné described the city as "hot enough to kill you," she spent hours in the Tuileries day after day.

Another guidebook suggested that on evenings when the city sizzled, visitors could join Parisians in cooling off with "a glass of lemonade" at one of the cafés that attracted clients by "lighting lamps and positioning them all over the ground." Such establishments continued the tradition that began during the Fronde, when chez Renard functioned as a gathering spot for rebellious nobles. These cafés in the Tuileries were among the first places where aristocrats ate and drank in public, as well as one of the first spots where women did so. They were also among the origins of the leisure industry that gradually developed to cater to the needs of the many who, in the words of an eighteenth-century observer, "came to the Tuileries to walk away their spare time."

Another public pastime originated in the Tuileries, a form of entertainment centered on the display of high fashion. As long as promenading took place in the Cours-la-Reine, carriages were on public view, but the outfits of those inside remained largely out of sight. But then two developments coincided: Le Nôtre's redesign transformed the Tuileries into the most popular garden in the city just at the moment when a true luxury goods industry was developing in Paris. When Parisians took to their feet in the Tuileries, they were thus able to show off typically Parisian garments and accessories just as soon as they had been invented—and to display them on a scale never before imagined. From then on, any style worn by well-heeled individuals in the most public display space in Paris was sure to start a trend. The entire modern spectacle of high style, every red carpet walk, has its origins in the daily parade that began in the Tuileries in the 1670s.

Already by the 1680s, shortly after Le Nôtre had completed his redesign, authors of guidebooks began to describe still another justification for a visit to Paris. As Charles Le Maire informed his readers in 1685, "crowds of foreigners gather in the Tuileries, because it's there that you can learn about the latest styles."

The visitors who flocked to the Tuileries may well have been hoping to copy more than just the latest dress on parade there. The clusters of stylish people walking in the garden represented a new development in the European city. To an outsider, the groups out in public together all appeared to know each other and to belong to the same circle: the Tuileries thus fostered the development of openly recognized fashionable sets. And those not part of these charmed circles were eager to emulate the ways of fashion insiders.

Inventions of various kinds were designed to help those not able to frequent the Tuileries on a regular basis achieve this goal. Just when guidebooks first discussed the impact of Paris' public gardens on fashion, a kind of engraving went into large-scale production for the first time: the fashion plate. In the 1680s and 1690s, thousands of these prints were produced in Paris; they depicted the fashion trends of the moment.

This image of a noblewoman by Nicolas Arnoult focuses in particular on the striped fabric of her dress, yards of which are billowing out behind her. During their much publicized visit to Paris in late 1686, the Siamese ambassadors had often appeared in striped textiles; in 1687, when this image was in circulation, Parisian fabric merchants had a banner year selling striped cloth of every kind. Arnoult specifies that the scene takes place "in the Tuileries," so that foreigners trying to imitate the ways of the stylish set would see such textiles as a way to blend in. The artists who created fashion plates such as this one had assimilated the essence of the Tuileries experience: they brought dress to life by showing it off in a precise context.

The image also promotes the kind of high-fashion accessories that were already a highly profitable sector for the luxury goods industry. The woman demonstrates to begin with how to hold a fan most fetchingly; fans were then becoming ever more widely favored by women all over Europe, and French fanmakers had recently achieved the preeminence they would enjoy for a cen-

Femme de qualité aux Thuilleries.

Se vend à Paris Chez N. Arnoult rue de la Fromagerie à l'image St. Claude aux halles. avec priv. du Roy.

Nicolas Arnoult's 1687 image depicts a noblewoman using one of the 101 new wooden benches that had been installed in the Tuileries the previous year.

tury to come. The noblewoman's décolletage and upswept hair show off in addition a tasteful choker and drop earrings; from her waist hangs one of the recently invented and highly prized tiny watches. It seems to read 4:55, which would indicate that she was waiting, at an hour when the garden was known to be less crowded, for a "private tête-à-tête." And thus it's fitting that the engraving also features another innovation then newly part of the Tuileries experience: the garden bench.

In October 1678, the royal account ledgers recorded a payment made to a Parisian carpenter named Barbier, for eight wooden benches designed specifically "for the Tuileries gardens"—the first for that garden and among the original public park benches. The experiment was a success: in 1686, the year before Arnoult depicted a lady of fashion posed on one of those benches, another carpenter, Pierre Guérin, "made and installed an additional 101 benches in the Tuileries, at a cost of four *livres* apiece"—not even half what an aristocratic household spent on meat every day; a song, when you think of the long-term impact that modest investment had.

Those benches—the very basic model depicted here—were installed in all three walkways. They, too, proved crucial to the formation of fashionable sets because of the kind of personal display that they made possible. They could function, as Arnoult's engraving demonstrates, as the ideal space on which a stylish outfit could be carefully arranged and shown off. They could also, as this image by Nicolas Bonnart illustrates, encourage other new leisure activities that in turn helped distinguish those able to indulge in them. The ladies shown here have taken a tiny dog for a walk in the garden; they are using the dog and one of the new benches to facilitate still another experience foreigners described as unheard of outside of Paris: intimate conversation and flirting in a public venue.

Guidelines were soon developed to help govern such novel forms of public behavior. Antoine Courtin's *Nouveau traité de la civilité qui se pratique en France parmi les honnêtes gens* (*The Rules of Civility, or Certain Ways of Deportment Observed in France in the Best Society*) was the best-selling etiquette manual of the age, reedited for nearly a century. It covered subjects ranging from table manners to personal hygiene. Its original edition from 1671, the moment of Le Nôtre's redesign of the Tuileries, contains six pages of rules for walking in a promenade space—everything from whether you can go on strolling if the person you're with decides to sit down on the grass (answer: you cannot) to the proper way to turn around when you reach the end of a walkway.

In the 1702 edition, that section was three times as long, evidence that public walking had taken on a much more prominent role during the decades when the "grand design" was being implemented. Newly essential regulations had been introduced: when, for instance, a gentleman meets a lady while walking, he should never kiss her unless she "extends her cheek," in which case he should merely "move his face closer to her hairdo."

Courtin's manual was quickly translated into English (at least six times), German, Italian, Dutch, and even Latin. Its success indicates how many for-

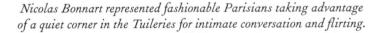

Dames en conversation aux Tuileries.

Dans ce lieu plein d'apas, ce jeune home amoureux, | Et l'on voit par le feu qui paroît dans ses yeux
Debite la fleurette, et presente une Rose; | Que s'il donne des fleurs, il souhaitte autre cho-se.

*Nicolas Bonnart represented fashionable Parisians taking advantage
of a quiet corner in the Tuileries for intimate conversation and flirting.*

eigners were eager to study the ways of the fashionable people who gathered
in the Tuileries. And because of his handbook, all over Europe, people could
learn to walk—and air-kiss—in the Parisian way.

Courtin gives the impression that the elegantly dressed people one encountered while promenading were aristocrats all—members of "the best society"—
whereas the raison d'être for his etiquette guide was that anyone could learn

to pass for noble and thus be taken for a person of distinction. Numerous commentators called attention to the fact that because of the Tuileries, something that previously had rarely if ever occurred had become commonplace: one encountered individuals who walked the walk and talked the talk and knew every dress code but hadn't a drop of blue blood. In 1684, Pierre Henry pointed out that many of the "superbly" dressed ladies promenading in Paris were mere bourgeoises flaunting "magnificent trappings." And Louis Liger informed readers of his guidebook that "there are many shopgirls whom you'd think were fine aristocrats, many bourgeois who are taken for great lords." In Paris' public gardens, or so it was widely claimed, the social mixing found on the Pont Neuf often became social confusion.

The fact that numerous authors quickly began to discuss the kind of social disorder fostered by the public promenade makes it evident that such confusion not only was an integral part of the experience but was integral to the novelty and the pleasure of the promenade—for aristocrats and bourgeois, Parisians and foreigners alike.

The most widely read French periodical of the day, the *Mercure galant*, frequently highlighted accounts of the goings-on in the Tuileries. The July 1677 issue includes two stories about socially dubious individuals. One "asks people to address him as 'Marquis' and could be taken for one because of his appearance and his manners"; the other "has just surfaced in the best Parisian circles." Day after day, they frequent the Tuileries in the hope of passing for aristocrats. The following July, the paper's featured story concerned an actual noblewoman who liked to dress down when she walked in the garden so that she could "have a little fun." She pretended to be a bourgeoise from the provinces ignorant of the big city; two Parisian gentlemen were taken in by her act. They offered to take her to the opera and to teach her all she needed to know—and were stunned to see "the servants and the magnificent carriage" waiting to take her home.

When English physician Martin Lister was leaving Paris in 1698 after a long stay, a Parisian noblewoman begged to know "his favorite sight in Paris." "The Tuileries in June, betwixt 8 and 9 at night," he replied. "I [don't] think there [is] in the world a more agreeable place at that hour, and that time of the year." And still in 1718, the very cosmopolitan Lady Mary Wortley Montagu pronounced the Tuileries "much finer" than any public recreation space London could offer.

The complete rampart around the entire city's rim was finally operational in 1761. Louis XIV's successor, Louis XV, saw the conclusion of ninety years of urban planning only late in his long reign. But the end result offered decisive proof of the wisdom of turning a broken-down defensive system into a vast complex of green spaces. Because of the rampart and the design that wove it into the urban fabric, Paris' famous gardens were never isolated but an integral part of the city's design. Paris therefore became a great walking capital, a center for urban leisure activities—and the premier spot in Europe for displaying and observing Parisian high fashion.

Already in the 1670s, Parisian journalists were reflecting on the impact of what one called "a completely new way for a king to prove his grandeur and the care he has for his people." One newsman contended that by reimagining his capital's design in such spectacular fashion, Louis XIV had done more "than any of our kings to beautify our city." And that opinion was still alive one hundred and seventy years later.

In 1844, well before Haussmann began his public works, Honoré de Balzac sang the praises of "the boulevards of Paris." Like all Parisians of his day, Balzac used "boulevard" and "boulevards" interchangeably, to refer to the original boulevard, the rampart that had been completed by the turn of the eighteenth century. "The boulevard," Balzac claimed, made all other European cities look "like a middle-class woman in her Sunday best." "Every capital has a poem in which it expresses itself, sums itself up, and is most fully itself," Balzac concluded. "No other city has anything comparable to the Boulevards of Paris."

CHAPTER SIX

City of Speed and Light: City Services That Transformed Urban Life

"Wait up, running man, what's your hurry?"

In a comedy by Pierre Corneille, one character reproaches another for racing by without greeting his friends. The "running man" is at a loss for words: he had hoped to slip by unnoticed. In his rush to get across town, he had been counting on a phenomenon made possible by the bustling urban crowd: anonymity.

As Corneille's man on the run indicates, Parisian walking was by no means only a leisure activity. There were many who walked because they needed to get around the city; these pedestrians wanted to get where they were going as quickly as possible.

The civil war years had awakened in Parisians a new appetite for faster communication and rapid movement. As soon as the war was over, private investors attempted to capitalize on those desires. They invented two revolutionary urban technologies focused on the circulation of information and people: public mail delivery and public transportation. With official royal permission, they put into operation innovations designed to help both Parisians and visitors alike find their way as the city added streets and neighborhoods, and to help them share news far more rapidly and frequently than ever before. Soon, a third urban technology, one instantly seen as a definitive mark of urban modernity—street lighting—made Paris a city where it was also possible to be on the go twenty-four hours a day.

The implementation of previously unknown city services indicates that Paris was more and more widely seen as a new kind of urban center, one that required never-before-imagined conveniences. Their invention also highlights Paris' role as an incubator of ideas that could revolutionize urban life. These novel city services combined to give Paris another new identity: as the City of Light, Europe's most innovative city and an urban center that attracted visitors with the excitement of the cutting edge.

The fifteen-year period during which these modern city services were first implemented was a heady era. By 1664, one Parisian periodical described "the age in which we live" as "the century of inventions."

The story of this facet of Paris' transformation began in August 1653, a memorable month for the city of Paris and for France in general. The traditional August holidays must have seemed far more festive that year, for France had finally emerged from civil war. The young Louis XIV had come home to his capital in October 1652, and Cardinal Mazarin had returned in February 1653, but the Fronde was officially over only late in the summer of 1653, when the last uprisings in the southwest were put down.

That August, the modern age for urban postal delivery began. Since the French national system carried mail only between different localities in France, prior to that time those who wished to send letters from one neighborhood in Paris to another either asked servants to deliver their correspondence and wait for a reply or hand-carried their own missives. But on August 8, 1653, Paris became the first European city endowed with a postal system. The new venture was the brainchild of one of the age's great inventors, Jean-Jacques Renouard, Comte de Villayer or Vélayer. (Later in the century, Villayer installed a prototype for the modern elevator in several royal châteaux.) On May 11, 1653, Louis XIV had granted him a royal privilege for the establishment of a mail delivery service "in our good city of Paris." On July 17, Parlement entered Villayer's monopoly in its registers.

The king gave Villayer "permission to establish people who will carry letters from one part of Paris to another." The monarch was taken with the idea of professional letter carriers, above all because of their potential usefulness for the business community. The new service, he reasoned, "will save businessmen much time." In addition, they will no longer have "to worry that letters and bills will be misdelivered by servants who don't know the city well enough."

The nuts and bolts of the system's functioning are laid out in the circular that introduced Parisians to the innovative service: "Instructions for Those Who Want to Send Mail from One Neighborhood in Paris to Another." The pamphlet advertises above all the speed of communication that would now be guaranteed: it would be possible to send a message and "get a prompt response two or three times in a single day." Public mail delivery would be especially useful, the circular explains, to "people who don't know the city well," to "those who are unable to be out and about," to "those who hate to walk," and to those who feel unable to keep up with the city's ever-accelerating pace— "those who are always in a rush and can't manage to do half the things they hope to do."

The brochure took Parisians step by step through the process of mailing a letter, beginning with the purchase of what Villayer called *billets de port payé*, or postage-paid tickets—the earliest known postage stamps. (London's Penny Post, a system by which the letter itself rather than a separate sheet of paper was stamped, began to function only in 1680.) Villayer's postal tickets were sold at a central location, an office in the Palais de Justice, for one *sou* or penny apiece; it then cost five *sous* to send a letter from Paris to Bordeaux or Avignon and ten to mail one to London. The year was preprinted on each ticket; the user wrote in the day and the month and then wrapped it around the letter to be mailed. The circular advised parents whose children were at boarding school to give them postage tickets so that "they won't forget to send news."

Next came postboxes, set up "at each end of every main street," so that "in an instant everyone in Paris will be able to find a mailbox." Users dropped off their letters and, three times a day (six A.M., eleven A.M., and three P.M.), mail was collected; delivery to an individual house address was guaranteed within one to four hours after each pickup. And thus, as a contemporary gazette pointed out, "life became easier" for all Parisians "whose friends and lovers live across town."

Only rarely do the first people to try out any invention leave an account of their experience. In the case of the original urban postal system, we have a detailed chronicle by a pair of enthusiastic letter writers. Madeleine de Scudéry and Paul Pellisson were authors both: Scudéry was already the most successful novelist of her generation and Pellisson was on his way to becoming a major historian. They were just beginning one of the most celebrated romantic friendships of the age, and they wanted to stay in constant touch. Since neither was wealthy enough to employ servants to deliver letters several times a day, they were the ideal clients for the new system.

Scudéry's and Pellisson's letters detail how what they called writing "*par la voie des boîtes*," by way of the boxes, had transformed communication. They rush to make the first pickup of the day. They write several times a day and at all hours. They experiment with another of Villayer's inventions: the greeting card. (Ten kinds of what were called "form notes" were for sale. You filled in the recipient's name and signed it; at the bottom there was space for a brief message.)

But Villayer's service barely lasted through the fall of 1653. He had undoubtedly attempted to inaugurate an unprecedented venture too soon after the war's end, at a time when Paris was nearly bankrupt, and few Parisians could afford *any* new expense—and neither the municipality nor the crown had the resources to provide funding. When public mail delivery within Paris finally returned in 1759, it was as a state-sponsored system.

The entrepreneurial instinct that had inspired Villayer's venture was, however, far from dead. A few years later, at the moment when Louis XIV began to implement his vision for his capital and just after the king's first street-widening projects in the Marais had been decreed, a pair of urban inventors realized that the new streets then being created would make it possible to move people across Paris with a previously unimaginable efficiency.

In the late 1650s, one of the age's most fertile minds, mathematician and philosopher Blaise Pascal, and an aristocrat with a passion for transportation of all kinds—by water as well as on dry land—Artus Gouffier, Duc de Roannez, began to collaborate on a system whose usefulness had never before been considered: public urban transportation. Until then, whereas cross-country voyagers could travel via public coach, no such service was available to the residents of Paris.

It was only after the civil war that carriages truly began to proliferate in Paris. During the decades when streets were made wider and therefore more hospitable to large vehicles, coaches and carriages increased in number until, by the end of the century, they had become a common sight.

All through the century private carriages remained hugely expensive status symbols. With the coat of arms of their owners painted on their doors, carriages were among the marks of social distinction most visible on the cityscape of Paris: these luxurious vehicles divided the city into haves and have nots as nothing else did. In the Marquise de Sévigné's letters, for example, she never failed to note that someone of her acquaintance had become a member of the carriage set or had been seen in a carriage.

In Paris, those who could not afford such luxury were first able to rent transportation in 1639, when the Marquis de Montbrun established a sedan chair rental service. His venture proved so successful that he was soon able to purchase a residence on the Place Royale. By mid-century, various vehicles were available for hire on a daily basis; this detail from a painting of the bustling Pont Neuf depicts the models of carriage and sedan chair then in use. Still, at a minimum cost of six *livres* a day, this service remained well beyond the reach of the vast majority of Parisians.

The new urban adventure of public transportation began just as Louis XIV's reign was shifting course dramatically. After Mazarin's death in March 1661,

Beginning in the 1640s, Parisians were able to rent carriages and sedan chairs similar to these.

the young king had decided to rule without a principal minister. Then, on November 1, 1661, Louis XIV's first child and heir was born, an event celebrated with public rejoicing and fireworks all over the city. The civil war must at last have seemed firmly in the past. Stability and prosperity were once again the order of the day.

In that same month of November, the mathematician and the transportation fanatic lined up investors and had contracts drawn up laying out the financing for a system of public transit for Paris. Soon after, they spoke to the king, and by January 1662, he issued the *lettres patentes* that gave them a monopoly. In early February, Parlement ratified his decision.

By February 26, Pascal and Roannez decided that it was time for a test run. With a team of rented horses, they set out at six A.M. on two consecutive days. As they reported to one of their major investors, Simon Arnauld, future Marquis de Pomponne, "it was a breeze" to complete four round trips along the route chosen for the original line before eleven A.M., "even though we were only crawling along and we ran into a good deal of traffic along the way." They repeated the experience both afternoons between two and six.

Finally, after much advance publicity and fanfare, urban public transit officially began on March 18, 1662. That same day, a contemporary gazette informed potential riders that basic information, from schedules to rules, had already been posted on street corners throughout the city; techniques developed during the civil war to attract a crowd were finding a new use.

Also visible all over town were posters advertising the new public service. They taught readers the basic rules of a public transportation system, to begin with, the fact that unlike vehicles for hire, public carriages would follow fixed routes—"they always have the same itinerary"—and a fixed schedule—"they always leave at a set time." The posters also explained that carriages would run often—every seven to eight minutes, still the norm at peak hours on frequently traveled bus routes in Paris—"so that it will always be quicker to wait for a carriage than to have your own carriage made ready." (Pascal and Roannez had expressed their hope that easily available transportation might convince those who did own private vehicles to leave them at home.) The posters also announced that service would begin at 6:30 A.M. and operate nonstop "even during the lunch hour" until 6:30 P.M. in winter and until nightfall in summer.

Twelve carriages eventually were deployed on each route, each of them drawn by four horses and thus able to carry eight passengers and two employees and to service its complete route ten times a day. Riders were promised vehicles "spacious and comfortable," "clean and in good condition," with "sturdy" curtains to provide protection from the elements. Carriages with glass windows were first seen in Paris in 1599, but windows only became common in the late seventeenth century. In 1684, such a large a pane of glass was still so expensive that a newspaper lamented the high cost of replacing a broken window.

As for the fare of five *sous*—twenty-four times less than the cost of renting the cheapest vehicle by the day—posters described it as "so modest . . . that everyone will be able to enjoy this convenience."

Gilberte Pascal Périer, sister of the mastermind behind the new system, immediately penned a detailed account of the first day of a new urban age. It seemed to her that most of Paris had come out to get a look at the latest mark of its modernity: "People were lined up on the Pont Neuf and all along the route to watch the carriages go by—it was just like Mardi Gras. Everyone was smiling and laughing with delight. They all want to have the carriages in their neighborhood . . . Already that first morning, many carriages were full."

Gilberte Pascal added that "from the start women rode in the carriages." "From the start," the women of Paris clearly realized that public transportation would provide still another instance of the kind of public gender mixing that so astonished foreigners newly arrived in the city. Within the safe space of one of the new carriages, they could sit in close proximity to Parisians male and female and from various ranks of society.

Gilberte Pascal was herself among the first women ever to use public transportation. In the spring of 1662, her brother was seriously ill—he died only months later—and the distance between their Parisian residences was long. She had no personal vehicle, so she usually walked. To avoid the fatigue of such a lengthy daily trip on foot, she decided to hop a carriage. Already by the afternoon of the first day, however, "the crowd gathered at each stop was so large that you couldn't get close, and the following days were the same." Days later, she lined up again and was "annoyed when five carriages passed me by without stopping because there wasn't a single empty place."

Just as her account indicates, the initial carriage line, which made the round trip between the rue Saint-Antoine near the Place Royale and the Luxembourg Palace, was an overwhelming success. As a result, within weeks, new posters announced that on April 11, "a second carriage line will go into service for the convenience of the inhabitants of Paris." Line 2 began at the Place Royale, made its way through the Marais following the route still used by today's 29 bus, crossed the merchant-class neighborhood near the rue Saint-Denis, before ending up near the Louvre on the rue Saint-Honoré next to the church of Saint-Roch. The two original routes crossed paths near the rue Saint-Denis. There, passengers traveling on one line, posters explained, could easily switch to the other. And thus the transfer was invented.

On May 22, still more posters announced the launch of a third route. This was the first north-south line, running from the rue Montmartre via the historic market area, the Halles, across the Pont Neuf to the Luxembourg Palace. "By royal command," on July 5 another north-south route was launched; it ran from the rue de Poitou in the Marais, via the rue Saint-Martin, passing in front of Notre-Dame, over the Pont Saint-Michel onto the rue Saint-André-des-Arts and the rue de Tournon to the Luxembourg Palace.

And on June 24, the pièce de résistance was inaugurated: by far the longest route of all, it was a circle line, "traveling around the perimeter of Paris" and divided into six zones. Passengers could travel across two zones on one ticket; as soon as they entered a third zone, however, they had to pay again. (Posters did explain that often only a short walk made it possible to avoid that additional fare.)

From north to south, east to west, and all around its rim, Paris' streets were now crisscrossed by a tightly organized system of carriage lines. The ambitious new venture naturally ran into snags, and regulations were put into place to deal with them. The organizers soon realized, for instance, that drivers

On May 22, 1662, this poster announced the first
north-south public transportation route in Paris: it
lists every stop the carriages made between the rue
Montmartre and the Luxembourg Palace.

might be in danger if they carried big sums. It was thus announced that they would no longer make change for large-denomination coins and that riders should try to have the exact fare. When users had complaints—about rude behavior from a driver, for example—they were instructed to make a note of the carriage's identifying "mark" (each was painted with a number and a fleur-de-lis; each line had a fleur-de-lis with a distinct design), to put their complaint in writing, and to take it to one of the company's offices.

The kind of privileged Parisians whom Pascal and Roannez had hoped to encourage to leave their carriages at home created a very different kind of problem. In 1662, the daily rate for a rental carriage with two horses was about seven *livres* (140 *sous*) and hourly rates were not yet available, so the five-penny carriages were a bargain for wealthy riders. They thus began to get on, to pay for all the seats in a carriage—and to instruct the driver not to accept other passengers. An ordinance was quickly issued to forbid this practice.

But the most serious difficulties of all arose because public carriages were intended to become, like the sidewalks on the Pont Neuf, great social levelers. The official documents drafted for authorities such as the Parisian Parlement, as well as the posters advertising the new venture, all confirm that those who invented public transportation aimed to provide reliable service at a price affordable to a broad spectrum of the city's inhabitants. Their target audience included not only wealthy aristocrats and professional men such as lawyers, but also *petites gens*, people of modest means.

The public carriages thus created a classic urban phenomenon: those Parisians who lined up to ride them were obliged to brush up against the flesh and limbs of strangers from across the social spectrum; they shared an intimate space with people with whom they would otherwise never have kept company.

Many, it seems, enjoyed this novel experience. One individual described being seated next to "a perfect stranger" and in the course of the ride learning "his name, where he lives, how much he makes, his father's job, . . . who his relatives are, . . . if he's an aristocrat and whether he owns a château and a carriage of his own."

Some Parisians, however, clearly found the proximity too close for comfort, hence the practice of paying for all the seats in a carriage in order to ride alone. Once this practice was forbidden, upper-class Parisians exercised pressure, and posters soon announced another regulation: "So that the bourgeois can feel more at ease, soldiers, servants, and unskilled workers will no longer be allowed to ride the carriages."

Those excluded from the city service struck back. The very day this ban was pronounced, carriages were attacked; one carriage driving down the rue des Francs-Bourgeois near the Place Royale was stoned by irate domestic servants. An edict making it a crime to threaten drivers was immediately issued; Paris' chief town crier, Charles Canto, toured the streets announcing "a public beating and a 500 *livres* fine"—the price of two thousand carriage rides—for anyone convicted of the offense. From then on, the original system of urban public transportation was no longer truly public.

And from then on, privileged Parisians were clearly "at ease" in the carriages. Paris' first true historian, Henri Sauval, noted that many used the carriages to get to work and that major court figures, such as Henri de Bourbon, Duc d'Enghein, eldest son of the Prince de Condé, "were not at all averse to taking them." In the summer of 1662, even Louis XIV, intrigued by all the hype, had several public carriages drive to his palace in Saint-Germain-en-Laye in order to see for himself how Parisians could now get about.

Other European capitals were not yet ready for this sign of urban modernity. In July 1662, Dutch mathematician Christian Huygens wrote his brother that when officials of the French company had come to seek his help in starting a similar venture in Amsterdam, he had replied, "Officials there would never allow so much commotion all through the city." His remark helps explain the dilemma of why great urban innovations are not always quickly exported to other cities.

Parisians were wild for the new carriages. In the fall of 1662, the story of public transportation was made into the hit play of the new theatrical season. *L'Intrigue des carrosses à cinq sous* ("The Intrigue of the Five-Penny Carriages"), by actor-playwright Jean Simonin, known by his stage name Chevalier, was staged at the Théâtre du Marais on the Vieille rue du Temple, just minutes from the Place Royale. When spectators entered the theater, which they could have reached via two of the carriage lines, they saw a set representing the Place Royale, the main office of the carriage company—and one of the new carriages.

Chevalier's play evoked the actual experience of the transit system operating just outside the theater's doors. It featured drivers wearing blue uniforms, just as the real-life employees did, and riders handing over exact change when they get on, just as the posters asked.

His play centers on two couples first driven apart and then reunited, all because of behavior that public transportation encouraged. One husband has become obsessed with the five-penny carriages because they make philandering so simple. "All day long he races from carriage to carriage" to meet and flirt with women at a previously unimaginable rate, relying on the anonymity of the system to pretend that he is not married. Curious to learn just how he has been spending his days, his suspicious wife adopts a fashion then common among high-born women when out in public and hides her identity behind a full-face mask. Predictably, the skirt-chasing husband is soon head over heels for the mysterious masked woman. When she removes her mask in the play's final scene, he declares, "Since I have fallen for her twice, surely I can love no one else."

Meanwhile, the husband of the second couple is taken with public conveyances for the ease with which they get him, once again anonymously, to the private gambling clubs then springing up all over town. He has already gambled away all his money and has begun to sell his wife's jewels. In order to find out where her treasures are going, she follows him "from carriage to carriage," and then to gambling clubs, successfully disguised as a man. (She alleges that it was "not uncommon to see cross-dressed women in the carriages.") She even manages to save some of her jewelry by picking her husband's pockets while they're riding next to each other. He is so impressed when he learns the pickpocket's true identity that he, too, falls in love all over again.

Chevalier's play continued to be staged for years. An English traveler, Sir John Lauder, saw it performed in February 1666 in Poitiers; he noted in his diary that his ticket cost twenty *sous*, four times the price of a ride in an actual carriage. Other English visitors left accounts of the carriages themselves. In

1664, Edward Browne described "the Carosses that goe about Paris"; in 1666, Sir Philip Skippon described what he saw as a most novel experience: "go[ing] about with other company" and paying the same price as "everyone else."

In 1691, the Duc de Roannez sold his stake in the company. The 1690s had much in common with the immediate post-Fronde years. The royal coffers were nearly empty, and few Parisians could afford anything beyond the bare necessities. The privately financed city service could hardly have been profitable, and state financing was out of the question, so the carriages ceased to run.

Europe at the turn of the eighteenth century, it seems, was not ready for public transit; Pascal and Roannez's venture was not carried on by others. Modernity's history is often discontinuous: great ideas can be forgotten for long periods and then reinvented. After Roannez's company failed, for example, Paris was without public transportation until 1828, when the first vehicles called omnibuses (from the Latin "for all") began to operate between the Porte Saint-Martin and the Madeleine. The omnibuses were actually a newer model of carriage, drawn by two horses and with room for twelve passengers—which meant that they were quite similar to, though probably slower than, the five-penny carriages.

In 1662, public transit, like public life in general, ceased at nightfall; after dark, Paris was a playground for *filous* and other thieves. Soon, however, this began to change. In October 1662, while Chevalier's comedy was playing at the Marais theater, a publicity flier circulated: it informed Parisians that it was no longer necessary to become fair game for cloak thieves by walking home through pitch-dark streets. For a fee, public torchbearers would now light their way. The brochure also notified the directors of the five-penny carriage company that, for a mere four *sous* a day, one of their carriages could have its route lit up by its own torchbearer.

Public transportation had thus made evident the need for a third convenience no city had ever known: street lighting.

Indeed, already in March 1662, the very month that carriages started rolling, Louis XIV had issued a royal patent to still another private investor, an Italian named Laudati Caraffa, known in France as Abbé Laudati de Caraffe, for a new public service: the rental of torchbearers. By August, when the transit system was fully operational, the Parisian Parlement had registered his monopoly. To Laudati de Caraffe goes the credit for the original formulation of an idea fundamental to our concept of a modern city: a city can only function as it should—that is, around the clock—if its streets are lit at night.

Prior to Louis XIV's reign, attempts at lighting up the night in Paris had been both sporadic and unsystematic. Beginning in the late fourteenth century, on official holidays and in times of danger, Parisian authorities had asked homeowners to keep a candle burning all night long in a window. The first attempt to make this practice permanent occurred in 1504, when Parlement ordered Parisians whose windows faced onto a street to keep a candle lit in them after nine in the evening. Similar laws were passed throughout the century, apparently with little success. In the early 1640s, a modest system of public lighting was initiated: lanterns were to be lit in certain streets and squares during the winter months. But that initiative, too, was soon abandoned. Until Louis XIV's reign, those Parisians obliged to be out after dark either carried a lantern or were accompanied by servants bearing torches; otherwise, they were at the mercy of the robbers who roamed their city's streets.

Then, on October 14, 1662, at the spot where the rue Saint-Honoré opens off from the city's traditional market area, Les Halles, the head office of Laudati de Caraffe's enterprise was inaugurated: the Center for Torch and Lantern Bearers of Paris. His employees wore uniforms so that pedestrians could recognize them at a glance; each was assigned a number. Torchbearers equipped with substantial torches (a pound and a half of "the best yellow wax") and lantern-bearers carrying oil lamps were stationed at strategic points in the most frequented areas of the city. You had only to show up at a designated location and for a set fee light-bearers would illuminate your way to any spot in Paris. As Laudati explained, this meant that those "without a personal servant could now return home whenever they liked."

Attached to the belts of Laudati's employees was an hourglass marked with the arms of the city of Paris; it timed fifteen-minute intervals. In the flier Laudati used to advertise his system, he claimed that "in the space of a quarter-hour one can get to any destination" in Paris. Pedestrians paid three *sous* for a quarter-hour of lighting; those with private carriages paid five *sous* per quarter-hour to have a light-bearer ride next to their coachman. Laudati de Caraffe thought big: he planned eventually to employ more than fifteen hundred light-bearers and to station them at each end of every major street and also in the middle of the longest streets, so that "wherever you go they will be available to light your way and escort you from street to street." Like the inventors of public transportation, Laudati de Caraffe intended his service to be truly public: he pointed out, "If you'll just follow someone who has paid for a torch-bearer's services, your way will be lit for free." From the start, public lighting was conceived as a way to reclaim the night for those without servants to light their way.

Street lighting was also seen as far more than a personal convenience. On this, the king and the inventor shared a commonality of vision that explains why Paris became the original city of light: they both realized that lighting could transform urban life.

In his letters patent, Louis XIV called attention to the high nocturnal crime rate "in our good city of Paris." That crime rate, the king affirmed, "is the result of insufficient light in its streets." "Businessmen are greatly inconvenienced," he added, "especially in winter when the days are short, because they are unable to do any work after nightfall, since they don't dare come and go freely in the streets." Public light-bearers, Laudati de Caraffe promised, would "make it possible for businessmen and merchants to move about as they wish; the streets of Paris will thus be far busier at night—and this will go a long way toward ridding the city of thieves." Their message was clear: in a modern city, public safety and commercial prosperity went hand in hand—and lighting was essential for both.

It's not known how long Laudati's company continued to function, though his idea lived on: light-bearers were for hire in Paris at least until the Revolution. Once, however, the king and his chief financial adviser, Colbert, sensed how radically Paris could be improved by increased light, they laid the foundation for a more ambitious and a truly public service. For the first time, a city service was to be state-sponsored, no longer dependent on the finances of a small group of private investors.

In 1665, a high-level commission was established under the direction of Colbert; the king himself presided over its initial meeting at the Louvre. Leaders of the Parisian Parlement, the chancellor of France Pierre Séguier, important magistrates—all gathered regularly during the following months to begin a major reform of city governance. Their most crucial decision was the appointment, in March 1667, of Nicolas de La Reynie to a newly created position, lieutenant general of the Parisian police. La Reynie remained in office until 1709, by all accounts governing the city brilliantly. The edict that established his position assigned a dual role to the Parisian police: "to purge the city of disorder and to create abundance for its inhabitants."

As soon as La Reynie took office, he set about making Paris safe and prosperous. Among his first initiatives was something no city had ever had before: true public street lighting. The members of that royal commission had been discussing this issue in the months preceding La Reynie's appointment—above all, how much such an operation might cost. A contemporary gazette indicates that they had already tested some form of street lighting in late 1666.

On September 2, 1667, barely six months after his job description had been formulated, La Reynie was thus able to inform Parisians that this innovative public service would soon be operational. Five days later, an edict was posted on street corners; Paris' town crier Charles Canto and royal trumpeter Hiérosme Tronsson marched through the capital announcing that the very streets on which they were walking would soon be lit at night. The October 29 issue of Charles Robinet's gazette boasted that "it is now as bright at night as at high noon." Lanterns—2,736 of them—had been positioned throughout the 912 streets that then composed the urban fabric. Small streets were allotted one lantern at each end, while a third one was added in the middle of longer thoroughfares. This was the original design for permanent, stationary street lighting.

Every aspect of the new service, and in particular its cost, had been ferociously debated by the commission—especially the two competing prototypes for the original streetlight, one in wood and the other in metal. Colbert in the end selected the metal lantern, for obvious reasons of safety, even though it was more than twice as expensive. Lanterns were composed of glass panels roughly two-feet square—at the time, a very large pane of glass indeed and thus another major expense. Each lantern cost about twelve *livres*, three times more than the original park benches on which Parisians would soon enjoy the Tuileries Gardens. And then there was the price of the candles: they were huge, designed to burn for eight to ten hours. It was estimated that it cost the city two *sous* every night to keep one such candle burning in each of those high-priced lanterns.

Different methods for suspending the lanterns were also tested. At first, some were hung about twenty feet off the ground in the middle of the street. It was later decided to attach them to the side of houses about one story off the ground and to raise and lower them by means of a pulley system. According to one English visitor's description, "the rope that lets [the lanterns] down" was enclosed in a metal tube attached to the wall of the nearest house; the handle that controlled the pulley was "locked up in a little trunk fastened onto the wall of the house."

All this created a system both visually and spatially discreet, as this image from the late seventeenth century shows. The man on the far right is walking through the streets ringing a bell to signal that lighting should begin. The individual behind him has already unlocked the "little trunk" and has used the handle to lower the lantern; a woman is ready to insert the special candle; the child next to her is getting the next candle ready.

The engraver, Nicolas Guérard the Younger, portrayed what was by then a well-oiled system. Homeowners were assigned responsibility on a yearly basis for a certain number of streets. They were issued keys to the pulley boxes and a basket large enough to contain ten to fifteen of the extra-large candles and were reminded by a nightly bell that it was time to set off on their rounds.

Nicolas Guérard the Younger's engraving illustrated the functioning of the original system of street lighting and depicted Paris as a city where brightly lit streets had created an active nightlife.

At the start in 1667, candles were lit between November 1 and March 1. Soon Parisians began sending delegations to beg La Reynie to extend the calendar. Lighting then became functional from October 15 until March 15; next, the date was moved back to March 30—and so it went bit by bit until, by the turn of the eighteenth century, the lights were on in Paris for nine months of the year.

There was also the matter of the daily schedule, the time at which the lantern-lighting bell was rung. This was soon fixed at six P.M. in October, 5:30 in November, 5:00 in December and January, 6:00 in February, and 6:30 in March.

Street lighting was a new kind of public service, run not by private investors but by the crown and the municipality and financed largely through the "mud and lanterns" tax, intended to pay for cleaning and lighting the streets. The city service was quickly seen by all Parisians as essential. Already in May 1671, concerned citizens called meetings in each of the sixteen administrative districts and voted to send a delegation to Parlement to express their willingness to contribute to the expense of an extended lighting calendar. Street lighting, however, was so exorbitant that covering its cost was always a struggle. At the end of the century, when the tax raised about three hundred thousand *livres* annually, candles alone ate up more than two hundred thousand *livres* of that total. From 1668 on, edict after edict tackled the question of how to raise the necessary funds.

Yet there was never any debate about whether the service was worth its considerable cost. The moment in late 1667 when those nearly three thousand lanterns were lit seemed to many the gesture that most openly symbolized the new and improved Paris.

Just as all those who had championed the revolutionary service had predicted, brighter streets had a notable impact on urban crime. Only months before lighting went into effect, a newsman complained that "no one dares go out" at night, whereas at the service's inception another journalist boasted that, "thanks to La Reynie and his beautiful lanterns, the gentlemen known as *filous* will soon be unhappy indeed."

Numerous regulations issued by the Parisian police during the months just after the new system went into effect indicate that La Reynie was targeting clothing theft in other ways as well: an edict from December 1667 shut down used-clothing dealers who had set up shop in close proximity to the Pont Neuf and who were suspected of selling goods stolen on the bridge. The contemporary press lavished praise on the new "exactitude" with which such regulations had been enforced since La Reynie had taken office.

La Reynie also tried to tilt the balance of power in favor of the officers of the law. He increased the number of officers assigned to the *guet*, the watch, the task of patrolling the streets at night on horseback. Laws went into effect to forbid those walking in the streets from having firearms, daggers, and knives on their persons—while a subsequent regulation authorized officers of the *guet* to carry "pocket pistols."

This aspect of Paris' transformation was widely celebrated. Already in 1671, author and journalist François Colletet announced in the first edition of his often reprinted history of Paris that France's capital was now "not only the most beautiful but also the safest city in the world." Because of the lanterns, Colletet boasted, "until two or three in the morning it's almost as light as in daytime." And because of increased police presence in the nighttime streets, "people are now so little afraid of robbers that, to my amazement, even on the Pont Neuf, where previously there was no security after dark, people now walk with as little fear as in daytime."

When royal painter Charles Le Brun decorated the ceiling of Versailles's monumental Hall of Mirrors with scenes commemorating the greatest accomplishments of Louis XIV's reign, he included one depicting "the police and public safety reaffirmed in Paris." This engraving by Nicolas Guérard the Younger advertises street lighting's role in reducing crime by dramatizing "the capture of a night thief." A robber is racing down the street, a stolen cloak still in his hand; he is easily outdistancing the cloakless nobleman coming

This engraving advertised the way street lighting could reduce urban crime—guided by lanterns positioned in Paris' streets, uniformed officers are closing in on a thief.

after him. The thief will clearly be no match, however, for the five uniformed officers of "the watch" who, guided by the radiant glow of the street lamp, are pursuing him on horseback.

Raymond Poisson's 1669 comedy *Les Faux Moscovites* ("The Fake Muscovites") centers on two Parisian thieves who tell of the hard times on which their profession has fallen. Because of the efficiency of "the watch," *filous* who "used to steal cloaks on the Pont Neuf," are "now as poor as street rats." "If we rob someone tonight, tomorrow we'll be hanged. Paris is now worthless for us; there are police everywhere." And all this began, they moan, about two years earlier—as soon, in other words, as La Reynie had taken up his duties. Indeed, times are so tough that Poisson's petty criminals have been forced to turn to new kinds of crime. Instead of fencing stolen cloaks, they have become cardsharps: disguised as wealthy Russians, they frequent gambling academies.

In 1694, a dictionary confirmed that times were hard for clothing pinchers. The examples that illustrate *filou*'s definition reaffirm both increased confidence in the police's ability to fight cloak pilfering—"last night the officers of the watch captured several *filous*"—and the notion that cloak theft was becoming a crime of the past: "*Filou* is now also used to refer to cardsharps and to all those who use their skill and shrewdness to trick others."

As La Reynie's mandate had predicted, this increased security went hand in hand with increased prosperity. Already in 1671, the delegation of concerned citizens who offered to help pay for additional hours of light emphasized that merchants were now able to take care of work "they were too busy to finish during the day." They added that the quality of life had improved for all, since Parisians "can now get together whenever they like."

And once the city's residents could socialize freely after dark, nightlife began. On December 4, 1673, the Marquise de Sévigné had dinner with close friends. The evening went on long past midnight, at which point a previously unimaginable experience took over, that of enjoying Paris after dark. "We thought it was great fun to be able to go, after midnight, to the opposite end of [town] just to bring someone home . . . We were laughing the entire time, certain that we would never be robbed—all because of the new lanterns."

Every one of the earliest Paris guidebooks promised foreigners an experience they could find nowhere else. Nemeitz assured readers of his widely translated introduction to the city that, because of "the public lanterns," the city no longer ceased functioning the minute night fell, as other European capitals did. "Many shops as well as most cafés and eating establishments stay open until ten or eleven P.M.; they keep lots of lights burning in their windows to make the streets even brighter." People now eat and shop "whenever they like," and as a result, there are "almost as many people out and about at night as during the day." This illustration from a 1702 guide to Paris' café scene and café society is the original depiction of nightlife: in a café brightly lit with candles, a varied group that includes a number of noblewomen is eating and drinking and enjoying life after dark.

Guidebooks included the public lanterns themselves among the "beautiful sights" that no visitor to Paris should miss. As Marana explained to Italian visitors, "Everyone must come and see . . . a spectacle so wondrous that even Archimedes, if he were alive today, could not improve on it." Nemeitz advised "positioning oneself at an intersection where several streets met." There, visitors could admire the spectacle of lights, "suspended at fixed distances from each other and extending out in all directions."

Street lighting became the first urban technology to spread widely across Europe. In 1669, a system was implemented in Amsterdam, created by artist and inventor Jan van der Heyden. (He had already redesigned the fire engine and invented the pump-driven hose.) In Berlin in 1680, the Prussian government began to erect posts on which to hang lanterns. Vienna was first lit at night in 1688. By the 1690s, London was sufficiently rebuilt after the Great Fire of 1666 for street lighting to become a priority. In 1691, candle makers protested to the Lord Mayor because Edward Heming was experimenting

*This view of an elegant Parisian café promoted
another advantage of street lighting: men and women
from across the social spectrum spending an evening
socializing in a public venue.*

with oil lamps; he was granted the right to install candle-based lamps in 1694.
Even then, however, London was lit only on moonless nights, something that
caused Lady Mary Wortley Montagu to affirm in 1718 that "Paris has the advantage of London in . . . the regular lighting of its streets at night."

French scientists also continued to try to find ways to improve the quality of the city service widely considered the glory of "the century of inventions." In 1703, the French Royal Academy of Sciences awarded one of their members named Favre a patent for the most ambitious street-lighting project yet conceived, a tower to be positioned on "the highest point in the city" and topped by four huge light sources—deep paraboloidal receptacles, each of them equipped with a reservoir containing oil and pipes for the evacuation of smoke. Favre contended that this gigantic tower of light—conceived nearly two centuries before Gustave Eiffel planned his structure—would be sufficient "to light an entire city throughout the night."

As Louis XIV's "grand design" was implemented and the cityscape was expanded, the original system of street lighting was also extended to keep the new streets safe and to help Parisians navigate new territory in their city. By 1702, 5,470 lanterns were positioned all through the city's streets. By 1729, that number had grown to 5,772; and by 1740, to 6,408. And when in the early

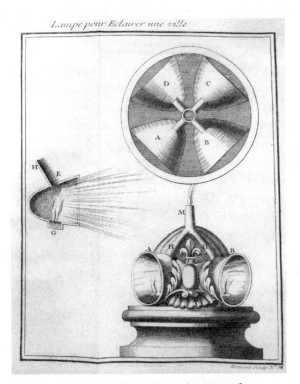

In 1703, an inventor obtained a patent for a
gigantic street light to be positioned on
the highest point in Paris.

eighteenth century the original boulevard on the Right Bank was at last complete, lighting was added there, too. The boulevard, the place where, in Balzac's words, Paris became "most fully itself," remained brightly lit until four or five in the morning. In his account of the ideal visit to Paris, Louis Liger encouraged visitors to become part of another of the original manifestations of Parisian nightlife, "the prodigious crowd of all ages and all ranks that came there to walk and to dance."

Over the course of three decades, street lighting had become as characteristically Parisian as the boulevard. It had become essential to the city's safety and its quality of life, as well as the most visible manifestation of Paris' status as the most modern of European capitals. It offered visible evidence that, under Louis XIV, Paris was defined not by isolated monuments but by its complete urban fabric. It had also proved key to Paris' transformation into Louis XIV's dream for his capital—"a place dedicated to pleasure," the kind of city where it was possible to eat and drink in public establishments until all hours, and even "to walk and dance" in public until four in the morning.

Technology has always been an engine driving urban change and development; it has always left its mark on cityscapes—the railway stations of the nineteenth century are an obvious example. And technology has also often been portrayed as the harbinger and even the cause of societal upheaval. It is therefore hardly surprising that the new Paris became a setting said to have fostered significant social change, as well as the setting chosen most often by the many contemporary commentators who wished to portray the French social fabric as evolving in decidedly dramatic ways.

Three images took shape and were used to conjure up the new pleasure city: Paris as the most stylish capital in Europe, populated by the best-dressed people on the continent; Paris as an urban center in which vast wealth was ostentatiously displayed by the parvenus whose gold ruled the city; and Paris as the most romantic city in the world with the most beautiful women anywhere to be found, the Parisiennes. All three originated with actual individuals and real-life experiences. But, as will happen when high-profile cases attract inordinate attention to a phenomenon, all three were probably blown out of proportion. As a result, they soon became true urban legends—legends that through the centuries remained part of the myth of Paris. More than any other ideas, these images make it possible to appreciate the interaction between the building of a capital in brick and mortar and the invention of a legendary city with an independent existence in the minds of those who conjured it up and those who dreamed of it. And the three are linked by a common obsession. Tales of the new world of fashion, money, and romance told at the same time a second story: the role played by these forces in reshaping French society.

Once Paris' new thoroughfares and new city services were in place, it became far easier to move about widely and at all times. From all accounts, this increased circulation played a crucial role in taking the social mixing that began on the Pont Neuf to a new level. Before the end of the seventeenth century, Paris was widely described in terms that would later be used for cities such as Gilded Age New York or Fin-de-Siècle Vienna, as a place where you could no longer tell who was who or what—or where they came from.

This social jumble was aided and abetted by the French luxury goods industry, an institution that could only have been successfully created in a city in which merchants and their clients could circulate easily and safely. Paris made fashion modern, and modern fashion in turn was key to Paris' transformation.

CHAPTER SEVEN

Capitale de la Mode

IN THE COLLECTIVE imagination today, Paris *is* fashion. And there is nothing new about this idea.

In 1777, an observer of contemporary manners concluded that "it is difficult for Europeans today to imagine what their counterparts in 1600 looked like." Between 1600 and 1750, he explained, they had been "transformed." Whereas in 1600, "Europeans knew nothing about style," by the end of the seventeenth century, people all over Europe had begun to dress fashionably—as the French did. "The French fashion industry works day and night" to create new styles, he contended, and as a result the French have succeeded in "making Europe French." Many factors contributed to this process, what a well-traveled Englishman had pronounced in 1701 "the Frenchifying" of Europe.

In seventeenth-century Paris, urban planning and the trade in luxury goods developed in tandem. A beautiful capital city was the ideal setting in which to commercialize beautiful things—hence Henri IV's vision for the Place Royale as simultaneously an architectural monument, a center of silk production, and the place where the new industry's products would be offered for sale. Hence also the fact that in an urban center like Paris, the act of walking could become far more than merely functional. It put the latest styles on public display; by showing off dress on real people and in precise contexts, it brought fashion to life and gave it glamour.

By the early 1670s, Paris was richly endowed with both revolutionary public works and the most remarkable residential architecture in Europe, and Louis XIV had begun a grandiose redesign of the city's thoroughfares as well as his project for an open city. Parisians could cross town using public transportation; at night, they walked by the light of publicly maintained lanterns—and they took advantage of the extended shopping hours made possible by street lighting. Paris was visibly a capital on the move, heading toward the novel and the cutting edge. The revitalized city jump-started the creation of a French luxury goods industry.

Over the course of the next three decades, France achieved a virtual stranglehold over this highly profitable trade. By 1700, English commentators were grumbling darkly that the French were exporting all over Europe, and to England in particular, vast quantities of very expensive and absolutely frivolous things—and since the English were producing nothing that the French coveted, all sales were pure profit for the French. The huge and very real trade imbalance thus created was the direct result of another key development of the late seventeenth century: all over Europe, people began to agree that a new force was now evident in their urban centers. They referred to it by its French name, *la mode*—everything that is stylish or fashionable. They also agreed that *la mode* originated in Paris, where the standards for style and fashion were now set. *La mode* was established in Paris; elsewhere, it was simply followed. Once this idea took hold, Europe was ready to "become French," and foreigners had found another reason to visit Paris: to learn about the latest trends and to acquire the novelties of the moment. In 1672, English poet laureate Thomas Shadwell referred to the French rule over fashion as "the Universal Monarchy for clothes."

Hand in hand with the development of style tourism went the transformation of the experience of acquiring luxury goods. The best Parisian merchants understood that *mode* and modernity worked in tandem: they thus took advantage of the latest urban technologies such as street lighting, as well as the city's attractiveness, and used Paris itself to help market their wares. Each of them also went all out to convince consumers that they were selling a unique product and that they, and they alone, were purveyors of the last word in Parisian style. In the city's newly modern streets, the shop was redesigned; novel marketing techniques were tried out, as well as innovative ways of displaying goods. Thus redesigned, the shop became another of the places where Parisian insiders might meet.

Together, these city planners, artisans and craftsmen, merchants, those responsible for their advertising, and surely their customers as well created a new urban amusement: we call it "going shopping." They took the simple act of buying something and reinvented it as a novel form of entertainment, still another social activity in which the fashionable set could indulge. Together, they worked out the new pastime's rules, from how to decide on the right price to how to determine value.

Never before had a modern city been so thoroughly and widely identified as a center for luxury commerce and for luxury commerce marketed in upscale settings. Thanks to the wholesale reinvention of the process of purchasing luxury goods, Paris acquired another facet of its identity, one that has remained through the centuries essential to its image: as Capitale de la Mode, *the* Capital of Style and Fashion. "Paris" then became a one-word ad for fashion.

Urban centers have always been centers of commerce. In every city, wares of varying quality are marketed in many ways. In this respect, seventeenth-century Paris was a city like any other.

Parisians still purchased many items as they had for centuries: at open-air markets and fairs and from itinerant peddlers who roamed the city's streets. This late-seventeenth-century scene depicts some of the goods and services offered by those peddlers described in a contemporary dictionary as carrying their shops "around their necks or on their backs." In the center, a woman demonstrates children's toys, a rattle and what she calls a "windmill." To her right, Dame Chiffon, "the Rag Lady," is an ambulant resale shop, offering used clothing and shoes. On the far left, a shoe repairman is in conversation with someone who fixes everything from pots to parasols.

The peddlers who roamed Paris' streets with their "shops on their backs" sold everything from used clothing to children's toys.

The stalls on the Pont Neuf were an extended open-air market featuring everything
from cooking implements to inexpensive fashion accessories.

Innovative kinds of public space, such as the Pont Neuf's broad esplanade, attracted less ambulant street traders. In their little stalls, they proposed both quotidian items and entry-level luxury goods such as ribbons, priced to attract a range of shoppers. More upmarket versions of these same items could be found at one of the original modern shopping venues: the Galerie du Palais or Palace Gallery. It was there that Parisians were introduced to the concept of indoor shopping.

In the sixteenth century, on each side of the walkway leading to the Grande Salle or Great Room of the Palais de Justice, the Law Courts, Paris' earliest shopping arcade was set up. In 1577, an Italian visitor described how "even the king himself and his court" could be seen there. "A great number of cavaliers and ladies" came, he added, some "for amusement and pleasure, others to shop." Thus began the process that, a century later, had completely redesigned the experience of shopping.

The original Palace Gallery was not unique. In the sixteenth century, Italy, Spain, and Flanders were vying for the high-end trade, and shopping arcades were established in all major European trading capitals, from Venice to London. But seventeenth-century depictions make it clear that the arcade functioned differently in each locale.

The second-floor gallery of London's Royal Exchange, for example, housed a range of shops, many of them practical (ironmongers, notaries), with some more exclusive trades (haberdashers, goldsmiths) mixed in. The exchange was a new experience for Londoners because so many stands were found in a single space. But the shops themselves were in no way a novelty: their design and the manner in which goods were displayed were quite basic. Women did work and shop there, but the gallery seems to have been, like the Exchange itself, where merchants met to cut deals, a heavily male establishment. Its French counterpart could not have been more different.

Just after midnight on March 25, 1618, an enormous conflagration destroyed Paris' Law Courts. A contemporary observer described how the gallery's shops "which were all built in wood, went up in flames and were quickly reduced to ashes." Queen Marie de Médicis's official architect, Salomon de Brosse, was responsible for rebuilding the Great Hall, so the Palace Gallery was reincarnated in a much grander setting. The new gallery was so distinguished architecturally that it soon became the first shopping arcade to be extensively recorded for posterity.

This engraving, produced not long after the gallery had reopened, gives a sense of de Brosse's elegant Renaissance architecture and of the arcade's distinctive blend of commerce: mainly book dealers and merchants who displayed such high-end fashion accessories as fancy lace collars. The depiction, like all other early views of the Palace Gallery, also highlights the innovations that earned it a place in the history of shopping. Each little stand has a counter— only a small one, but a real counter nonetheless—on which merchandise is laid out for customers to examine. Each stand has some method of storage clearly visible, indicating thereby the availability of additional stock. And each one has a few samples of key merchandise displayed in a manner designed to catch the eye of visitors. All these features combined to make the small stands in the Palace Gallery the first true precursors of modern shops. And the shopping experience found there was also modern in one final way. Although book dealers were often male, women also "manned" these stands, just as men as well as women sold fashion accessories. Women sold to male shoppers, and men to female shoppers. Unlike arcades elsewhere in Europe, the Palace Gallery encouraged complete gender mixing.

The Gallery remained such a popular destination all through the seventeenth century that it was enlarged several times; by 1700, it housed one hundred and eighty merchants. Each redesign aimed to make it more attractive and to keep it up to date: new shops were built "in symmetry" with existing ones and "in the most agreeable architecture possible."

Parisians and visitors alike were drawn there just as their successors in later centuries would be to the arcades of the Palais Royal, to indoor *passages*, and, beginning in the 1820s, to the original *grands magasins* or department stores—which were organized like multistory versions of the Palace Gallery. Once there, they looked around, strolled, talked to friends and made

*In Paris, public shopping for high-end merchandise began in the
covered arcade known as the Palace Gallery.*

new acquaintances. Dozens of merchants in close proximity showing off vari-
ants of similar goods also introduced Parisians to a phenomenon previously
impossible in luxury commerce: comparison shopping. The Palace Gallery
thereby gave consumers an early lesson in the art of desire.

Because of those little stands, Paris began to take over from other European capitals and to win the reputation it enjoyed by the second half of the

seventeenth century: as the place to find both the biggest assortment of goods and absolutely to-the-minute styles. On his first day in Paris, November 11, 1664, Sebastiano Locatelli, member of a wealthy Italian merchant family and destined for the priesthood, started his tour of the city at Notre-Dame Cathedral ("as I felt obliged to do"), followed by the Sainte-Chapelle, to which he devoted all of six lines in his travel diary. He then stopped by the Palace Gallery—and that got two full pages of comments. He raved about the "vast number" of shops "full of every kind of merchandise imaginable" and in particular about the "unusually attractive women" running most of them.

Locatelli's account foretells a major way in which seventeenth-century Paris transformed the experience of foreign travel. Even a future priest was more susceptible to the allurements of shopping Parisian style than to those of one of Europe's greatest cathedrals. Locatelli's diary shows how successfully the marketing strategies developed at the Palace Gallery attracted the attention of consumers and even taught them new ways of evaluating and acquiring merchandise. All the factors he pointed out combined, as Locatelli repeated several times in his account, to transform shopping from a mundane experience into "a pleasure."

Europeans from many nations would soon come to feel as Locatelli did, that, in Paris, you would find more choice and the entire experience would be far more beguiling than anywhere else. And in 1664, the transformation of high-end commerce in Paris was only just beginning.

In January 1664, Louis XIV gave Colbert, his right-hand man for the next twenty years, his first major role: Surintendant des Bâtiments, Arts, et Manufactures, Superintendant of Buildings, Arts, and Manufactories. Behind that unwieldy title lay immense powers. In his new capacity, Colbert oversaw the financing of all projects involving French royal buildings, including the Louvre and later Versailles. He also became the equivalent of a modern minister of culture, with the power to shape the development of the arts in France. And last but far from least, he was in charge of the creation and development of all of what were known as manufactories, the Gobelins tapestry workshop, for example. In this capacity, Colbert played a defining role in the reorganization of existing French industries such as the Lyon silkworks and in the creation of new ones for the production of everything from mirrors to lace. This was the official origin of what would become by 1700 the all-powerful French luxury goods industry.

Colbert orchestrated this French takeover of the production of luxury goods with Louis XIV's active participation. Notes in Colbert's handwriting that date from 1664 illustrate perfectly the closeness of their collaboration.

In about 1600, Henri IV posed before a panorama of premodern Paris.

This detail from a c. 1640 painting is the earliest image of the newly completed Île Saint-Louis.

To convey a sense of the Place Royale's importance for Parisians, this 1612 view makes the new square so large that it dominates the city.

By 1655, the Place Royale was depicted as an elegant residential square and promenade space.

A 1660s view shows Louis XIV crossing the Pont Neuf, both taking in and becoming a part of the spectacle of Paris.

Another scene of the Pont Neuf in the 1660s depicts everyday life on the bridge.

Souvenir fans, such as this one featuring a painting of an open-air market on the quais of the Seine, allowed visitors to bring their favorite images of Paris home with them.

Scenes of the open-air theater on the Pont Neuf presenting Paris as a culturally and socially vibrant city are among the most frequently encountered seventeenth-century souvenir images.

Bird's-eye views of the Seine and the grandeur of Paris such as Abraham de Verwer's from 1640 promoted the appreciation for urban beauty to which the Pont Neuf introduced Europeans.

Two men take advantage of one of the Pont Neuf's innovations: balconies from which visitors could enjoy the panorama of Paris.

The Pont Neuf gave Parisians good reasons to be out and about and many new things to see. Paintings depicted those who visited the bridge as actively engaged with the city and the people around them.

New public works helped turn Paris into a spectator city. The balconies that appeared on residences in the 1640s allowed Parisians to take in the urban display and to put themselves on display for each other.

Early in the seventeenth century, less fortunate Parisians transformed the riverbank just below the Pont Neuf into a very public beach.

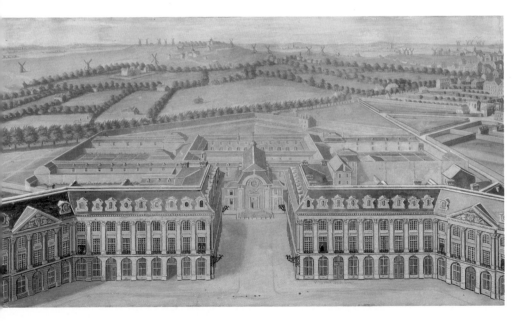

At the century's end, the city's wealthiest residents put their fortunes on display by building grand homes on the newest residential square, the Place Louis-le-Grand.

Early in his reign, Louis XIV was portrayed, accompanied by his mother, passing the Place Royale on one of his regular inspection tours of Paris.

Fifty years later, Louis XIV was still inspecting Paris' monuments, here the newly completed Église Saint-Louis at the Invalides.

Experts believe that these notes, which lay out a new vision for French economic policy—a revised tax system, the creation of the East Indies Company
and West Indies Company—were likely dictated by the still-young king. Two
lines stand out:

Revitalize manufactories in France.
The king wears and distributes fabric to every member of his court.

The king of France strategically made his actions reflect his words. For
official appearances, he would arrive clothed in textiles produced by state-
sponsored workshops, the very manufactories he and Colbert wanted to "revitalize." And by personally distributing French-made textiles "to every
member of his court," he obliged them all to follow his lead. He knew that when
the most closely watched Parisians of the day were seen in public showing off
the finest new fabrics made in France, his court would serve as a walking advertisement for his nation's luxury goods. He thereby put into place a strategy
that helped guarantee French dominance over the world of style.

Colbert is given credit today for crucial tactics that rebooted the French
economy. His interventionist policy—called protectionism, mercantilism, or
simply *colbertisme*—imposed heavy taxes on all imported goods. Colbert also
ordered French manufacturers to copy the foreign products French consumers most desired. He even established standards, and this strictly enforced
quality control guaranteed the superiority of French-made goods.

But equally important was Louis XIV's instinctive understanding of the
mechanics that drive style and fashion. For instance, providing samples to
prominent tastemakers is a marketing strategy that proved essential to the
development of the luxury goods sector—and one that is still used today. The
single-minded collaboration between monarch and minister made it possible
for fashion to become a state industry for France.

In 1672, the king authorized the publication of a new periodical, one that
was to play a crucial role in making Paris the capital of fashion. Its editor, Jean
Donneau de Visé, was given official permission to publish, with one precise
caveat: he "would make no mention of politics." In the decades that followed,
Donneau de Visé often ignored that prohibition and included coverage of everything from war to diplomatic missions. From the start, however, he carved
out a niche never before covered by the periodical press: the world of style.
The *Mercure galant*'s Parisian edition was reprinted in Amsterdam as well as
in several French cities; the new periodical thus soon attracted a pan-European
readership. From the start, Donneau de Visé was an unabashed spokesperson

for all things French; for nearly forty years until his death in 1710, he relent-lessly promoted Paris as the new world center for everything fashionable. Over the course of those four decades, the publicity he gave French luxury commerce helped bring about this state of affairs.

From his inaugural issue in 1672, Donneau de Visé included coverage of the French scene from an angle previously unexplored in journalism: a segment devoted to *la mode*—among the earliest examples of that particular usage of the term. In the 1673 issue, Donneau de Visé made fashion coverage a central part of his periodical's mission. He re-created a conversation he had allegedly had with two women of his acquaintance, whom he ran into while walking in the Tuileries gardens. This was the first time that the recently redesigned public garden was identified as a privileged showcase for the latest in French fashion. The women had given him a crash course in all the areas in which stylish Parisians felt they had to be up-to-date. They began with dress, men's as well as women's, then discussed furniture, interior decoration, and textiles (in particular all the latest French silks, such as a "speckled brocade that could be mistaken for real ermine"), before concluding with the latest culinary trends (even the stomach follows *la mode*, one remarked).

After some forty pages, the ladies ended on this note: "Everyone agrees that nothing has greater appeal than styles that originate in France, and that ev-erything made in France has a certain air about it that craftsmen elsewhere never manage to give to their work. This explains why countries all over the world are importing French-made goods." The *Mercure*'s informants on style then made clear exactly how it had come to be that, for example, "German ladies are so mad for French-made shoes that two shipping containers [four thousand pounds] of them recently left for Germany." To hear them tell it, it was all so very simple: a fashion no sooner appeared at the French court than it quickly spread through Parisian society, from noblewomen to rich bourgeoises to shopgirls. The same trickle-down effect next took place in French provincial cities before the latest style finally reached women across Europe—by which time, the ladies of the French court had of course long since moved on, and the whole cycle had started up again.

Prior to the 1670s, there was little sense of international fashion: for the most part, women from different European countries respected their country's na-tional dress. Styles changed very slowly, and luxurious garments conveyed a message of wealth and power more than a sense of style and fashion. The transnational migration of fashion trends began in earnest with Paris' ascent to European capital of style. Fashion began to be exported; styles began to travel quickly from one country to another. From this moment on, fashion was poised to become an international business.

At first, style travel was strictly unidirectional. Just as the ladies interviewed in the *Mercure galant* had predicted and just as their monarch had hoped, men and women all over Europe began to imitate any look that originated in Paris. But this did not happen merely because someone from Germany caught a glimpse of a lady or a gentleman in Strasbourg. The pan-European reign of *la mode* also depended on advertising, as Donneau de Visé well understood.

The *Mercure galant* was unabashedly devoted to promotion. In the same issue in which the ladies explained the workings of *la mode*, one of them plugged the wonderful silk stockings ("the most attractive in the world") she had just seen in the shop of one of the first fashion merchants to become celebrated, Jean Perdrigeon. Perdrigeon, a *bonnetier* or specialist in fine woven textiles and fashion accessories, was said to have the most discerning eye in Paris. Shoppers went to his establishment aux Quatre-Vents, To the Four Winds, situated near the Palace Gallery, as they might visit a concept store or an exclusive boutique today, with the belief that Perdrigeon's product was unique. While other merchants also sold silk stockings, the ones he featured were sure to be the model everyone just had to have that season. When a character in a comedy by Molière held up a ribbon bought at Perdrigeon's, another immediately remarked, "C'est Perdrigeon tout pur"—"That's *so* Perdrigeon." By featuring this shop, Donneau de Visé was teaching his readers not only what to wear, but about the difficulty of knowing just the right place to find the merchandise of the moment. And the answer was always: in Paris.

By 1678, the *Mercure galant* had become so popular that it was being published on a monthly basis. That year, it also became the earliest periodical to include images illustrating the fashion trends of the current season. Plates depicted new outfits in precise detail so that readers far from Paris could see how to pull them together. This image illustrates men's high fashion for winter 1678: the captions call attention to the most important elements, such as the fact that truly stylish cloaks that season would be scarlet lined in black.

These illustrations in the January 1678 issue of the *Mercure galant* marked the first time that images of stylish dress were used to advertise fashionable attire available at that moment for purchase.

Images like these quickly became common; they then became known as *modes*. That same January issue of the *Mercure galant* made clear the relationship between such illustrations and the marketing of *la mode*: it included this image, the original depiction of the kind of place where the clothing featured

*The illustrated fashion press began with this image, an engraving that explained
in detail how fashionable men should dress for winter 1678.*

in fashion plates could be purchased. This was an institution that soon became
essential to Paris' identity as the capital of style, the upscale shop.

Donneau de Visé spared no expense in promoting the new Parisian way of
shopping. This image was drawn by Jean Berain, the king's official designer
and the chief decorator for the Paris Opera Ballet. Berain portrayed a fashion-
conscious couple; their outfits correspond exactly to models illustrated in the

Jean Berain's 1678 image of a high-end shop is the earliest illustration of modern fashion marketing. Displays on walls and counters present a selection of merchandise far larger than a merchant could have brought to a private home.

Mercure that same year. They are shown in an interior every bit as to-the-moment as their clothing. It's the establishment of a high-end merchant with a range of goods much like that found chez Perdrigeon. Fashion accessories are arranged artfully on shelves. Luxurious fabrics flow down over the display counters in all their visual and tactile glory, allowing customers to imagine how they might look in an actual outfit.

Berain enticed the *Mercure*'s readers with this view of the Parisian shop as a proto-department store, an early exercise in the selling of emotion. The new kind of shop, as it was defined in January 1678, was a place where customers would find a large selection of highly desirable merchandise showcased in an elegant setting and laid out with flair. It was the kind of abundance of choice designed specifically to make shoppers "greedy," as one eighteenth-century German lady put it, to overwhelm them with something retail has showcased ever since: the sheer accumulation of all the stuff that money can buy.

Berain was not advertising the precise shop of an actual merchant. He depicted instead his view of the perfect emporium, the model Parisian boutique.

During the decade that followed, various artists and printers—Claude Sim-
pol, Alexandre Le Roux, Nicolas de Larmessin, Veuve Le Camus—followed
Berain's lead and produced images of ideal shops, the kind of shops never
previously seen, in Paris or anywhere else. In their hands, the shop itself became an art form and shopping inside a shop was promoted as the modern
way of acquiring luxury goods.

Prior to Louis XIV's reign, merchants would take samples directly to the
homes of wealthy clients for their selection, so only minimal shopping took
place in actual stores. Indeed, a merchant's shop was mainly a storehouse for
his inventory. Shopwindows that opened onto the street were closed with
horizontal shutters, the bottom half of which folded down to form a makeshift
presentation space for a small selection of goods from which passersby could
choose; display space was thus always minimal and rudimentary.

Berain and other artists highlighted the ways in which, in the modern shop,
merchants were able for the first time truly to market desire and thus to entice
their clients to leave their homes in order to shop in public. In all these original images of upscale shopping, merchants were shown presenting a range of
their wares in a manner designed to capture shoppers' attention, to make them
want to linger and make a purchase. These artists might well have been train-
ing both merchants and their clients in the ways of shopping inside a shop.

These images from the 1680s and 1690s testify to the fact that a new age was
dawning for shopping: merchants were becoming for the first time aware that
in order to sell shoes and fabric in the modern city it would be necessary to
surround these commodities with an aura. Luxury goods became an industry
for France because all involved, seventeenth-century merchants as much as
their monarch, recognized the added value of promoting the dream of Paris
and the reputation of its stylish inhabitants—the aura of things French.

Alexandre Le Roux's vision of a high-end cobbler's establishment, for instance, depicts a shop now completely separate from the storeroom and shows
how to make it appealing to a well-heeled clientele. The image highlights the
kind of personal service such customers required. By portraying a world of
greater choice and the process of selection, it also highlights the advantages
for customers of this new environment. An elegant noblewoman, the epitome
of the fashionable Parisienne, has removed one shoe and is ready to try on a
fancier model—striped and with an elaborate bow much like those on her
sleeve. Other models are lined up on shelves in the background; an assistant is
at hand to take the necessary measurements and to make any needed adjust-
ments. To give clients a sense of the process of fabrication, and to emphasize
the quality of the cobbler's materials and of his work, a sample skin, wooden

Le Cordonnier

Pour estre bien chaussée, il faut être en posture | Et apres que j'auray manié vôtre bas
Vous pancher en arrier, et vous mettre un peu bas | Vous aurez un Soulier fait comme une peinture
A Paris chez le Roux au bas de la rüe de launcrie chez un peruquier   Avec privil du Roy

This is the earliest image of an upscale shoe shop. The cobbler has adopted the wig and dress of a nobleman in order to put an aristocratic clientele at ease.

molds, and a few tools are laid out on shelves and on the counter, the presentation space that took over the role of the folded-down shutter and that came to symbolize the modern shop. Le Roux even shows the owners of high-end shops how to dress in a way designed to make their upper-class clients feel at home: just as they did.

La Coifeuse

*These hairdressers have added a large window to make their premises
brighter. An elaborate display shows off the range of accessories
they use to create styles.*

A contemporary image depicts another kind of shop then becoming fashionable in Paris, that of a *coiffeuse* or hairdresser. Here, the hairdressers have in-
vested their efforts in something not possible with the in-home shopping
experience: the fine art of display. Instead of a simple counter, they use an elegantly carved table, an example of new models of fine furniture then being

IE AN MAGOULET Brodeur Ordinaire de Seü la Reine
Demeurant Rue S.Benoistalhôtel deBruxelle,porte de l'abaye S.ᵗ
Germain des prez , fait et vend toutes sortes de Broderies
en Or, Argent et Soye tant pour Hommes et Femmes que pour
meubles et Esquipages des plus a la mode.

*Royal embroiderer Jean Magoulet advertised his shop as the height of
comfort. He uses glass everywhere to let light in; his customers are seated
in deep, plush armchairs.*

invented in Parisian workshops. They have added another recent innovation
of French architects, built-in drawer-based storage and, above it, have arranged
various implements for adorning or propping up elaborate hairstyles in an eye-
catching pattern. Expansively sized windows are fitted out with the large
panes that French glassmaking technology had only recently made possible.
These were crucial, as perhaps the greatest disadvantage faced by those who
first moved the shopping experience inside was the lack of natural light. Windows with large panes of glass made shop interiors far brighter, at the same
time as they opened them up to the city outside. The view from this window
suggests that the coiffeuses have located their shop near either the boulevard or
one of Paris' public gardens and thus that the experience of visiting such an
establishment would be, like that of spending time in a public walking space,
a new urban recreational activity. Finally, the image suggests that stand-alone
shops might do well to exploit the Palace Gallery's big selling point and have
attractive young women market their wares.

This ad lists goods available at The Royal Lamb,
a furrier located in the Marais.

Shortly after the first scenes inside modern shops were produced, Jean Ma-goulet, official embroiderer to Queen Marie-Thérèse until her death in 1683, used this image to promote his establishment on the rue Saint-Benoît, near Saint-Germain-des-Prés, for once thus a real rather than an imaginary empo-rium. Magoulet thereby informed potential customers that he had created a space fully up to the latest standards. His shop, as he advertised it, was spa-cious and well lit, a place that facilitated in every way the process of looking over patterns and samples of his wares. To encourage clients to linger, Ma-goulet has positioned around the shop another kind of furniture also recently invented by the best Parisian workshops: oversize, comfortable armchairs. To make his premises lighter and brighter, Magoulet has added not only a double window with large panes but also a half-paned French door. He, too, uses a handsome large table as a display space; he has covered it with a fine cloth. Magoulet shows the clientele he hoped to attract that they would be fully at ease in his shop, waited on by people dressed like nobles and in a setting as elegantly appointed as any aristocratic dwelling.

Magoulet's ad took the form of what was known as an *enseigne*, literally a shop sign. These were large sheets of paper on which a merchant's shop sign was reproduced; they served to wrap up customers' purchases. In the 1690s, when Magoulet used his *enseigne*, merchants were promoting their wares widely, with ads in periodicals and with trade cards that listed their shop's address and the goods in which they specialized. This card for L'Agneau Couronné, "the Royal Lamb," the establishment of furriers Beguet and Serire on the rue Saint-Catherine in the Marais, enumerates the models of muffs and bonnets shoppers would find there. By then, such widespread advertising had become one of Paris' most remarkable features.

When English physician Martin Lister arrived in the French capital in 1698, he was quickly struck by the fact that compared with London, "there is very little noise in this city of public cries of things to be sold." In Paris, he went on to explain, advertisement was no longer primarily handled in the age-old manner, by people who walked the streets crying out the news, but in other ways, all of which involved print. In Lister's account, the walls of Paris had become a sort of diary that recorded the way the city was evolving. The walls talked, and people went along reading in the streets, reading what the city had to say. Lister mentions "printed papers upon the corners of streets . . . in great letters," "bills printed in great Uncial [an inch high] Letters." "This sure is a good and quiet way," he concluded of the manner in which imaginative advertising techniques were taking over in Paris—in giant letters and everywhere you looked.

In 1716, another periodical was launched, *Les Affiches de Paris* ("The Placards or Posters of Paris"). In its inaugural issue, its editor explained that he "had seen more than one French ambassador who had collected copies of all the posters in Paris and planned to bring them back with him as the most telling monument to the grandeur of the capital of this kingdom." By the early eighteenth century, the official representatives of the French state had understood that advertising was helping do their work for them by making foreign visitors such as Lister aware of the ways in which Paris was leading the way.

This image, produced at exactly the moment when Lister was reading the streets of Paris, depicts walls alive with print. On the left, a man is spreading glue, preparing to attach another placard or poster. The caption on top begins, "Absolutely everything is posted or advertised these days." On the far left, we read the thoughts of the man who posts the ads: "I put up placards all over the streets . . . in order to give the public wild and unreasonable dreams." The artist, Nicolas Guérard the Younger, suggests that those who walked through the first heavily illustrated streets understood even then that the reality behind those bold claims was hardly the point. All those "printed papers" posted "in great letters" were selling dreams—among them, the dream of shaking one's past and starting afresh, the notion that if you bought the right clothes and wore them correctly, people might indeed look at you in a new way. And this was one notion that, it seems, was not totally "wild and unreasonable" in the Capitale de la Mode.

By the early eighteenth century, even dictionaries of the French language were pushing this dream. Usage examples for the word *mode* informed readers that "more than any other nation, the French have the honor of seeing their styles and fashions imitated," and also that "foreigners follow the style set by the French."

Histories of Paris such as Charles Le Maire's in 1685 taught readers that "Parisians dress better than anyone else in Europe." In his account of his travels in India, François Bernier declared Parisians simply the most stylish urban population in the world. Bernier, a tireless promoter of exotic cities, nevertheless advised his readers that if an elegant urban scene was what they were after, they should set their sights on Paris rather than Delhi. In Delhi, Bernier explained, one sometimes came upon "Rajahs . . . beautifully turned out, covered with gold . . . , atop superb elephants." In general, however, "for every two or three beautifully attired individuals, you find seven or eight miserably dressed beggars," whereas "for every ten people you see in the streets of Paris at any time of day, seven or eight are always well dressed and seem to be of some standing."

This is artist Nicolas Guérard's view of the way publicity was invading the streets of Paris. The caption at top announces that "absolutely everything is advertised on a poster these days."

When he described the beautifully turned-out people one encountered in Paris, Bernier was careful to specify that they "seem to be of some standing." He thereby subtly warned his readers that, for all the talk of fashion being dictated by those in the highest social rank, in Paris there was no longer a necessary relation between fine dress and fine status.

Previously and still in places such as India, fashion served as an absolute marker of station. Because styles did not change very quickly, an expensive article of clothing retained its value as a status symbol for some time. But as long as fashion moved at a stately pace, the production of luxury goods could never develop on a large scale. For that to happen, fashion had to change frequently. Proactive merchants and manufacturers thus saw to it that styles, as the 1673 *Mercure galant* was the first to report, had begun to evolve so rapidly that "you can barely keep up with them." In addition, for something worthy of the name "industry" to develop, high fashion had to be adopted by an ever growing segment of the population; it could no longer be reserved for those in the highest rank. A fashion industry had to promote democratized fashion open to all.

To say this openly, however, would have been to destroy what Louis XIV had immediately seen as a major selling point for French luxury goods manufacturers: the notion that styles began at the court of France. Instead, everyone involved in promoting Paris simply defended these contradictory views as though they were perfectly compatible. Donneau de Visé was doing just this in the earliest coverage of the fashion scene. On the one hand, he introduced a concept that proved key to the marketing of French fashion—*le bel air* or *le bon air*, the right style—which he presented as the exclusive preserve of the French court and those who knew its ways well. *Le bel air* was "that certain air that outsiders and foreigners could never come up with on their own." On the other hand, he explained just how styles that began at court were now immediately passed down through the ranks—from the women of the court to all the women of Paris, even those lovely shopgirls—and spread geographically as well, to the French provinces and then abroad. If the original garment featured, say, buttons set with real gemstones, it could be copied using fake stones—and a relatively inexpensive knockoff of the same outfit could be produced by substituting golden buttons.

This contradictory double message—that high fashion was simultaneously exclusive and available to all—was the basis for the promotion of Paris as Capitale de la Mode. Guidebooks similarly insisted that people of quality in Paris were unique and had to be seen: "They carry their whole Fortune upon their backs," one author announced. But they also claimed that a foreigner who traveled to Paris could "be completely transformed"—if necessary, "within hours." Visitors strapped for time or for cash could buy off the rack, ready-to-wear garments both old and new; they could rent an outfit for a special occasion such as a ball. They would thereby have obeyed what Nemeitz proclaimed as "the first rule for any foreigner in Paris: you should never be different; you should always adhere strictly to the fashion of the moment." In a big city where people often made judgments based on appearances, they would no longer instantly be identified as outsiders, and they could be taken for what their clothes proclaimed them to be. *La mode*, or so guidebooks encouraged readers to believe, thereby promoted social mobility. As one guidebook claimed, when picking clothing off the rack, "you could simply choose your rank just as you choose your size."

With such enticements, these travel books took it for granted that their readers would come to Paris to enjoy a pastime so new that no language had a name for it: shopping. In French it was sometimes referred to as "running from shop to shop"—which one author described as "an exhausting experience." Some guidebooks, Nemeitz's in particular, concentrated on teaching international tourists the rules of this emerging form of urban entertainment; he even chose this focus as his guide's subtitle: "How to Spend Your Time and Your Money Well in Paris." Others such as Marana's cautioned readers that the ready availability of such a range of luxury merchandise could make newcomers positively "dizzy" and encourage them to "spend every cent they had and pay more for things than they are worth." Marana thereby issued the original warning against what has been ever since the goal of modern shopping techniques: to encourage the overstimulation and momentary loss of self-control that increase the likelihood of impulse purchases.

While all guidebooks prepared their readers for the fact that shopping in Paris was an expensive proposition, Nemeitz added this advice: "One should spend one's money in places where one does so happily and with pleasure"—and, from that perspective, no other city could match Paris and "the French ways." He considered "really fine clothing" the best investment a visitor could make, and his concerns were simple: helping them to find the best quality and to get it for a fair price—what Parisian merchants had only recently begun to refer to as *le juste prix*, the right price. The new phrase indicates that, in upscale boutiques, fixed prices were beginning to replace the age-old market practice of haggling. It also indicates that Parisian merchants of luxury goods had decided on a niche for themselves: as purveyors exclusively of merchandise of the highest quality and in the very latest style. This added value would justify *le juste prix*, both a price higher than those found in shops elsewhere on the continent and a set price.

And Nemeitz concurred with their reasoning. He knew that he was writing for travelers who were appraising the same goods in several European capitals, and he thus took the concept of comparison shopping for granted. Nemeitz explained that in some cases the best price should be all that counts—it didn't really matter where you acquired your underwear, for example; it was just as well to buy it in Holland or England where cheaper models were available. High-fashion merchandise, however, was altogether another proposition: merchandise that was truly up-to-date necessarily cost more because it couldn't be found in just any shop. To make his point, Nemeitz introduced readers to the best-known luxury goods merchant of the turn of the eighteenth century: La Frénai.

"*L'opinion fait tout*," Nemeitz explained: "what other people think is the most important thing." By this he meant that in Paris "nothing is considered attractive and stylish unless it comes from La Frénai's shop." You might find elsewhere goods that you considered similar, but you couldn't fool fashion insiders, who would know at a glance if your purchase came from La Frénai's boutique. And to have someone recognize that your outfit came from there or to be able to say that you owned something purchased from La Frénai—that was beyond price.

La Frénai was among the first merchants to be aware of the monetary value of what would now be called his brand, among the first merchants to understand that his name could add value to the merchandise in his shop and even to merchandise sold under his name outside his legendary original emporium on the prestigious rue Saint-Honoré. He thus opened shops in several locations in Paris, including a stand in the Palace Gallery, creating in effect the original chain of stores. La Frénai even shipped goods to other countries for sale under his name, and he easily recouped the cost of shipping. Nemeitz informed his readers that "Mr de La Frénai sells abroad with a mark-up."

Indeed, La Frénai was so confident of the value of his name brand that he became one of the first merchants to take a stand against the age-old practice of offering goods for sale with no price on them and bargaining with each customer. Elsewhere in Paris, Nemeitz explained to travelers, one might still be able to bargain, whereas La Frénai "names his price and never budges." His shops were thus among the first anywhere to instate an innovation that astonished Martin Lister when he arrived in Paris in 1698: fixed pricing. Lister considered the practice "a very quick and easie way of buying" and described it as "writing explicit prices upon every thing in the Shop." In all his marketing strategies, La Frénai was banking on the value of *la mode*.

Nearly two decades before Nemeitz explained La Frénai's ways to the international set, in 1695 playwright and journalist Laurent Bordelon staged a dialogue in which a character asks how to acquire that elusive quality, *le bel air*. The answer: you have to "frequent La Frénai's [shop] assiduously." La Frénai's discerning eye could drape you with more than simple clothing. He could give outsiders *le bel air*, make them look as if they "belonged at the court of France." And this prospect unsettled many.

Soon after Bordelon wrote, English pamphleteer Erasmus Jones published a diatribe against the manner in which the French fashion industry was changing the long-established way of the world, a pamphlet that shows how seriously the claims about *la mode*'s powers found in seventeenth-century guidebooks and periodicals were taken by many. In and because of big cities, Jones contended, fashion no longer functioned as a guarantee of status. Now "fine feathers make fine birds, and People where they are not known are generally honored according to their Clothes and other Accoutrements they have about them." The new fashion system devised by French merchants, Jones warned his readers, "encourages every body, . . . if he is in any ways able, to wear Clothes above his Rank; especially, in large and populous Cities, where obscure Men may hourly meet with fifty Strangers to one Acquaintance, and consequently have the Pleasure of being esteemed by a vast Majority, not as what they are, but what they appear to be." In the Capitale de la Mode, anyone who could afford it could acquire instant status.

The spectacularly successful methods of merchants such as La Frénai provoked more than social anxiety. La Frénai was only one of many Parisian merchants who made their goods available in other European capitals. To do so, he relied on a network of French merchants who, in the seventeenth century's closing decades, had begun to establish all over Europe shops in which they offered for sale only Parisian luxury goods. The wealthiest Europeans still continued to place orders directly with shops in Paris whenever they felt the need to replenish their wardrobes; at times, the quantities they ordered were so impressive that they received coverage in the pages of the *Mercure galant*. But once French-run boutiques became common in foreign capitals, a far broader public had access to the latest styles from Paris. As the century drew to a close, the amount being spent on these ever more available luxury goods became a subject of great concern to many informed observers outside of France.

In a 1701 account of his extensive travels through Europe, Cambridge graduate Ellis Veryard berated his fellow countrymen for their "infatuation with . . .

whatever bears the name of French." He ranted about "the multitudes of [the French] who follow their trades abroad." He claimed that "Italy, Spain, Germany, England, and Holland are full of them" and added that French merchants who set up shop abroad manage to "fill their pockets . . . in ten years time." Such is "the dexterity of the French in getting an high value on their goods," he concluded, and such is the "dementation" of Europeans that they now only desire things "far fetcht [imported] and dear bought."

Others tried to estimate the value to the French economy of this European "dementation." Already in 1679, a pamphlet signed only "J. B." (probably by Slingsby Bethel, a wealthy English merchant and proponent of free trade) warned all the European slaves of "Madam la Mode" that, even though "France hath no mines of gold and silver . . . as other places have, yet but . . . their stock of money doth not fall much short of the money of the rest of all Europe." His assessment was part of a major shift in public opinion that began in England in the early 1670s at the same time as the French takeover of the luxury goods industry. As a result, the English turned massively against the French and began to blame them for having corrupted the English court. And this assessment of the economic consequences that resulted from the French takeover of high fashion was still being repeated in the 1760s by Italian silk merchant Antonio Zanon, who called "that very word *mode* a veritable treasure for France, both immense and enduring, . . . a most precious capital."

In 1673, Donneau de Visé summed up his introduction to the new world of French fashion by naming it *"l'empire de la mode"*—the empire of style and fashion. A century later, Europeans took this phrase at face value and contended that the French had made *la mode* into a real empire, one unlike all others in that the French themselves had manufactured the commodities that made them rich, rather than finding treasures in distant colonies. When you factored in all areas over which *la mode* reigned—French "silks and fripperies," as well as France's "Wines and Brandy"—it became clear that French exports were as good as gold: because of them, all commentators agreed, the French were "draining out of the rest of Europe prodigious sums." Estimates of the magnitude of the trade imbalance thus created varied, but all said that the scales tipped heavily in France's favor. One commentator contended that, already in the late 1670s, England was importing on an annual basis 1.5 million pounds more than it exported to France.

All observers also agreed that the credit for having turned "ribans, lace, perfumes, and . . . other toyish commodities" into a national treasure belonged to Louis XIV, for having "encourag'd and improv'd trade as well as manufactures," and to Colbert, for "not permitting any foreign commodities to be imported into France, but such as are incumbered with such great duties," thereby creating the spectacular trade imbalance that was the envy of all. To prove this point, Zanon quoted at length the words of the master strategist Colbert himself on how he had managed "to prevent money from leaving the kingdom of France."

Nearly a century after Colbert's death, Europeans were thus still desperate to understand how he had managed to turn fashion into a gold mine. Even understanding his strategy, however, proved useless. As the numerous critics of the French stranglehold on luxury commerce all recognized, no one could slow, much less stop, the relentless invasion of *la mode*. That acute observer of the eighteenth-century European scene, the Franco-Italian writer Louis Antoine de Caraccioli, contended that the forces unleashed by Louis XIV and Colbert had taken on a life of their own. "Since commerce is the tie that binds nations together, it's hardly surprising that it is making Europe French," he began—before adding that "a European child can barely walk when he is taught to stammer that precious word 'Paris' and [learns] that this is the name of a delightful city where all the most elegant and marvelous things are made."

If any of those trained at a young age to serve the empire of fashion later made the voyage to Paris, what they found there would have confirmed those early lessons in style. By the mid-eighteenth century, Paris had become so literally a capital of fashion that, according to a contemporary almanac devoted to the city's merchants and craftsmen, fully half of its shops sold luxury goods and clothing: there were more than fifteen hundred *couturières* (seamstresses and dress designers) in Paris but only three hundred merchants selling fruit; more than two thousand *merciers*, haberdashers selling high-fashion clothing, but only two hundred and eighty *vitriers* to cut glass and replace windows. "French industry worked day and night" churning out one new fashion after another; because of street lighting, Parisian shops were able to stay open until ten or eleven at night. Like the modern city, fashion no longer slept.

In still another respect, Paris had thus become the place it is today, an urban center in which visitors find the marketing of style and fashion all around them. No city more than Paris has enjoyed such a constant and deep association with the world of style and high fashion. And ever since the late seventeenth century, luxury commerce has been excellent business for the French.

But the true legacy of *la mode* is found outside of Paris. Every major urban center now has a fashion scene, and every modern fashion scene is indebted to the manner in which the French fashion industry was invented and first marketed its goods. Paris in the seventeenth century defined shopping as we still know it—comparison shopping, indoor shopping, shopping in an attractive store with seductive displays of merchandise and seductive employees, paying more for the very latest styles and for the most coveted brand names, shopping as a leisure activity. It gave us the first fashion advertising, the original fashion magazine, and the very idea of fashion trends. In the seventeenth century, it was widely believed that Paris simply *was* shopping—and in many ways, it still is.

CHAPTER EIGHT

City of Finance and New Wealth

IN VILLAGES AND small towns, signs of individual wealth and social distinction are rarely ostentatious. But in urban centers, the divide between haves and have nots is often brutally evident. And the phenomenon is not new.

To become conspicuous, consumption required the kind of urban center that could supply a sufficiently broad range of sufficiently luxurious goods. Consumption also had to spread well beyond the traditional clientele for such costly possessions, for this clientele of royal and princely courts and great aristocratic families enjoyed its possessions only in the relatively private contexts of palaces and stately homes. In addition, the new clientele for luxury had to refuse discretion and choose instead to display the signs of its wealth with ostentation. Finally, consumption could only become conspicuous in a city populous enough to provide a large and constant audience, as well as an audience aware of the value of what was on display.

In the seventeenth century, all these factors came together, and Paris became the European capital of conspicuous consumption when a new kind of wealth began to be very ostentatiously exhibited. In the course of the century, ample opportunities to make one's fortune public were being created in the French capital—from mansions grander than any previously seen there to the ever more luxurious clothing shown off in upscale boutiques and on the backs of those promenading in public gardens. On the boulevard, the most fashionable people were immediately recognizable.

In many cases, however, those visibly stylish and wealthy individuals were not the sort anyone might have expected to reign supreme in Louis XIV's Paris.

Seventeenth-century Paris is often portrayed as an aristocratic domain, a socially rigid city under the sway of the long-established fortunes of wealthy nobles. But while old money did play a role as the French capital was acquiring its modern face, the new Paris was overwhelmingly a construction financed by the freshly minted riches of individuals who were complete outsiders to the traditional circles of power. All through the century, incalculably ostentatious displays of opulence were rolled out by non-Parisians of humble birth. The most publicized cases involved young men from poor families in the French provinces who, once they reached the French capital, had managed to amass fortunes. To a man, they owed their rags-to-riches stories to their instinct for the workings of the age's equivalent of high finance.

In all the major urban projects of seventeenth-century Paris, from the Place Royale to the Île Saint-Louis to the Place Vendôme, and in all the most visible spots in every fashionable neighborhood and along every newly constructed or newly widened thoroughfare, innovative and attention-getting architecture was likely to have been bankrolled by individuals who occupied what Louis XIII's chief minister, Cardinal Richelieu, termed "a separate sphere" in French society. He had in mind the members of a new and newly powerful financial elite who gradually came to ever greater prominence in France in the course of the seventeenth century. Richelieu viewed these men as inhabiting a place or sphere of their own in French society because, although they often lived as nobles did, enjoying a level of influence and a lifestyle traditionally the exclusive preserve of great aristocrats, many were decidedly not to the manner born.

Guidebooks presented this financial elite's impact on the cityscape as a noteworthy feature of modern Paris; their authors never failed to point out when a residence they recommended as particularly fine belonged to a man of finance. And indeed more than half the homes new to Paris in the seventeenth century and considered then and now to be of architectural significance were built by men who had made their fortunes in finance rather than inheriting them. These men, who early in the century became known as "financiers," were more than three times as likely as the scions of the great old families to build a home in seventeenth-century Paris and thereby to have helped create the original modern French architecture. And, as a 1707 work explained, this was evident to all: "Everyone knows that it's because of the financiers that [Paris] has the special glow for which it is so renowned at present."

The financiers were not the only group responsible for the "special glow" with which memorable modern architecture enveloped the city. A second profession also made a meteoric rise to prominence in the city on the move: the real-estate developer. Those who speculated in real estate, like financiers, were often outsiders, non-Parisians of quite modest extraction. Like the greatest financiers, the most prominent developers managed to shake off their past and amass impressive fortunes with astonishing speed.

The financiers and the developers were a powerhouse driving the reinvention of Paris. Without their massive loans and investments, their considerable appetite for risk, their business acumen and their vision, no traditional authority, whether monarch or municipality, could have made it all happen.

Their phenomenal success stories were naturally much talked about, and an iconic urban figure thus surfaced: the self-made man. In the new city Paris was becoming, anyone could become anything, or so people began to say. A poor boy from a village on the other side of France could arrive in the capital without a penny to his name, and within a few years begin dealing in real estate or finance—and could end his life with one of the largest fortunes in the capital.

The notion of the penniless outsider become lord of finance was, however, never viewed in a positive light. On the contrary, the same Parisians who so gleefully took to social mixing on the Pont Neuf and social confusion in the Tuileries were less content when confronted with this particular spectacle of social change.

In the seventeenth century, Paris became a city in which to many the lure of money seemed omnipresent—a city that, as commentators observed, "abounds with opulence and wealth," a city that was "paradise for the rich and hell for the poor" because everywhere you turned you saw "infinite numbers of shops full of beautiful things you were dying to buy." Paris also became a city in which the power of money often overturned the long-established applecart of hierarchy and influence—a place that allowed those who knew how to make money fast to become masters of the urban universe that Paris was so widely proclaimed to be. As one commentator put it in 1694, "Gold is everything in the century we live in; its absolute power makes it the master of all men . . . Gold confers titles of nobility on even the lowest born."

Many people did not take easily to the notion of lucre's supreme rule in Paris.

In texts ranging from political pamphlets to memoirs, from legal treatises to novels and comedies, financiers were often and extensively reviled. Writers of every stripe—low-born as well as high, judicious magistrates as well as anonymous satirists—spoke of men of new wealth in the same way, as "leeches" who were bleeding the country dry and making paupers of honest citizens.

Seventeenth-century authors created a vocabulary to describe members of the social sphere whose emergence was essential to the invention of the modern city. Even today, these terms appear in French in other languages: nouveau riche, parvenu. This is also true of what is today the most common name for any individual involved in large-scale financial dealings, financier. In the word's inaugural appearance in English, in the 1652 *The State of France*, John Evelyn explained the workings of "the king's revenue" and described "the great Financiers who suck the very blood of the French people."

For the first time, Europeans could use words invented with the objective of classifying individuals according to their financial status and of singling out persons of new wealth. Such individuals had existed before but evidently not in sufficient numbers for a society to bestow official linguistic recognition on the phenomenon. And whereas previously, in European cities such as Venice and Amsterdam, most recent wealth had been accumulated through trade and the overseas trade in particular, the parvenus of seventeenth-century Paris had amassed their fortunes by dealing not in goods but solely in money.

The emergence of the financier began in about 1600, when the French monarchy first encountered fiscal problems that have ever since plagued the modern state.

Prior to the seventeenth century and early in that century, the French state lived mostly within its means: Henri IV even built up a small surplus (Adam Smith claimed he was one of the last rulers ever to do so). Then, during the first quarter of the century, spending began to outstrip revenue. As a result, the bankers, especially Italians, who had ruled over the finances of all European nations in the sixteenth century gradually ceased to play a preeminent role in France. The individuals then known as bankers dealt in foreign currency exchange and transferred funds throughout Europe. When, for example, a monarch had to pay soldiers stationed on foreign soil, he would call on a banker. But once French monarchs began to spend on a previously unheard-of scale, the need for another type of financial agent became evident. Lyon, formerly the nucleus for French finance because of its association with Italian bankers, thus lost its centrality. And by the 1630s, Paris—home to the financiers, the new financial agents on whom the crown increasingly depended—had become the country's uncontested finance hub.

Whereas in the sixteenth century the French monarchy's revenue had remained stable, in the range of eight to twenty million *livres* annually, during the first half of the seventeenth century this situation changed dramatically. Between 1590 and 1622, for example, revenue rose from about eighteen million *livres* to an estimated fifty million a year; by 1653, the total had grown to roughly 109 million, and it stayed well over a hundred million throughout Louis XIV's reign. This meant that the French monarchy had access to resources that vastly outstripped those of its major European rivals. A noted eighteenth-century economist estimated that during Louis XIV's reign France's revenue was four times greater than England's and nearly three times superior to that of the Dutch Republic.

Relatively little of that was spent on keeping up appearances: between 1600 and 1656, court expenses rose only from three million *livres* to six million. However, whereas in 1600 court expenses accounted for thirty-one percent of the budget, in 1656 they represented only seven percent. During that half-century, the cost of war changed the face of French finance.

France was at war with foreign enemies for sixty of the years between 1615 and 1715; it was torn by civil war for another five. In addition, Europeans had begun to wage war on a scale without precedent. The Thirty Years' War (1618–48), the War of the Grand Alliance or of the League of Augsburg (1688–97), and the War of the Spanish Succession (1701–14) made armed conflict more costly than ever before. As a result, the French military machine never ceased growing. Whereas, for example, in the 1590s the French royal army was only forty thousand strong, less than a century later Louis XIV maintained a force of about four hundred thousand. Since France's main rivals, England and Holland, were maritime powers and the French had no navy to speak of, the country spent on a colossal scale to acquire one: in 1661 its entire "fleet" consisted of eighteen near wrecks, but soon one hundred and twenty vessels sailed under French colors.

Such transformations were possible because those in charge of the finances of France had begun to follow a logic later presented by Adam Smith as "the necessity of contracting debt in times of war": "An immediate and great expense . . . will not wait for the gradual and slow returns of new taxes. In this exigency government can have no other resource but in borrowing."

The French government's bookkeeping divided expenses into "ordinary" (court expenses) and "extraordinary." Due to the rising cost of war, between 1600 and 1656, extraordinary expenses ballooned—from just seven million *livres* to over a hundred million. When budget deficits began to surge, the state began to borrow as never before and thus had recourse to a type of financial agent who surfaced in the late sixteenth century: the financier.

The original financiers signed *traités*, tax or loan contracts, with the crown; they also bought, sometimes at auctions organized by the crown, *charges* or offices that made them part of a private fiscal administration with close ties to the government, an administration that vastly expanded in size in the course of the seventeenth century. In return, they acquired the right to collect a new tax or import or export duty from which they guaranteed the government a fixed income—and from which they were allowed to retain a sizeable share of the profits. Contract terms varied with supply and demand, but financiers always lent money at a cost far above the official rate of between five and eight percent. At moments when a war was going badly and the monarchy's need was therefore most pressing and money most scarce, a rate of twenty-five percent became standard—hence the steady rise in "extraordinary" expenses, a category that included the interest on loans.

Tax contracts were especially useful to the crown because the deal was closed and money changed hands very quickly. Contracts for five hundred thousand *livres* were soon common; many involved far larger amounts. Naturally, few financial agents were able to deal for such stakes: it's likely that, at any moment in the century, fewer than a hundred individuals virtually controlled the financial fate of France. As the monarchy became ever more dependent on credit because its needs were growing, that number shrank. And thus it was that the first gigantic modern fortunes in Paris originated not with the profits of commerce or industry but from high finance. Indeed, by the middle of the seventeenth century, the French word for business, *affaires*, came to mean solely financial affairs. If someone was *dans les affaires*, literally "in business," everyone knew that his business was high finance. And the business of high finance was to keep the monarchy afloat: in French, the original meaning of the verb "to finance" was "to supply the king with money."

French soon had a range of words to designate financiers: *traitants* (from *traité*, a tax or loan contract), *partisans* (from *partis*, another word for such contracts), *fermiers* ("farmers," since the process of collecting taxes was called "farming"), *maltôtiers* (from *maltôte*, an unjust tax). It was in Paris that most financiers were in business and that their fortunes were on display. Every stage in the city's reinvention was made possible by them—by their willingness to invest in public works and to accept financial risk.

The inescapable refrain in real estate today—"location, location, location"—would have made sense to those who financed the construction of the original modern city. In 1600, a wealthy individual who wished to build in Paris had few options indeed. Land was easily available but not a location—a prime spot that would set off a new home and increase the property's value. By 1700, Paris was rich in locations: Left Bank and Right Bank alike now featured freshly designed neighborhoods up to the latest standards in urban planning.

It was on the Place Royale that the economy of the modern city first became visible. Two of those chosen by the king to receive lots facing the square were emblematic of the new Paris: Charles Marchant and Jean Moisset.

Marchant, the only real-estate professional among the square's original inhabitants, had just completed his most ambitious undertaking by far: the first privately financed bridge in Paris. He had assumed the entire cost of what he called Pont Marchant or Marchant Bridge (its official name was the Pont aux Marchands or Merchants' Bridge), which connected the Île de la Cité to the Right Bank. (The wooden bridge went up in flames in 1621.)

The largest investor of all was an individual who had only recently begun to be known as Jean *de* Moisset. Moisset was the self-made man par excellence. He had been raised to the ranks of the nobility by Henri IV "because of his investments in the economy." Indeed, Moisset had begun to sign loan contracts soon after Henri IV began to rebuild Paris. Moisset, however, was hardly the sort of individual usually found in the corridors of power.

Born into extreme poverty near Montauban in southwestern France, Moisset traveled to that city in about 1585 to look for work. He became a domestic servant in the household of the Baron de Reniers, who gained such confidence in his abilities that he arranged for him an apprenticeship with a Parisian tailor. Moisset didn't have the money for a public coach, so in 1592 he walked all the way to Paris, a full month's journey. In his will, Moisset described himself in 1592 as "penniless and in dire need." But once in Paris, the apprentice quickly became a successful tailor. He got his big break when he accompanied a client traveling to Florence to negotiate Henri IV's marriage. There, Moisset used his savings to buy fine fabrics that he sold in France at a sizeable profit, a profit he put into loan contracts.

Moisset became notorious among his contemporaries for his dishonesty and "illicit" activities. On one occasion, he was to have been executed for theft from the royal household and was saved only because of the intervention of one of Henri IV's mistresses. Despite all this, Moisset made himself so useful to the king that he became a trusted adviser, whose counsel the monarch sought out. In 1603 Henri IV even made it possible for him to assume a lucrative position in the municipal financial administration. The penniless young man of 1592 made such a spectacular financial ascension that by 1605 he was able to pay out well over four and a half million *livres* to purchase a post in the national tax administration. And by 1609, Moisset was affluent enough to build not only that townhouse on the primest spot on the Place Royale—the so-called "grand pavilion" or the "royal pavilion," now the "queen's pavilion"—but another townhouse near the Louvre and a magnificent château near Paris where the king and queen were his guests. Even Richelieu took note of Moisset's metamorphosis from "humble tailor to wealthy financier."

In 1634, royal financial ledgers recorded an unprecedented leap: from seventy-two million in 1633, expenses rose to one hundred and twenty million—and the following year they jolted up to more than two hundred and eight million, a figure never repeated in the decades to come. In 1634 and 1635, the Thirty Years' War took a decisive turn when Richelieu decided that France would enter into direct conflict with the Habsburgs. This entailed vastly increased military spending—and more loans from financiers than ever.

In the early 1630s, one of the greatest ages of Parisian real-estate development began. In 1633, the first major sale was made on the newly completed enchanted island in the Seine; the finest residences on the Île Saint-Louis were all constructed by the early 1640s. And simultaneously, on each bank of the Seine the state turned over to developers a vast expanse of largely virgin terrain—a phenomenon unique in the history of Paris. These projects marked the last time that the city center was built up; from then on, Paris could grow only by expanding outside its existing limits. And most of the clientele for all the new properties consisted of individuals whose fortunes were tied to the Thirty Years' War.

The Left Bank neighborhood then created comprises most of what are now the sixth and seventh *arrondissements* or districts, while the terrain on the Right Bank is roughly equivalent to today's second *arrondissement*. Just as remarkable as the magnitude of these undertakings is the fact that, even though in each case a consortium of developers was officially in charge, one man accomplished the lion's share of the work. It's incomprehensible that Louis Le Barbier is virtually unknown today: he may well be the private individual who most significantly shaped modern Paris.

Le Barbier was born in Orléans into a family of very modest means. He arrived in Paris early in the seventeenth century and soon married the daughter of a wealthy man who had engaged in some small-scale real-estate speculation; in about 1610 Le Barbier began to make his mark as part of the first generation of financiers. By 1622, he became a partner in the consortium that purchased from the state the right to develop a highly visible area directly across from the Louvre. It was then that Le Barbier found his true calling: as the first great modern real-estate developer. For the next twenty years, he turned over property, most often at a dizzying rate.

That initial development across from the Louvre was a lengthy enterprise that really paid off only in the 1630s. It was also very costly: hundreds of thousands of *livres* were tied up in it, and no partner outspent Le Barbier. He had brilliant architects build grand homes on spacious lots, so that buyers could acquire a finished property, a practice that vastly increased his profits. To add value to his properties, he financed amenities: a bridge (the Pont Rouge or Red Bridge, ancestor of today's Pont Royal), a massive pump to supply water and copper piping to distribute it, an embankment (part of which is now the Quai Voltaire), a covered market called the Barbier Market, and, above all, modern-style streets—the rue du Bac, the rue de Verneuil, the rue de Belle-chasse, the rue des Saints-Pères—that are still among the most prized addresses in the city. Le Barbier's work was the foundation for a new neighborhood, the Faubourg Saint-Germain.

In the 1630s and 1640s, Paris expanded at a pace and on a scale never before seen, and the first financiers were responsible for more than half the residences constructed. At that moment, eighty-four percent of financiers lived in private homes, many of which were at least as grand as any aristocratic residence: a quarter of them featured between six and ten bedrooms, sixteen percent more than ten—and one an astonishing thirty bedrooms.

The Faubourg Saint-Germain had its share of residents from the city's financial elite. In general, however, financiers chose to live in closer proximity to the seats of power, the Louvre and Richelieu's Palace, the Palais Cardinal (today's Palais Royal). They thus acquired almost all the land in Le Barbier's other major venture, a new urban enclave that took shape on the Right Bank. It was known informally as "the Richelieu neighborhood" since its southern limit backed onto the gardens of the Cardinal's palace.

This Le Barbier development filled in the last remaining large open terrain in the vicinity of the Louvre and was the first significant development on Paris' Right Bank since the fourteenth century. Today, it stretches from near the Paris Opera almost to the Halles, from the Palais Royal garden virtually to the boulevards. In 1632, a consortium purchased the rights to expand the cityscape to the north. Le Barbier won the contract to relocate several entrances to the city, notably the Saint-Honoré gate, and to build a new entrance near the Louvre. The plans for the development, initiated by Richelieu himself, called for an ambitious and visionary infrastructure to include a navigable canal and a major innovation, a covered sewage system to be kept clean by using water from the canal.

While some of these projects were never carried out, what was accomplished was impressive indeed. Le Barbier almost completely bought out his associates and proceeded to lay out fine streets, among them today's rue des Petits-Champs and rue Sainte-Anne. True to his style, he piled on amenities: in 1636, he planned a *boucherie* or meat market on a grand scale, with room for eighteen stands—he rented each out for five hundred *livres* a year. To lure tradesmen to the new neighborhood, Le Barbier built modest rental properties: locksmith Jean Despotz, mason Simon Boucher, tailor André Tissèdre, and master brewer Henri Brocard were among the first to relocate.

Le Barbier also combined small plots, acted as general contractor, and worked with architects such as Louis Le Vau, who in 1637 completed the area's first grand home, and François Mansart. As this image of a design by Mansart indicates, the residences thus produced were huge, entire worlds unto themselves, closed off from the street behind grand entrances. Both Mazarin and Colbert, who in 1665 acquired Le Vau's 1637 residence, lived on lots drawn up by Le Barbier. Everyone who was anyone in the burgeoning financial industry was drawn to the area, and this remained true for decades. Even at the turn of the eighteenth century, when one of the greatest financial minds and wealthiest men of the age, trusted royal adviser Pierre Crozat, decided to build a home to house his fabled art collection, he chose the rue de Richelieu.

Le Barbier's speculations brought him a handsome fortune: in 1639, when his daughter married the son of an important member of Parlement, the proud father settled on her a dowry of two hundred thousand *livres*—in cash. Then in early 1640, the tide suddenly changed. Financiers issued various financial instruments, bills and notes that guaranteed that the person holding them would be paid a certain sum. As soon as one person defaulted, a chain reaction would

In the new neighborhood that developed near the Louvre where many important French financiers acquired land, the residences built by leading architects were among the largest Paris had ever seen.

set in, usually leading to a serious crisis when others found themselves saddled with worthless bits of paper. A business associate's bankruptcy left Le Barbier in such a situation; in his high-stakes life, things quickly spiraled out of control. When he died in early 1641, Le Barbier, too, was bankrupt. Two decades earlier, Jean Moisset had lost his colossal fortune of some twelve million *livres* in similar fashion.

But Moisset and Le Barbier were the unlucky ones. As the century progressed, others exercising the same professions accumulated unprecedented wealth, fortunes that at the time could have been amassed in no other way. Paris' first great historian, Henri Sauval, was an eyewitness to it all. He estimated that, by the 1660s, "there were more than 400 people in Paris worth at least 3 million."

And from 1685 on, war made possible windfalls more spectacular than ever before. The late seventeenth century was an age of great economic theorists, all of whom made virtually identical estimates of financiers' profits. Sébastien Le Prestre de Vauban concluded that during the six years leading up to the War of the League of Augsburg (1685–90), financiers cleared more than a hundred million *livres*; Pierre Le Pesant de Boisguilbert put it closer to one hundred and seven million—and this from contracts that had brought the crown only three hundred and fifty million.

Just when financiers' purses were at their fattest, the Richelieu neighborhood was expanded with the century's final development, a residential square today known as the Place Vendôme. The square was a fitting counterpart to the Royal Square that had inaugurated the golden age of Parisian real-estate development.

The square, first planned by Louis XIV around 1685, was initially to be called the Place de Nos Conquêtes, the Square of Our Conquests, in commemoration of the great military victories of his reign. From then on, however, victorious celebrations were few and far between, and royal finances were always stretched thin. In 1699, the original project was abandoned.

The project was soon relaunched by a consortium of private investors, who gave it a new name: the Place Louis-le-Grand, Louis the Great's Square. Like the Place Royale, as this engraving dating from the time of the development's completion shows, the new square was surrounded by townhouses with identical façades behind which each owner was free to choose his home's design. But whereas land around the Royal Square had been given away in a gesture of royal largesse, this time the municipality was in charge of the process, and the lots were sold.

This is the Perelle brothers' view of the newly completed Place
Louis-le-Grand where almost all the townhouses were
owned by financiers.

Since the sales took place during what may well have been the worst moment for the French economy during the two centuries of the Bourbon monarchy's rule, only one clientele was able to step forward. Pierre Crozat's even wealthier older financier brother Antoine was the first to complete a home on the square. He was soon joined by two of the most important "tax farmers" in the land, as well as other financiers. And when Antoine Crozat married his daughter to the Comte d'Evreux, the scion of a great but impoverished family who was himself heavily in debt, Crozat not only paid all his son-in-law's bills but gave his daughter a dowry of a half million *livres*. He then acquired the lot next to his own and had an even more spectacular residence built for the young couple. The newest location in Paris was beyond the reach of all but financiers and the aristocrats they bankrolled.

Indeed the sole residents of the Place Vendôme who were neither financiers nor relatives of financiers were two great architects newly flush because of the role they had played in developing the area and from designing many residences on or near the square: Paris mapmaker Pierre Bullet and Jules Hardouin-Mansart. Small wonder that even Germain Brice, whose multivolume guide to the wonders of Paris contains hardly a negative comment about the way the city was evolving, characterized the Place Louis-le-Grand's first inhabitants as "a few wealthy individuals who, thanks to the blind, unjust, and grotesque twists of fate, were able, even during these recent years of war, to acquire homes worthy of great lords." Brice also included this laconic put-down of the ostentatious décor, "everywhere sparkling with gold," of Antoine Crozat's mansion: "Bad taste reigns in certain circles."

In no time at all, as a contemporary urban historian noted, "the new streets in the square's vicinity were covered with lovely homes"—the lovely homes of the city's financial elite. Still another neighborhood, baptized "the Louis-le-Grand neighborhood," had been added to the map.

It was situated at what was then the very boundary of the city. A 1705 image depicts the homes along the square's upper edge: immediately beyond them runs a newly completed section of the tree-lined boulevard that defined Louis XIV's Paris. And behind that, fields stretch into the distance. The financiers who built their grand homes as France teetered on the edge of bankruptcy thus inhabited a sort of gated community, surrounded by members of their own sphere and well removed from the misery that then reigned elsewhere in the city.

Indeed, the years that saw "homes worthy of great lords" going up around the square were not kind to most Parisians. In the 1690s, the daily wage of a manual laborer in Paris was twelve *sols* a day (a *livre* contained twenty *sols*); the glazier who maintained the windows of the home on the rue de Richelieu of a financier with an annual income of two and a half million *livres* was paid one hundred *livres* per year. Many Parisians in those years depended on bread

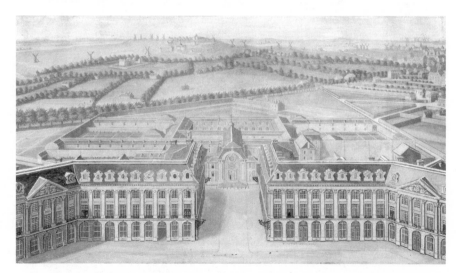

The Place Louis-le-Grand was situated at the city limit. The great promenade space known as "the boulevard" ran just behind the new square's north side.

In the 1690s France was nearly bankrupt. Starving Parisians waited every day for loaves of "the king's bread." In this 1693 engraving, two lucky ones are exiting the turnstile; a man presents his rationing card. Supplies may be running out, for soldiers are pushing back all those gathered behind him.

rationing to survive. As this contemporary image shows, mobs gathered at distribution points every day and fought to get a loaf of "the king's bread" before supplies ran out.

And yet, at birth, many financiers would have seemed destined for those bread lines. Among those active in the first half of the century whose social status can be documented, sixty-six percent were noble; sixty-nine percent of those, however, were brand-new aristocrats who had purchased their titles. Among all financiers, eight percent began their careers as household servants, including ten who had worked as liveried footmen in noble households, and twenty-five percent began as lowly clerks who had lived in the homes of financiers and had been constantly at their beck and call. Eight percent were the sons of manual laborers. Later in the century, one in two financiers had purchased their nobility—and by then, many no longer bothered to follow established procedure and simply displayed fraudulent documents "proving" their aristocratic standing.

As surprising as their social mobility is the fact that over the entire century financiers felt the direct wrath of average underpaid and overtaxed Parisians only once: during the civil war.

In the late 1640s, contemporary observers began for the first time to call attention to the idea that financiers now "possessed all the state's fortune." The Fronde was thus, in part, a financial revolution, a revolt against the monarchy's fiscal policy. When a coalition of members of Parlement and the aristocracy came to power, they decided to confiscate wealth accumulated by financiers in order to keep the city government running, and a true witch hunt began. During the siege of Paris in 1649, the Parlement's deputies discovered in one financier's home "25,000 *livres* hidden under floor boards," as well as "a strand of pearls worth 20 to 30,000 more." From then on, rumors of "millions hidden in their homes" drove bands of marauders to break into residences all over the city. Financiers naturally offered to lend huge sums to help the monarchy crush the opposition.

Once this moment of actual danger was past, however, financiers typically suffered only the kind of attacks that break no bones: visual satire and verbal abuse.

Fashion plates normally proposed models of elegance and sartorial style. But financiers were portrayed instead as the epitome of bad, nouveau-riche taste. In this image from the late 1670s, a financier is depicted as ridiculously overdressed—too many ribbons, too much lace, a wig too long and with too many curls. As the caption explains, "all the gold that can't fit in his pockets is displayed on his person."

Political pamphlets, newspapers, novels, and plays reviled men of finance: in Paris all through the century, the financiers inspired a true urban legend. That legend suggests that the same individuals who had welcomed social mixing and even social confusion were no longer as tolerant when confronted with an unprecedented phenomenon: because so much of the old money was drying

Le Financier.   1678.

Les Guerriers ont moins de resource   Ceux cy mettent l'or dans leur bource
Que ceux qui font dans les partys;   Et les autres sur leurs habits.

*Henri Bonnart portrayed a financier as the height of nouveau riche
fashion, so eager to wear all his most expensive things at once
that he is hopelessly overdressed.*

up, the formerly reassuring line between old money and new was disappear-
ing. Recent fortunes increasingly reigned supreme, and outright and dramatic
change of station had become available to the highest bidders.

The political pamphlets that blanketed Paris during the Fronde told of "these
big men who didn't even own shoes when they left their village to come to

Paris" and now "only two years later are rich." Another called attention to the Île Saint-Louis and "all its enchanted palaces built by thievery and plundering." Still another promised "a full list of all financiers along with their genealogy, their life story, and their net worth"—and it delivered on that for two hundred men of finance, from how they got their start to the dowry of each of their children. Those who lived through the Fronde contended that Parisians could often "talk of nothing but the huge fortunes accumulated by one financier or another," that "they say, even when it isn't true, that major financiers had begun life selling used clothing."

Early comedy often mocked stereotypical financial figures, misers and usurers. But the modern depiction of the world of high finance began on the Parisian stage in the 1680s and 1690s. In comedies whose titles frequently play up their Parisian setting—*Les Enfants de Paris* ("The Children of Paris"), *Le Parisien* ("The Parisian")—playwrights Florent Carton (aka Dancourt), Jean-François Regnard, Charles Chevillet de Champmeslé, and Alain René Lesage considered the ways in which new money was rewriting the rules of the game in Paris. Their plays from the 1680s and 1690s featured the first realistic men of finance, modeled all on the Parisian financiers who inhabited the best addresses in town. Regnard called them *modernes seigneurs*, "modern lords"—the lords of finance.

No play offers a more sober view of a society under the sway of instant wealth than Dancourt's 1687 comic gem, *Le Chevalier à la mode* ("The Most Popular Knight"). In Dancourt's Paris, "you can recognize people of quality by the large number of creditors pounding at their doors from dawn till dusk." They go about "in broken-down carriages" attended by servants whose livery is "in tatters." The title character, the Chevalier de Villefontaine, allegedly the impoverished scion of an old family, courts wealthy women and lives off their largesse. He's found a gold mine in the person of Madame Patin, the widow of "an important financier who made two million in the king's service." She freely admits that her husband "didn't acquire his fortune through legitimate means" and is seeking to use it "to buy her way into the nobility." Madame Patin runs around Paris making a very public show of those ill-gotten gains—"as bedecked and bedizened as possible . . . shinier than a carousel."

In the masterpiece of French financial comedy, Lesage's *Turcaret*, the play's title character, still another financier "who came from nothing," uses his dirty money to purchase the affections of a penniless aristocrat, the Baroness. Staged in February 1709, when the War of the Spanish Succession was going particularly badly and the financiers' power was thus at its apex, during a legendarily harsh winter that was causing widespread suffering, *Turcaret* must have delighted all who blamed France's misery on those who had signed tax contracts with the crown.

One after another, the play's characters—Turcaret's valet Frontin, the Baroness' maids Lisette and Marin, assorted aristocrats, and even the financier's own sister—announce that they'll do whatever it takes "to ruin Monsieur Turcaret," to cause "his destruction, his annihilation . . . to fleece him, to pluck him, to gnaw at him, to skin him alive." In the course of the play, they conspire to clean him out—two hundred here, thirty thousand there. In the end, "the law" helps them finish him off: "legal proceedings because of crooked financial dealings" have been initiated; Turcaret's remaining cash (three hundred thousand *livres*) has been confiscated. The play closes, however, not on this catharsis but on a warning: Frontin announces that he "is no longer a servant" but "*dans les affaires*"—in the business of finance. "Monsieur Turcaret's reign is over," he says in the play's last words. "It's my turn now."

By the turn of the eighteenth century, tract after tract, as libelous as the most extreme tabloids today, denounced "the reign of the financiers over Paris." The 1707 *Les Partisans demasqués* ("The Partisans Unmasked"), for example, justified the king—"he is obliged to tax his subjects to defend his crown against all the enemies who have joined forces against us"—while condemning as "savage and inhuman" the methods used by the "bloodthirsty" financiers to extract ever greater sums from an impoverished population. Its anonymous author contended that "three to four hundred individuals, all living in Paris" were bringing an entire nation down. The following year, *Pluton maltôtier* ("Pluto the Financier"), described financiers as intending "to slit the throats" of all Frenchmen and declared that they won't be happy until "they've burned the entire kingdom to the ground." As the anonymous author concluded: "*C'est le style ordinaire des financiers*"—"that's exactly how financiers operate."

There were even pamphlets modeled after the new guidebooks to the city: they took readers on room-by-room tours of the city's great homes—in this case those of the wealthiest financiers. Anti-financier guides imitated Brice's style to show that "financiers have laid their hands on all the money in France" and have used it "to gobble up everything in sight"—from old master paintings to rare porcelain.

Meanwhile, *vaudevilles*, those songs based on current events first prominent during the Fronde, soon had Parisians humming refrains such as "may the infamous *maltôtier* Bourvallais rot in prison," or "let the hangman string them all up."

Late seventeenth-century dictionaries included the inaugural appearances of several terms for financiers, every definition reflecting the rabidly anti-financier mood. The entry for *partisan* in Pierre Richelet's 1680 *Dictionnaire français*, for example, announced that "*partisans* are all rich, and . . . they are far from the most honest men alive." A decade later, Furetière's *Universal Dictionary* explained that *partisan* is now less used "because everyone hates them so much." In his definitions of *financier*, *partisan*, and *traitant*, Furetière noted that official tribunals were "investigating abuses" and "punishing people for embezzlement." In 1694, the French Academy's dictionary confirmed this view: "*traitants* have become excessively rich," and "the lifestyles and business dealings of rich *financiers* are under investigation."

The stories of Parisian financiers inspired the creation of other new words that were soon transplanted into many European languages. Along with the word "financier" itself, they remain today a highly visible reminder of the original modern men of finance.

First came *nouveau riche*. By the 1670s, its usage had become widespread: lawyers Olivier Patru and Claude Le Prestre denounced the "*nouveaux riches*" as "the plague of our century" and described Paris as "absolutely teaming with *nouveaux riches*, flaunting the fruit of their plundering of widows and orphans."

Next came *parvenu*. The French dictionaries of the 1690s explain that because of the get-rich-quick ascension of financiers, the verb *parvenir*, to achieve, had acquired a new meaning, *faire fortune*, to make one's fortune. A noun soon existed to designate such individuals: *parvenu*, "those who raise themselves suddenly from the lowest rank to a great fortune"—as in this reference to "the extravagance of new parvenus and tax collectors." In *Le Paysan parvenu* ("The Parvenu Peasant"), novelist Pierre Carlet de Marivaux, nephew of Bullet, the architect responsible for many of the most ostentatious *parvenu* residences in Paris, fictionalized a *parvenu*'s rise—"one day a servant, the next, master of the house."

Last but surely not least, the archetypal figure of modern wealth was first named: the millionaire. *Millionnaire* was initially a synonym for *nouveau riche* and *parvenu*, an individual of humble origins whose vast wealth was both sudden and ill-gotten. The word appeared in the early eighteenth century and was first widely used by Lesage, the author of *Turcaret*. In the original version of *Beauty and the Beast*, Beauty was the daughter of "a rich millionaire."

When these words later appeared in English, the phenomenon they evoked, of low-born individuals quickly amassing vast wealth, was always described as inherently French. Maria Edgeworth's letters from Paris in 1802 feature early appearances of "nouveau riche" and "parvenu," both used in the context of French society: she contrasts the poor taste of the newly wealthy with that of the old nobility. In 1816, Lord Byron described an acquaintance as "what is called [in France] a 'millionaire.'"

The story of these three words neatly sums up the inability of all who first commented on the financiers to view them with anything but suspicion and scorn. By the end of the century, economic theorist Vauban calculated that roughly ten percent of the population was living in dire poverty, that "not even 10,000 French families were comfortably off," and that most of these were either "men of finance or related to them by marriage." Neither he nor anyone else, however, pointed out that while the financiers became wealthy because they had successfully exploited this system, they bore no responsibility for it. And no one mentioned that their fortunes had served the Bourbon monarchs well. Without them, France could not have become the premier power in Europe—and Paris the continent's most brilliant capital. Finally, financiers were always scorned for what were described as their origins "in the dregs of society," but no one recognized their rise as a sign of a new openness in French society.

The financiers offered proof that the city Paris had become was no longer exclusively a society of entitlement: an opportunity society had been born along with the new neighborhoods, the new streets, and the new mansions. The extreme mobility that marked their trajectories showed that in a new kind of city it was possible to break out of one's allegedly fixed place.

Although Cardinal Richelieu's *Testament politique* was not published in his lifetime, numerous contemporary manuscripts survive. For the section in which Richelieu described the new men of finance, three different transcribed versions exist. In the first, financiers occupy a "separate place" (*place*) in French society. In the second, they constitute a "distinct political body" (*partie*). In the third, they form a "separate class" (*classe*) in French society. There is no original manuscript in Richelieu's hand, so it's impossible to say which idea reflects his actual intention.

It's understandable that this passage so troubled Richelieu's seventeenth-century editors. The first financiers were an early warning signal of the manner in which the combination of modern finance and the modern city could remake society. But no one was yet sure how, or to what extent. Still in 1741, David Hume did not know how to classify financiers: he called them a new "race of men."

In France, the evolution from a caste-based society in which honor and prestige were the dominant values to a class-based society in which great wealth could determine an individual's social station began with the seventeenth-century financiers. Their stories demonstrated that an individual's rank could be made rather than inherited, that it could be determined by economic status. Many of the monuments on which Paris' reputation as the most beautiful city in the world has always rested are a highly visible reminder of the possibilities for self-invention that modern cities have consistently provided.

Prior to the seventeenth century, in France only the Catholic Church had offered a young man of modest birth a means of changing his place in society. But in seventeenth-century Paris the new world of high finance that came into existence as the city was reinvented began to create never-before-imagined opportunities for social outsiders and to allow them to become self-made men, "modern lords" or lords of finance. It was then that it first became evident that, in the modern city, money and financial influence would increasingly trump all traditional forms of social status.

CHAPTER NINE

City of Romance

M OST OF THE facets that through the centuries have remained essential to Paris' identity have traveled through time with striking continuity: the terms in which Paris' role as Capitale de la Mode is evoked today are remarkably similar, for example, to those with which seventeenth-century observers greeted its inception, and the same is true for the experience of walking its streets. Indeed, only one image of Paris has recently taken on a surprising new spin: the city's link to love and romantic involvement.

Today, Paris is often presented as the most romantic city in the world. Couples from all over the globe flock to the city for their engagements and honeymoons because it is so often repeated that love pledged in Paris will last forever. Paris first became known as a romantic city in the seventeenth century, at the same time as it acquired its many public display spaces—its parks and its boulevards, its arcades and its upscale boutiques. Those who saw the city evolving before their eyes were the first to say that the new Paris was made for romance. But none of them would have understood why anyone could believe that bonds of love forged in the modern city might be lasting—much less last forever.

"Love in Paris is totally unlike all other kinds of love," Honoré de Balzac declared in 1835, before adding "love there is above all . . . a charlatan . . . Love soon passes, but . . . likes to leave a trail of devastation to mark its passing."

This was already the commonly held view of love in Paris one hundred and fifty years earlier, when the city originally became known as a center of romantic intrigue. Like Balzac, those who first portrayed the experience described it as fleeting; like him, they agreed that on the road to romance in

Paris you encountered many illusions. Eternal? Hardly. And that was essential to its mystique. In Paris, romance was an experience shrouded in mystery, with a hint of danger. It was fun; it was exciting and sexy, an adventure one could find nowhere else—but it was definitely not for keeps. And this was true in large part because of the women of Paris.

Foreign visitors to seventeenth-century Paris were constantly amazed at the freedom women enjoyed there, at what a visible presence they were in every new public venue then created—behavior that was clearly unfamiliar in other European capitals. As the Sicilian Marana remarked in the early 1690s, "*Elles vont par la ville comme il leur plaît*"—"[The women of Paris] go about the city absolutely as they like."

The many descriptions of the women one encountered in the new Paris make it clear that seventeenth-century observers believed that a new kind of woman had come onto the scene in the new type of city. The Parisian woman, the Parisienne, was more beautiful, more seductive, and more sophisticated than women elsewhere—so knowing that she was always a menace to the men who fell for her. "Love in Paris [was] totally unlike all other kinds of love" mainly because it was such risky business. Again and again, the beautiful women of modern Paris were the ruin of all those who were seduced by their charms.

Women's unrestricted participation in the spectacle of the city was first evident on the Pont Neuf's broad esplanade. There, attracted by street theater

Foreign visitors were surprised that in Paris women of all ranks were seen walking about anywhere and anytime they pleased.

*When foreigner visitors shopped at the Palace
Gallery, they always commented on how many
women they saw there—merchants and clients alike.*

of many kinds, as long as they were in the company of gentlemen, even noblewomen joined the crowd: they watched actors perform; they took in the
river views; they shopped for trinkets at open-air stalls.

At the Palace Gallery, the space was more contained and the shopping
more upmarket, which undoubtedly explains why, even without a male escort,
women seem to have felt completely at ease being seen there. It was also there
that the women of Paris first began to be perceived as flirts, and very public
flirts at that.

And this seems to have been still another way in which the Palace Gallery
was unlike shopping arcades elsewhere in Europe. Comedies set in London's
Royal Exchange featured shopgirls trying to protect themselves from the advances of men who assumed that women who chose to work in a public setting
must be as readily available as the goods on display. But the numerous accounts
of the Palace Gallery make it clear that neither female merchants nor female
clients had anything to fear there.

Sources as varied as Pierre Corneille's 1633 comedy *La Galerie du Palais*, Berthod's 1654 chronicle of Parisian life, and accounts of foreigners such as Locatelli, the wealthy young Italian destined for the priesthood who visited Paris in 1664, all present women's behavior at the Palace Gallery in similar fashion. Attractive shopgirls interacted easily with potential clients; their upper-class counterparts, young unmarried women visiting the Gallery because of the unique commercial opportunity it presented, shared close quarters there with eligible young men. This behavior was presented as one of the things that made Paris special—and never as in any way inappropriate or unseemly.

The women of Paris were so attached to their independence that they adopted a fashion that allowed them to circulate freely in places less hospitable to their presence than an exclusive shopping arcade. High-born women took advantage of what Nemeitz described as "the privilege of going masked at all times." This "privilege" was not unique to Paris: noblewomen in other European capitals also donned masks when in public to protect their privacy. Only in Paris, however, did an otherwise quotidian practice evolve into an elaborate and often flirtatious ritual: Nemeitz pointed out that the women of Paris decide "to conceal or show themselves when they please." Only in Paris did these masked women take on an aura of mystery and even glamour. It was in Paris that a new term, *incognito*, was first used to describe this fashion—and it was there that the phenomenon of masking began to spread well beyond personages of the highest rank.

The word *incognito* was created to describe a practice that began in Renaissance Italy and then gradually developed throughout Western Europe. When dignitaries of the very highest rank, from cardinals to kings, wished to avoid being openly recognized, they traveled *incognito*. This meant that they used an assumed name and kept their servants and retinue well out of sight. They thus spared those in the territory through which they were passing the obligation of receiving them in a manner befitting their rank—with great pomp and costly ceremony.

In the early seventeenth century, the word *incognito* was imported into French from Italian. And by the century's second half, the practice of going about in public in Paris without advertising one's rank was becoming an ever more common occurrence. Some great aristocrats began to appear *incognito* simply because they wanted to avoid the fuss and to enjoy the city like average Parisians: the Marquise de Sévigné describes the wonderful time had by two princesses of the French court "running about the streets [of Paris] *incognito*." Others, such as Peter the Great on a fact-finding mission to Paris while planning his model city on the Neva, "wanted to be able to see [Paris] exactly as he pleased, without himself being a spectacle for others, to be able to take public transportation if he felt like it." The modern city had created the desire for more casual, more modern ways of visiting it, and *incognito*'s spread was the expression of that desire.

From 1650 on, Parisian periodicals and gazettes were chock-a-block with references to ambassadors who chose to avoid a state visit and see the capital just like an average visitor. The notion that so many VIPs preferred to conceal their status undoubtedly gave far less important people ideas, for by the late seventeenth century, *incognito* was no longer being used to describe only princes but "anyone who didn't want to be recognized." And there appear to have been a great many people "running about the streets of Paris" as though they really needed to preserve their anonymity.

In 1689, artist Jean Dieu de Saint-Jean recorded for posterity recent inventions of that particularly Parisian tyrant, *la mode*. This man of quality shows off the newest trends for that winter—just the right trim on his beaver muff and so forth. In addition, he wears his highly desirable cloak in the up-to-the minute manner: pulled up high to cover the lower half of his face and his nose. This was not done for any reason so practical as keeping warm. In Paris by the 1680s, a man out walking with his cloak over his face was announcing instead his intention of concealing his identity. Men did not wear masks, but in Paris when a man pulled up his cloak, he was officially *incognito*, just as the image's caption proclaims. For the first time, a high-fashion accessory was being used not simply to call attention to its owner's status but, as sunglasses can function today, to proclaim his wish not to be recognized—with the implication, of course, that an individual thus camouflaged was so important that his identity needed protection.

In a companion image, this noblewoman is dressed, as the caption indicates, for "going about the city" in a then highly fashionable three-quarter-length coat with a well-lined hood. She wears heavy gloves and, on her right wrist, a tiny muff is visible. Over her mouth, she has positioned a full-face mask undoubtedly made of black velvet, as was the style. Women who donned such masks were, just like men with their cloaks pulled high, officially *incognito*. But this noblewoman is not trying to hide her face, as women elsewhere in Europe did when out in public. Indeed the noblewoman's coy pose makes you question whether the purpose of her alleged disguise was really to conceal her identity.

In numerous late-seventeenth-century depictions of high-born Parisian women going *incognito*, they, like this one, toy with their masks rather than use them to cover their features. It was just as Marana said: "They decide when to hide their faces and when to reveal them exactly as they please." In their hands, *incognito* was transformed from a technique used to preserve privacy

Dessiné par J.D: de S: Iean 1689.   *avec privilège du Roy*   *F.Ertinger Sculp*

Homme de Qualité allant incognito par la Ville

*When a Parisian pulled his cloak up to cover the lower half
of his face, he was announcing his intention of concealing
his identity, a practice known as "going incognito."*

Femme de qualité allant incognito par la Ville

When women wished to "go incognito" in Paris, they used a mask as men
used their cloaks: to cover only the lower part of the face.

into a means of coquettishly flirting with those around them and deciding when to let the mask drop, something that added to the mystique of the new women of Paris.

The full-face mask this noblewoman carries with her was a model considered typically Parisian. It was not attached in any way; to keep it on, women put their teeth around a small button that protruded from the back. In his 1690 dictionary, Furetière explained that women had nicknamed this form of camouflage a *loup*, a wolf, "since it could frighten young children." This image, also by artist Dieu de Saint-Jean, depicts a *loup* firmly in place, and proves that, with her visage thus covered, a woman would truly have been *incognito*. In Chevalier's comedy about the five-penny carriages, the wife who managed to ride with her philandering husband without being recognized was, for example, wearing a *loup*.

Of all the many images of women described as *incognito* in Paris, in this one alone has she actually donned her *loup*. And in this lone image, the woman is identified simply as a "*dame*," which means that she was almost certainly not a lady of quality. With this detail, the artist thereby warned his audience that you could never be sure who was hiding behind those mysterious new masks.

In seventeenth-century Paris, an early form of celebrity culture emerged. Some visitors came for the express purpose of gawking at famous figures as

*This particular model of
full-face mask for women
was known as a* loup *or
wolf, "since it could frighten
young children."*

they went promenading about, and guidebooks such as Brice's encouraged this new type of tourism by indicating the addresses of important court figures and wealthy financiers. Going *incognito* allowed nobles to avoid being "a spectacle" for these celebrity watchers. Soon, however, individuals without a famous identity to protect had begun to adopt the camouflage of the rich and famous, in the hope that those they encountered would believe them to be a distinguished person trying to slip by unnoticed. The cloak and the mask thus became the perfect disguises for those who wanted to be seen.

Already in his 1643 comedy *Le Menteur* ("The Liar"), Corneille exposed the lengths to which an individual could be driven by the desire to be important enough to have to disguise one's identity. His hero is a lowly student and a mere bourgeois who so desperately wants to be part of the smart set in the Tuileries gardens that he begins dressing above his rank and telling tall tales of his romantic exploits—tales in which he always stresses that he is *incognito* when he calls on his conquests. But there were no mysterious married women in love with Dorante. There was only an unknown young man longing to become a player in the new world of mystery that Parisians accessorized with masks and cloaks.

A half-century later, the game of masking had become just what Corneille had predicted, a device most often used by those hoping to become famous for being famous. And from then on, it was no longer always such innocent fun.

The stakes began to change with the emergence of a figure seen ever since as iconic, the Parisienne. Prior to the seventeenth century, the women of Paris were widely appreciated as more sophisticated than women elsewhere in France. But in the seventeenth century, it became a commonly held view that the women of Paris "surpassed in beauty all other women in the world," as one foreigner wrote in the 1690s. The Parisienne was granted this new status only after the rise of the French fashion industry: from the start, *la mode* and the Parisienne were seen as inextricably bound together. Still today, English speakers refer to the women of Paris with their French name; all through the centuries that word, "Parisienne," has been associated with style and fashion. And the supremely beautiful and supremely stylish Parisienne was soon being defined not only by her physical attributes and her fashion sense.

Dancourt staged the first full-scale exposé of her ways in his 1691 comedy, *La Parisienne*. His heroine Angélique, among the original incarnations of the beautiful Parisienne, has three lovers. Her credo? While "it's complicated to deal with three men at the same time . . . it does seem to me that it's wise to take the proper precautions so that you always have one when you need him." This was increasingly seen as characteristic behavior for the Parisienne. As the Sicilian guidebook author Marana put it, "she loves neither long nor enough." Or, in the words of poet Jean-François Sarasin: "She's a woman, and a woman of Paris, or to spell it out for you: a coquette."

Prior to the seventeenth century, the women known as coquettes were usually ridiculous figures—at times prudes, at others too old to attract the men at whom they threw themselves. Early in the seventeenth century, the coquette became ridiculous in a new way: she was the original fashion victim, overdressed and chasing after every fad.

And by the 1680s, the coquette had been redefined once again: she had become synonymous with la Parisienne, like her, an arbiter of *la mode*, and thus no longer ridiculous; she made others ridiculous instead. Artists advised on fashion plates that coquettes "make fools of everyone." Dictionaries defined them as "fickle, inconstant," and warned that while they "want others to commit to them, they can never commit to anyone." They "allow men to love them" but only "feign love for others." Around 1690, a slew of comedies with titles such as *The Summer of the Coquettes* depicted them doing just this. Cidalise, the coquette in a 1687 comedy by Michel Baron, is chided by her uncle because she is encouraging three suitors and "unfaithful to all of them"—to which she replies, "Today it's no longer a crime to string many men along, but rather a crime *not* to do so."

At the same moment as Baron's coquette was entertaining Parisian theater audiences, this engraving by Nicolas II de Larmessin was in circulation: it could have been a depiction of Cidalise and her three suitors. The caption alleges that "capricious behavior" like Cidalise's has now become common among the women of Paris. The image is presented as a warning about the "wiles" of "beautiful women who are conscious of their charms" such as the fashionably dressed lady it portrays. Men should be on their guard, for today's "inconstant, faithless" women want "a retinue of suitors" rather than just one.

By the late seventeenth century, or so it was widely rumored, these fickle coquettes were using their fashion sense to add a new level of social confusion to Parisian society. In Paris, it was said, you could find the female equivalent of the parvenu: women of humble birth but so beautiful and with such an exquisite sense of fashion that anyone could have been fooled into thinking they were great ladies.

No one satirized the Parisian coquettes and the social confusion they helped create as mercilessly as journalist and author Eustache Le Noble. He depicted a city in which rich and poor, noble and non-noble alike mix so freely in the new public spaces that low-born women have the chance to reinvent themselves. In a 1696 periodical, Le Noble published "Le Luxe des Coquettes," "The Expensive Tastes of Coquettes." Two friends out for a walk in the place

Larmessin's engraving satirized the fickle behavior of Parisian coquettes who refused to be faithful to one man alone.

always presented as the coquettes' playground, the Tuileries gardens, spot a pair of phenomenally fashionable women, every detail of whose outfits would seem to indicate that they are of the very bluest blood: the embroidery with a thread of real gold, the actual gemstones "that glisten on their bodies." One friend hazards an estimate of their social worth. They are surely "at least Marquises"—to which the other scoffs: "Are you from the stone age?" "To-day," he explains, "everyone is all jumbled together. People are no longer confined within the limits of their birth rank [*condition*]."

And thus it was said that the mingle-mangle society of a fashion-obsessed big city had fostered the rise of this new woman named a coquette, low-born but using her fashion sense to pass for noble and taking advantage of the landscape of modern Paris, its new public gardens and promenade spaces, to show herself off. "Professional coquettes," Le Noble warned, "know the art of siphoning off bit by bit a credulous man's fortune." Their "magnificent display" attracted "lots of birds they can pluck"—and "with the cash from a patsy's pocketbook, they can develop even more expensive tastes." By the end of the century, one satirist proclaimed coquettes "all powerful in Paris."

And the coquette was merely a prelude to the truly dangerous Parisians of the seventeenth century's final decades: the *aventuriers* and *aventurières*. While there was, at first, a *coquet*, a male serial heartbreaker, the idea never generated much traction. *Aventuriers*, on the other hand, could be male as well as female. And, whereas contemporary critics were always rather vague about the toll taken when coquettes fleeced their victims, the crimes of which their successors were accused were set forth in often lurid detail.

In 1687, Dancourt introduced the French to the first of a new breed. The impecunious hero of *Le Chevalier à la mode*, the Chevalier de Villefontaine, is characterized as an *aventurier*. That word, which had previously designated those "who go off to war in search of glory," was acquiring a new meaning in French: "those who have no money," who "seek wealth by unscrupulous means," and who "without being in love with any woman, try to win the good graces of all of them." Dancourt's Chevalier is very much just such a new-style knight; he strings five or six prosperous older women along, taking money from each to pay his bills. Dancourt leaves audiences with this vision of Paris: "Many of today's young lords behave like scoundrels in matters of love" because they so desperately need cash to keep up appearances.

Soon, these modern knights, also known as *chevaliers aventuriers*, had a name in English: "adventurers" or "fortune-hunters." And fortune-hunters were presented as fixtures of the Parisian scene. One periodical, *École du monde nouvelle* ("The New Way of the World"), featured an exposé of the young Chevalier de Cardone who had just married "a much older and very wealthy widow" and was spending her fortune as fast as he could—on, for example, "superb outfits" in which to "dazzle" other, younger women.

In 1697, Le Noble told the tale of the ultimate "adventurers of love," Ponsac and Caliste, the heroes of his novel *La Fausse Comtesse d'Isamberg*. We first watch the low-born rake Ponsac as he works his way through the French provinces convincing wealthy marks, and one very prosperous widow in particular, that he is of noble birth and fine intentions. But it is in Paris that Caliste is able to come into her own. Playing the role of a countess, she becomes the first of a long line of French heroines both dangerously beautiful and deeply attached to the fine things and the high life that Paris offered in such abundance.

Ponsac and Caliste set up two households, one in the Marais, the other across town in the Faubourg Saint-Germain. The city's populousness and its size allow them to operate on a scale possible nowhere else. They maintain double identities; they shift goods between the two residences; they disguise ill-gotten finery and porcelain with fraudulent monograms and coats of arms.

Everyone takes Caliste for the Comtesse d'Isamberg, and she wins the affections of both an English lord and an individual named Gripet who, "from the dregs of society," had risen through the ranks of the royal financial administration to become one Paris' wealthiest financiers. The lord believes he is paying court to a lady of his station, while the financier is convinced that he will be able to use his "five or six millions" to acquire a noble wife and thus a measure of social respectability.

Were there truly so many strikingly beautiful Parisiennes? And was time spent in their company really such risky business? While we'll never know for sure, many kinds of evidence suggest that those dangerously beautiful *aventurières* were not merely the stuff of fiction. Similar stories crop up in sources ranging from letters and memoirs to periodicals and guidebooks. The contemporary press entertained readers with tales of mysterious women appearing in the Parisian fashionable set and managing to convince even young aristocrats of their blue blood—and then taking them for all they were worth. An authentic chevalier and member of an old aristocratic family, Louis de Mailly, published a tell-all volume about the individuals one encountered in Paris' public gardens. He informed readers that all the rumors being bandied about were "absolutely true."

Fashion plates contributed to the impression that *aventurières* had become a highly visible presence on Paris' public promenades. This image from the 1690s depicts the most famous of them all, the Loison sisters—great beauties of very humble birth and the subject of much gossip because of their alleged romantic entanglements in the highest echelons of French society. The sisters—as everyone knew, one was a blonde, the other a brunette— are shown strolling arm in arm in a Parisian walking space, almost certainly the Tuileries, dressed in the height of fashion. (These most celebrated *aventurières* of all do have one thing in common with the absurdly overdressed financiers portrayed in other such images: they have adorned their faces with far too many *mouches*, patches or beauty-spots.)

The big city, aided and abetted by the luxury goods industry and by the development of a fashionable set, had given shelter to women who a century later would all be lumped together under a single name: the *femme fatale*. Like the coquette and the *aventurière*, the *femme fatale* was a woman both beautiful and seductive, one likely to be the downfall of any man who came under her sway.

A second vision of the seductiveness of the women of Paris was also first promoted in the seventeenth century. In 1655, a book without precedent appeared, a slim volume called *L'École des filles* ("The School for Girls"). It was the

Mesdemoiselle Loison.

The Loison sisters, shown here strolling in a public garden, were known as the most notorious Parisian coquettes.

original work of modern erotic fiction. After Cardinal Mazarin pronounced it "a most wicked book," those in charge of censorship sought to destroy every copy they could find; in so doing, they helped make it an underground classic.

The oldest surviving copy of *The School for Girls* dates from 1667; this is the edition that began to torment Secretary to the Admiralty Samuel Pepys the minute he spotted it at his favorite bookseller's. In his diary, Pepys recounts his struggles: terrified that he might die suddenly and that the book would then be found in his library, he resisted its purchase for some time. Finally, Pepys decided on this compromise: he bought a copy, read it several times that very evening—and then burned the book.

L'École des filles tells the story of two young Parisians, offspring both of prosperous merchants. Sixteen-year-old Fanchon is totally inexperienced; her suitor Robinet takes her sexual education in hand. Her older cousin Suzanne explains all the necessary terminology, and Fanchon quickly has a thorough grounding in theory as well as practice; soon, she is firmly committed to the joys of sex.

The School for Girls was the first of a long line of books that established Paris' reputation as the center for the production and the publication of erotic literature of all kinds. This connection with books seen as steamy or smutty also contributed to the image of Paris as a city where, as in the original modern erotic novel *The School for Girls*, sex was more freely discussed and more openly a part of everyday life than elsewhere.

But *L'École des filles* was not just a garden variety Parisian sex romp: it conveyed a highly practical message along with its titillating content. Her cousin makes Fanchon aware of everything then known about contraception, information that in the seventeenth century was available nowhere else. It was also information of which the young women of Paris were obviously in dire need.

It had long been commonplace in cities all over Europe for unmarried mothers simply to abandon their infants on the steps of a public building, often a church. But in seventeenth-century Paris, as Louis XIV recognized in the August 1670 decree that established the city's first publicly funded and administered Foundling Hospital, "the number of these children has risen rapidly." In fact, in just six decades the abandonment of children increased nearly nine-fold. The city's population grew during these years, but at nowhere near this rate. When that new Foundling Hospital opened its doors in 1671, it welcomed 928 infants; only two years later it housed more than 1,600.

These sad statistics represent the all-too-predictable consequences of a quickly growing population in an urban center endowed with an ever-increasing variety of leisure spaces where the city's inhabitants were jumbled together. The far less predictable consequence of the indiscriminate mixing was the rise of the new, characteristically Parisian self-made woman.

Through the centuries, this vision of the dangerously beautiful and stylish self-made women of Paris lived on, as inherently linked to the city's modernization and to the mystique of "Paris" as was the spectacle of the city's boulevards and its public gardens. In 1731, by the time the Champs-Élysées had been completed and the boulevard was beginning to circle around the Left Bank, Abbé Prévost published *L'Histoire du chevalier des Grieux et de Manon Lescaut*, "The Story of the Chevalier Des Grieux and of Manon Lescaut." Prévost chose the Paris of Louis XIV as the setting for his account of a modern knight and the gorgeous, low-born woman who became the gold digger to break the mold. Manon's Paris is recognizably the Capitale de la Mode, the city of money and high finance, the city of speed and light, and "a place dedicated to pleasure." She spends a fortune transforming herself into one of the most visibly stylish women in the city; Paris' public promenades become the setting for many of her conquests—and her expenses are bankrolled by some of Paris' most important financiers.

All through the following decades, as the edges of neighborhoods that had originated in the late seventeenth century were filled in, and then as the city gradually expanded beyond the limits fixed by Louis XIV's original beltway of green, novels continued to promote this image of Paris as a place where it wasn't necessary for a woman to bring birth or money to the table in order to succeed as long as she was beautiful and ruthless. In 1880, Émile Zola's novel *Nana* concluded the saga that Le Noble had begun nearly two centuries before.

Nana stands for the Paris of 1870, a city beginning to emerge from the remodeling efforts of Baron Haussmann, a city still adjusting to its new design. Haussmann tried to trump the Sun King's efforts in all the urban works new to seventeenth-century Paris: more boulevards and wider ones, the biggest promenade space the city had ever seen (the Bois de Boulogne), and a *place*, the vastly expanded Place de L'Étoile, that made the Place Vendôme and the Place Royale seem mere relics of a genteel age. In similar fashion, Nana makes the gold digging of the seventeenth century's coquettes and *aventurières* look like child's play.

Zola's heroine epitomized the then most recent incarnation of the dangerous Parisian woman: the *cocotte*. Like her predecessors, the *cocotte* dressed in the height of fashion and wanted to be surrounded by every kind of luxury that Paris could provide. Like the coquette, she ran through the fortunes of one admirer after another to finance her taste for expensive things.

But what sets their successors definitely apart from the original Parisian gold diggers is their stories' end. Manon is reduced to poverty and rags before she dies in the Louisiana "desert." Zola lingers over Nana's death from smallpox, which he describes to the last, lavishly repulsive detail. True *femme fatales*, Manon and Nana spelled the downfall of many men, but in the end were fatal only to themselves.

By contrast, in real life as in fiction, the *aventurières* of seventeenth-century

Paris come out unscathed: their creators refused to kill them off; their contemporaries apparently felt no need to delight in their downfall. One of the
notorious Loison sisters married into an aristocratic family. And in Le Noble's
"The Expensive Taste of Coquettes," when we last see the former opera singer
Perrine, whom Le Noble satirizes as the most devastating coquette of all, the
woman who has ruined a marquis "and countless others" is back at the Paris
opera—only this time she's sitting in the best seat in the house, "trying to
make the real ladies realize that they can't compete with her magnificent attire
and her pricey necklace."

And this was perhaps the most modern aspect of seventeenth-century Paris'
new sexiness: these women who learned how to manipulate *la mode* in order to
skew the social order were not punished for their ability to refashion their des-
tinies. Instead, the coquettes and the *aventurières* were allowed to enjoy their
rich admirers' many gifts, and those rich admirers were described as "dupes,"
fools or idiots, rather than victims. It was understood that these grown men
were able to take care of themselves. It was also understood that they, too, had
their ulterior motives for maintaining these relationships.

As Le Noble explained it, men able to afford these dangerous women were
not put off by the amounts they demanded: "The vast expense these coquettes
necessitate does not terrify those who give themselves over to such spending—
this financial ruin is a big part of their pleasure." The more a coquette makes
them pay, "the more faithful they are." In Paris, the ability to spend a fortune
keeping a fraudulent countess in the height of fashion had become a status
symbol, a way for a rich man to stand out in the urban crowd.

As soon as Paris began to become Paris on the sidewalks of the Pont Neuf,
women had been part of the mix. It must have seemed natural that they par-
ticipate just as fully in the social confusion that by the end of the seventeenth
century was destabilizing socioeconomic boundaries that had formerly seemed
fixed.

Ever since their creation, the French words used to describe the self-made
women of Paris—coquette, cocotte, femme fatale—have been adopted by
many languages. And through the centuries, wealthy foreigners in search
of romantic excitement made their way to the French capital with the hope of
meeting a notorious coquette or cocotte and being seen with her at the opera
or in a public garden; the successful transgression of social boundaries by
these women became an essential aspect of what one early-eighteenth-century
guidebook called "the freedom of Paris."

Countless English lords and German barons, American financiers—and even
Sigmund Freud—understood just what Baron Pöllnitz meant when he remarked

in 1734 that "most people know what sort of place Paris is." In its role as the European capital of romance, Paris was long seen as "the sort of place" where love was simultaneously risky and risqué, an experience far more exciting than what passed for romantic intrigue anywhere else—"the sort of place" that Europeans believed would be less confining and less conventional than the more oppressive societies of their home countries.

In Paris as it was reinvented in the seventeenth century, nouveaux riches, lady-killers and gold diggers, financiers, ersatz aristocrats as well as a great many genuine marquis and comtesses were all part of the urban spectacle and on public display. You could never be sure exactly whom you were dealing with because so many truly looked the part. A few complained or warned that a way of life was ending, that the world of the old aristocracy would never be the same. For the most part, however, French and foreigners alike seem both to have been aware of how much the modern city was shaking things up and to have felt that it was a good ride.

It's often said that the world in which social distinctions were of supreme importance was a casualty of the First World War. After its demise, the kind of extreme social confusion that helped define the romance of Paris became simply the way of the world. And in our permanently socially confused age, the bond between Paris and romance has been redefined. The danger and the risk that for centuries were essential to the story of love forged in Paris have been eliminated, and the Parisienne is famous only for her sophistication and her style and no longer for her fatal charms. The city of light has been recast as the most romantic of all cities, a place that should be essential to the story of every modern love story—true love, that is, rather than romantic intrigue. And so much talk has even had a very visible impact on the cityscape.

In the early 2000s, two of Paris' famous bridges were transformed into what are called "Love Bridges," their railings completely covered with "love-locks," padlocks on which couples from around the world carve their initials before attaching them and then throwing the keys into the Seine as a declaration of undying passion. From the Pont Neuf to the Love Bridges, the romance of "Paris" has changed along with the times.

Making the City Visible: Painting and Mapping the Transformation of Paris

I N THE MID-1850S, exactly two centuries after Louis XIV initiated his grand design for the French capital, a new remodeling of Paris began, mandated by Napoleon III. To carry it out, the emperor appointed not a noted architect or urban planner, but an administrator and technocrat, Baron Georges Eugène Haussmann. Like the first, this second refashioning changed the city's face dramatically. But while Haussmann's urban works were bigger than the originals, they can hardly be described as better: the projects realized under Haussmann's direction were largely derivative of models created in the seventeenth century.

In order to echo the public gardens such as the Tuileries at the center of Paris, additional recreational spaces—notably, the Parc Monceau and the Bois de Boulogne—were added near the city limits. A new boulevard—this time with a north-south axis—was planned as a central thoroughfare, much as the original boulevard had been imagined to allow Parisians to circle around their city's periphery. The city's boulevards were lined with buildings now often described as typical of Parisian architecture, though many defining features of Second Empire architecture—from mansard roofs to the use of the stone known as *pierre de taille*—had in fact already become characteristically Parisian in the seventeenth century. Even the Place that served as a pivot for the new Paris dictated by Haussmann, the Place de l'Étoile, was not an original idea, but a vastly expanded version of l'Étoile, conceived in 1670 to link the Champs-Élysées to the Bois de Boulogne.

Since the Paris of the nineteenth century hewed so closely to the city invented in the seventeenth, it is hardly surprising that many institutions

considered essential to the boulevard culture of the nineteenth century—
from the Parisian café to the shopping arcade and the department store—
similarly expanded on models created in the seventeenth century. Nor is it
surprising that figures seen as representative of Haussmann's Paris—the new
man of finance, the banker; the cocotte; the stylish Parisienne—can be seen
as larger-than-life incarnations of characters who had first become characteristic of the Parisian scene two centuries before.

However, the response of those who witnessed the nineteenth-century
renewal of Paris could not have been more different from that of their
seventeenth-century precursors. Whereas the Parisians who strolled the original boulevard had enthusiastically greeted the transformation of bulwarks
into a vast promenade space, their counterparts in the nineteenth century in
no way shared their appetite for change.

In 1857, poet Charles Baudelaire responded to Haussmann's initial inroads into
the cityscape with "The Swan." "*Le vieux Paris n'est plus,*" "Old Paris is gone,"
the poem begins, before concluding with a one-word exclamation: "*Hélas!*"—
"Alas!" Baudelaire's melancholic "*hélas*" and the "sadness" he expressed at the
fact that "Paris is changing" represent well the reactions of many who watched
the city being transformed by Haussmann. They regretted the old and feared
what was to come. They were terrified that Paris as they knew it would be
destroyed forever by the new boulevards and the new kinds of public life
those boulevards would bring with them.

Nothing highlights the difference in response more clearly than the fate of
the maps that guided the two plans for urban renewal. Haussmann followed
Louis XIV's example and had plans drawn up; he decided on two separate
views, one of Paris in its then current state, the second including the projects
he had planned for it. Like the Bullet-Blondel map, these plans were put on
display in City Hall. The Bullet-Blondel map was carefully followed for decades and revered as a symbol of the revitalized city Paris was becoming.
But in September 1870, when an angry mob burst into City Hall during the
uprising against Napoleon III that culminated in the Paris Commune of 1871,
its leaders cut Haussmann's maps to pieces—a gesture that accurately reflected the vehement and generalized opposition to the vision for the French
capital that those plans represented.

It was of course easier to greet the seventeenth-century urban upheaval that
set the standards for Haussmann's work because it was carried out without the
wholesale destruction of existing urban fabric that Haussmann implemented;
to lay that north-south boulevard, for instance, it was necessary to bulldoze

through long-established and densely populated neighborhoods on both banks of the Seine. It was also surely easier to welcome the original boulevard because the beltway created under Louis XIV would open up to the world outside a city that could afford to give up its defenses, as the king proudly proclaimed in 1670 when he ordered Paris' walls torn down and replaced by a walkway. The extraordinary new system of fortifications the king was having erected around France's borders would help protect the French capital from invasion for nearly one hundred and fifty years.

In contrast, by the time Haussmann's work came to an end in 1870, Paris was under siege, about to fall into the hands of the Prussian army. At a moment when the city desperately wanted to shut itself off from the world outside, fear of change was rampant. Author and art critic Edmond de Goncourt was echoing the commonly expressed view of Haussmann's just completed thoroughfares when he evaluated them apprehensively as "these new boulevards without turnings," a sight that "make[s] one think of some American Babylon of the future." And when contemporary artists such as Edgar Degas and Édouard Manet depicted what Paris had become, their paintings often suggested that alienation was characteristic of the public life that had resulted from the Haussmanization of their city.

Two centuries earlier, eyewitnesses to modernization appear to have experienced no apprehension at the idea that their city was changing around them. Instead, they seem to have been so exhilarated by the prospects they saw opening up that they were eager to broadcast the story of Paris' rebirth and to celebrate the revolution brought about by modern urban life.

Those with front-row seats for the moment when Paris became Paris used media of all kinds to spread the news of urban transformation. For the first time, the inhabitants of a city left an amount of information, both visual and verbal, so considerable that it became possible to observe the effects of city planning on those who lived through the process. Beginning in the 1680s, visitors could take virtual tours of the redesigned cityscape in the new type of city guidebooks that Brice pioneered. And long before then, Manet's precursors had begun to produce images of various kinds—from maps to paintings—that showcased a city in flux. Just as soon as every pathbreaking monument was completed, artists created a visual record, highlighting the monument's innovative features.

These seventeenth-century depictions of Paris' reinvention were the first images ever conceived in an attempt to represent an urban fabric as it was transformed. They portrayed new public works—for example, the sidewalks of the Pont Neuf being negotiated by a crowd of pedestrians—and they thereby helped teach Europeans not only about recent developments in Paris but also how to negotiate an unprecedented kind of city.

Before the seventeenth century, cities had very seldom been depicted, and only as a backdrop to the main subject. In miniatures found in medieval manuscripts, in fifteenth- and sixteenth-century portraits, a skyline can sometimes be glimpsed in the distance, most often that of a generic rather than an actual city. In the sixteenth century, mapmaking became far more precise and more widespread than ever before. The first relatively accurate maps of the most important European cities began to circulate shortly before the mid-sixteenth century. Prior to this moment, few people could have had a remotely exact sense of even their own city; almost no one could have contrasted the aspects of different cities.

In 1572, the first volume of *Civitates orbis terrarum* ("The Cities of the World") was published. By the time the work's sixth and final installment had appeared in 1617, this atlas had provided readers access to maps of 546 major cities from the four corners of the earth. Largely edited by Georg Braun and engraved by Franz Hogenberg, the compilation set the standards for cartography for decades to come. For the first time, Europeans could compare the cities of the

Georg Braun's 1572 atlas The Cities of the World *reinvented cartography: it included this influential view of Paris.*

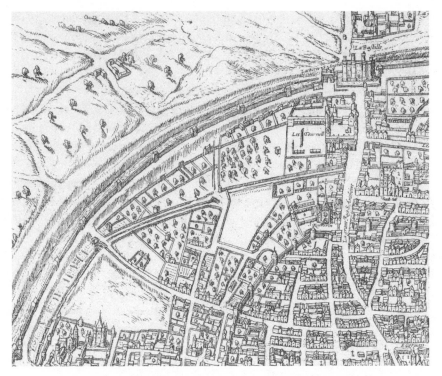

*A detail from Braun's map depicted the unremarkable terrain later
to become the Marais. In 1572, the area had no distinguished
architecture; much of it was completely undeveloped.*

globe. They could judge relative size and shape, the position and flow of rivers. Parisians got their first sense of what Amsterdam was like, and Londoners their initial image of Paris.

Volume one featured this view, perhaps the finest of the early maps of
Paris. It highlights the city's distinctive shape, produced, as Braun and Hogenberg indicate, by the fortifications that, in 1572, still encircled the capital's
perimeter.

But, as is evident in this detail from Braun's map, the urban layout found
inside those walls was not equally distinctive. In 1572, Paris had the air of an
overgrown village. A great deal of its terrain was only lightly built up; on
much of it, there was no construction at all. It had relatively few streets, and
most of those were meandering and short, alleyways serving only the immediately surrounding area. Most residential construction, of various sizes and
scales, was random and in no way distinguished. Only two monuments—the
Bastille fortress and a royal palace, the Palais des Tournelles (referred to by

Braun as "les Tournelles")—and one famously broad thoroughfare, the rue Saint-Antoine, identify this as a view of Paris rather than another contemporary capital such as London. Braun's map offers decisive proof that in 1572 Paris had not yet begun to take on its modern identity.

And three decades later the situation remained unchanged.

At the very end of the sixteenth century, Henri IV chose to be depicted in front of a panorama of the city he had just conquered. The Seine flows immediately behind the king: across the river, two royal palaces are visible, the Tuileries (destroyed in an 1871 fire) and the Louvre, still with its medieval tower.

Blank spaces in maps and paintings tell their own story. In this case, they prove that at the dawn of the seventeenth century, Paris was distinctly non-urban, a capital remarkable for the absence of construction. The canvas depicts greenery everywhere—not planned green spaces in the form of public promenades, but acres and acres of undeveloped terrain. This was space ready and waiting for the great builder kings, Henri IV and Louis XIV, who would soon turn those fields into built forms and an urban design.

When Henri IV commissioned a panorama of the newly conquered city in which churches were conspicuously absent and only royal palaces were featured, he was announcing that, with the age of religious conflict behind it, Paris was about to become a great secular city. And when he chose a panorama in which the cityscape appears largely undeveloped, the king could well have

This 1600 painting portrayed Henri IV with a view of his newly conquered capital city that focused on its many empty fields.

been proclaiming his intention of taking up the challenge of those blank spaces.

The meadow on which the king's horse proudly rears up remained free of construction until the 1630s, when Louis Le Barbier began to develop it. All through the century, as that huge open space was filled in, new names were added to the map of Paris: among them, rue du Bac, rue des Saints-Pères. By the early eighteenth century, meadows had been transformed into what is today an iconic neighborhood, somewhat larger than the district now referred to as Saint-Germain-des-Prés, Saint Germain of the Fields.

In 1707, the area received its crowning touch, a paved walkway that completed the embankment at the edge of the Seine. That walkway was called the Quai d'Orsay, a name that was among the final marks of the Bourbon monarchs' conquest of what had been undeveloped terrain at the heart of Paris. Visitors to today's Orsay Museum find themselves standing in roughly the same spot from which Henri IV began planning the city's transformation.

A similar story can be told about sites all over Paris.

This detail from Bullet and Blondel's 1675 map depicts the area that appears so unprepossessing on the Braun plan of 1572. By 1675, the district was no longer villagelike; it had become distinctly urban. It had acquired many new streets, often long and straight, thoroughfares designed to connect this area to the city at large.

Not all of the many fine private homes that had been built along those modern streets are depicted. Those that are shown share a similar, impressive scale; they are built around inner gardens and are called *hôtels*. These were the original Parisian townhouses, examples of characteristically French residential architecture. They were among the earliest private residences in the city built with the large blocks of white stone, *pierre de taille*, that quickly came to be considered a typically Parisian construction material. Because of such residences, the city had begun to acquire a uniform architectural façade, and certain areas—notably the Marais, the Île Saint-Louis, and the financial district near the Louvre—had begun to look like one vast palace.

Bullet and Blondel also record monuments that had been added since the Braun view: the Jesuit church, Saint-Louis, on the rue Saint-Antoine; and above all the original modern city square, the Place Royale, built on land occupied in 1572 by the Palais des Tournelles and thus a gesture of royal largesse, a king's palace transformed into residential architecture and public recreational space. What was in 1572 a largely undistinguished urban layout had by 1675 become a model of contemporary city planning—and the neighborhood still known as the Marais.

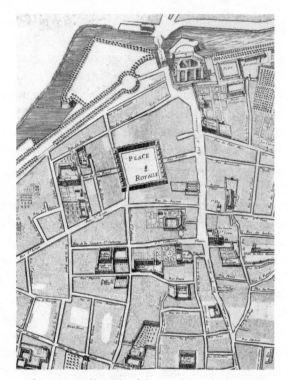

*The 1676 Bullet-Blondel map shows that in just a
century the area known as the Marais had been
endowed with wider, straighter streets and new
kinds of residential architecture. A broad new
public walkway has replaced the fortifications
shown in Braun's map.*

In 1572, on either side of the Bastille stretched those fortifications that closed
the city off from the world outside. Bullet and Blondel's map represents instead
rows of carefully planted trees, the elms that bordered the grandest public
walkway ever conceived. Their 1675 view was the earliest depiction of the
original boulevard that allowed Paris' inhabitants to admire their city while
they walked on this novel kind of esplanade.

A quickly changing urban fabric attracted cartographers eager to record
each transformation. Only twenty-one maps of the city had been produced in
the sixteenth century. Then, in the following century and in particular during
Louis XIV's reign, the French replaced the Dutch as the premier cartographers in Europe, and they proceeded to transform the process of mapmaking.
As a result, in the seventeenth century, a new view was published almost every

year—eighty-four in all. The production of so many maps in rapid succession makes it clear that a large audience was actively following the redesign of the French capital.

Maps could record the creation of infrastructure; they could not show how the city's inhabitants interacted with that infrastructure. But more accurate mapmaking helped inspire the original generation of artists interested in painting the city. As a result, in the seventeenth century, representations of urban centers became common all over Europe, and the city came into full view for the first time in the earliest stand-alone urban scenes ever painted.

A tradition of city painting emerged at virtually the same moment in several European capitals, in Amsterdam, London, Paris, and Rome in particular. These were the first paintings focused exclusively on urban centers and urban life. The canvases now known as cityscapes played an important role in Europe's first great age of secular painting.

All early city views are aspirational canvases: they highlight the very different goals and ambitions guiding each urban center's development. The artists thereby provided the original urban images, paintings designed to reveal both the reality of a cityscape and the way the actual city was thought of by its inhabitants and foreign visitors. Though these canvases are surely not absolutely accurate depictions, they can teach us a great deal about life in the great cities of the seventeenth century. More important still is what they can teach us about how the inhabitants of Paris and London and Amsterdam wished their city to be seen by the world outside and how travelers wanted to remember the city they had visited.

The seventeenth-century paintings that depict cities such as Amsterdam and Haarlem are glowing testimonials to the beauty and prosperity of these urban centers during the heyday of the Dutch Republic. Numerous views of Amsterdam feature its latest monument, Town Hall, and the Dam, the spacious square in front of it. These paintings depict the city as calm and never crowded: people walk alone or in small groups separated by expanses of open space. Everything is pristine; every burgher's dress a demonstration of wealth and status. Nothing is out of place or order; people are neither unruly nor rushed.

The canvases sent a message that Dutch cities were prosperous and that their inhabitants had everything they wanted—and therefore no reason to be on the move. Monuments seem to be signs of guaranteed stability and continued prosperity.

The original images of Paris stand radically apart from contemporary urban images such as these. They give a sense of a city aspiring to be innovative and different, a city where the unexpected (a chance encounter, a sight never before seen) was the order of the day. Paris, these paintings tell us, was a capital driven by dynamism, creative energy, and potential for change, rather than by the desire for economic prosperity above all.

The vast majority of these representations highlight urban phenomena then found nowhere else in Europe: the Pont Neuf's sidewalks, the uniform residential architecture of the Place Royale. They focus on innovative recent monuments such as these, and not merely to bolster civic pride.

In depictions of other European capitals, the city's inhabitants seem merely incidental. They are seen walking in the vicinity of the landmark depicted, tiny figures who seem to have been added solely to call attention to the monuments' impressive size. They are never shown interacting with their city in any way. In contrast, views of Parisian monuments tell a story in which the individuals depicted are active participants. They engage with each other in ways newly possible. They also engage with their city in ways possible only because of Paris' unprecedented monuments; some of them are even clearly enthralled by the signs of urban change taking shape around them. Views of Paris in the seventeenth century are the first paintings to give a sense not only of the city itself but of people's place in the city.

The Place Royale's inauguration inspired what may be the earliest true Paris view (color insert). The anonymous artist focused attention not only on the spectacle staged in the square in April 1612 and on the crowd that gathered to witness it, but also on the architecture that was publicly unveiled on that occasion. The painting is the original depiction of residential architecture and the impact it could have on an urban center.

By highlighting the pavilions' blue slate roofs and by making them nearly the same color as the sky above, the artist seems to announce the central role the newly completed square would play in shaping the city: the Place seems monumental, easily overshadowing the cityscape around it. And by accentuating the unbroken roof line as well as the continuity of the façades surrounding the square, the artist provided the original illustration of the way in which a uniform architectural façade could contribute a sense of visual unity to urban fabric.

The Royal Square was represented again and again: it's thus possible to follow, image by image, the Place's evolution over the course of the seventeenth century. A scene from the middle of the century is another first for painting: the original depiction of the functioning of urban recreational space (color insert).

The canvas shows how Parisians walked in the Place Royale: only on the sand and never on the grass. It also indicates how, in Paris, recreational space inevitably became display space. A couple seated on a park bench is observing the activity around them; they are in turn being observed by some residents of the Place, who have stepped out onto one of the first balconies in the city in order to follow everything happening on the square below. Louis XIV is seen passing by in his carriage: he is on display for his subjects, just as they are showing themselves off to their king.

But it was the first public works project undertaken by Henri IV when he became master of Paris that most completely captured the imagination of contemporary artists. In the seventeenth century, the Pont Neuf was the most frequently depicted monument in Europe.

The fact that so many views of this one monument can now be found in museums and collections all over Europe indicates that painters saw the Pont Neuf as the best way to market the essence of the Parisian experience and that travelers who had made the trip to see the French capital in the process of taking on its modern identity felt that these images were the best reminder of what the city stood for.

A few of these paintings depict the Seine as a working river packed with boats of various kinds, while others portray a more sedate river and an unobstructed view out over the water. And nearly all canvases feature individuals using the bridge not to cross the river but to contemplate it. Pont Neuf views demonstrate the ways in which a bridge could encourage the discovery of urban beauty.

Some people stand simply at the edge of the sidewalk; others take advantage of the balconies (color insert). They all clearly understood that the New Bridge had made it possible to see Paris as never before, as an urban panorama worthy of contemplation.

These river spectators stand quietly to the side of what are above all scenes of noisy confusion: at the center of each painting is an illustration of the way in which the original sidewalks functioned as a social leveler. Each Pont Neuf view represents the crush of vehicles fighting for space on the bridge, as well as different aspects of the street life that developed there, from buying books to buying apples. In every case, they show off a true urban crowd, in which people from across the social spectrum brush up against each other in close proximity.

In one view from early in the century, two women in a carriage have stopped to chat with two noblemen, one of whom is traveling on foot, while the other is on horseback (color insert). The crowd milling around them is for the most part definitely not of their station. Several of the least fortunate Parisians, one of whom is a cripple, share the sidewalk with clerics and street venders as well as other aristocratic pedestrians. On the riverbank in the background, men are stripping off their clothes, preparing to go for a swim.

In these early scenes of social hodge-podge, there is never a trace of the detachment and isolation that painters portrayed as inherent to Parisian life in the wake of Haussmannization. Rather than avoiding eye contact as Manet's and Degas' nineteenth-century Parisians do, in seventeenth-century views of the city every individual depicted is an active spectator: they stare at the bustling scene taking place around them; they look each other straight in the eye.

In one such scene, two carriages share the same space. While the first crosses the river, its passengers lean out the window gawking unabashedly, and the driver stares not at the road ahead but sideways, at the goings-on in the Pont Neuf street. The owners of the second carriage have given up all pretense of mere transportation: they have ordered their vehicle to pull over to the side and turn around; it is parked there, facing the urban throng.

There were also reminders of the social and gender mixing that so amazed residents of other capitals that were less costly than a large painting: souvenir fans. This one was created in about 1680 to commemorate the new open-air poultry and bread market that was first held on the Quai des Augustins (today's

A new open-air market on the banks of the Seine began in August 1679. This image shows Parisians of all ages and all ranks mixing easily and seems designed to advertise the quality of urban life in a beautiful, well-designed city.

Quai des Grands-Augustins) in August 1679. (This fan was painted but was never cut down to the characteristic fan shape, which suggests that some visitors preferred to return home with a small image that they could put on display instead of a lady's fashion accessory.)

By 1680, the work of paving the river's banks was nearly complete. The fan advertises the pleasures and the practical advantages of those new paved river promenades. In this redesigned bit of cityscape, the market has attracted Parisians from every walk of life. Aristocrats mix freely and with no concern for their safety or for protecting their status. Accompanied by a male companion, elegantly dressed noblewomen are there to look for the freshest poultry. Some, such as the lady buying bread on the right, even shop alone. No one has bothered to have servants along. In the right foreground, an aristocratic child and his small dog try to frighten the birds; his parents are not afraid to let him play by himself. And on the far left, a female merchant is even trying on a man's hat for size. It's all as if the anonymous artist wanted to encourage those who purchased this souvenir of their trip to Paris to consider how comfortable people could become with diversity of various kinds when they encountered it in a setting as carefully thought out and as appealing as this one.

Some images, such as this fashion plate from 1687, advertise more upscale urban entertainment, in this case, Paris' role as a cultural capital. Like the nobleman portrayed here, waiting at the entrance to the opera, wealthy Parisians could show off the finest fashions available in the most elegant shops on the continent when they attended performances staged at the Paris Opera-Ballet. But the open-air theater on the Pont Neuf was equally famous and, like the balls held late at night on the boulevard, these performances were free and open to all.

The many maps and paintings combined portray an urban center's transformation from overgrown village to modern city—from the creation of essential infrastructure to the creation of a significant mass of people interacting in ways that would encourage many to break free of their familial and communal roots. The original images of Paris—its high life as well as its low—depict it as an environment in which self-made individuals could shine in ways never before possible.

What do great cities and their urban design stand for?

From the very beginning of the seventeenth century, Paris' influential new urban works addressed this question head-on. In Paris, public architecture became significant only when it was more than simply monumental. The first paintings of the French capital teach us again and again that Paris was noteworthy because it was far more than a collection of major buildings,

Homme de Qualité sur le Theatre de l'Opera.

Se Vend A Paris Sur le quay Pelletier, a la pomme d'Or, au troisiéme apartement.

*A 1687 engraving portraying a nobleman waiting at the entrance
to the Paris Opera promotes two things for which the city had
become known: the public display of high fashion by its
residents and noteworthy performance arts.*

far more than a center of commerce. Paris was instead a revolutionary kind of
capital, one whose built fabric encouraged residents to step out of their homes
and spend time in its streets. There, they mixed and mingled, Parisians all and
part of the same urban crowd.

No image suggests that the new Paris was an ideal city. The affluent are never shown sharing their wealth with less privileged Parisians; the high-born do not open their arms to those not of their rank. But all residents share the same space—and usually on an equal footing.

It's often said that pictures speak louder than words. But surely words and pictures together speak more resoundingly still. Here are some of the words that were either invented or first used in their modern meaning in French in the seventeenth century: sidewalk, city square, pedestrian, traffic jam, balcony, boulevard, avenue, embankment—even street. Contemporary views of Paris depict all these phenomena—from aristocrats stepping down from their carriages and becoming pedestrians to the experience of using a sidewalk. Together, pictures and words called attention to the invention of concepts, behavior, and conveniences without which it's hard to imagine the functioning of the city as we know it. Together, they allow us to take stock of what the invention of Paris meant for the history of Paris and for the history of urban space.

There were also other new words: financier, nouveaux riches, millionaire, fashion, coquette, gold digger. These terms make it plain how much it was all of a piece. Wars gave France new frontiers that, once fortified, helped protect Paris so that its walls could come down and be replaced by a grand boulevard. The same wars created the financiers and their new wealth. From the Île Saint-Louis to the Place Vendôme, residences financed by nouveau-riche fortunes became essential to Paris' reputation as the capital of modern architecture. Parvenu wealth also helped support the luxury goods industry without which *la mode* could never have gained the traction necessary to found "the empire of fashion" that was soon a force to be reckoned with in cities all over Europe.

The new words of seventeenth-century Paris also make it clear that the urban culture that took shape on the boulevard and in the public gardens had made room for dramatically new social trajectories. The aristocratic world in Paris was already beginning to fade, long before the Revolution of 1789. A truly aristocratic city could never have become a modern city.

Today, for many from all over the globe, Paris is without question the most beautiful city in the world. Books and films, blogs and websites, define the spell Paris casts in similar terms. The uniformity of Paris' architectural façade is unequaled, you read again and again. Its parks and gardens seem to be made for romantic walks. The bridges of Paris are depicted as essential to its charm, as are its squares, especially the arcades of the Place des Vosges. Walks along its boulevards and by the Seine are described as key to its romance, and the same is true of nighttime strolls through the City of Light—in particular, in the streets of the Île Saint-Louis.

Today's websites and bloggers thus prove that the innovations of urban planning that Henri IV, Louis Le Barbier, and Jean-François Blondel—as well as the Sun King himself—considered crucial to the transformation of the French capital from barren fields to a new kind of cityscape, the public works that Colbert believed would "make foreigners recognize [Paris'] grandeur" and its status as the modern Rome, accomplished all that those who planned and financed them intended and far more. They gave the city an identity, an identity clear to both its inhabitants and to outside observers. They made Paris a model city, an urban wonder appreciated and copied both widely and repeatedly. They invented both Paris as we know it today, a capital in mortar and stone, and "Paris" as tourists have thought of it ever since, the mythic city that for more than three centuries has attracted visitors with the same promise of wish fulfillment that led Freud to dream of "set[ting] foot on its pavement."

Over those centuries, cities have come and gone, and both cultural and financial capital have been asserted in various locations. But Paris remains the first great city of the modern age—the city that introduced Europeans to a new idea of the city and to cities as ideas, and even as characters. Paris caused urban planners to invent what a city could be, and it caused visitors to dream of what a city might be.

ACKNOWLEDGMENTS

This book would never have taken shape as it did without two museums: the Musée Carnavalet, Museum of the History of Paris, and the Museum of London. Their collections of seventeenth-century city paintings or cityscapes were essential in helping me think about the impact of changing cities on their inhabitants. Anna Sparham of the Museum of London toured their reserves with me and was an insightful and a generous interlocutor. At the Musée Carnavalet, Jean-Marie Bruson opened galleries that sadly were long closed to the public and allowed me to spend time with the paintings that most influenced my view of seventeenth-century Paris. I am very grateful to him for his time, his patience, and his erudition. Also at the Musée Carnavalet, Gérard Leyris showed his generosity in many ways: by pulling endless dossiers in the museum's print room, by lighting the way through the seventeenth-century painting collection, and by taking wonderful photos. Every museum should be lucky enough to have a photographer as talented as Gérard Leyris.

A number of people helped this project along by reading parts of it at various stages. My agent, Alice Martell, was my first reader and, as always, right on the mark with her suggestions. My editor, Kathy Belden, responded immediately and enthusiastically to the first pitch for the book. And no one was more patient than Jerry Singerman. He read sections in draft and provided great suggestions as well as much-needed encouragement.

Lance Donaldson-Evans answered numerous questions about sixteenth-century precedent. Christian Jouhaud discussed the *mazarinades*, provided information, and suggested sources. Lesley Miller from the Victoria and Albert Museum brought some key references to my attention and gave advice on images. At the Bibliothèque Historique de la Ville de Paris, Geneviève Morlet introduced me to their collection of early merchants' cards. Liliane Weissberg and Fabio Finotti helped with questions about the evolution of German and Italian. Christophe Madelelin followed the trail of nouveau riche in Dutch. Joe Farrell and Ralph Rosen were always willing to answer questions comparing Paris and ancient Rome. James Amelang generously shared references and information on early modern cities. Caroline Grubbs and especially Matt Pagett provided excellent research assistance, often using the Internet in ways that still escape me to help track down difficult references. Matt also provided creative and much-needed help with editing and managing images.

Lynne Farrington and John Pollack of the University of Pennsylvania's Van Pelt Library obtained scans of sixteenth- and seventeenth-century maps. Lynne was also willing to discuss and even to speculate about the printing of *mazarinades* with me. Chris Lippa and Elton-John Torres worked digital magic. Karen Cook of the University of Kansas' Spencer Library Special Collections graciously had details scanned from their copy of the Turgot map. And Alan Chimacoff was my photo guru. Alan taught me (via e-mail, no less) how to take certain tricky shots; he repositioned images, and he always knew just what adjustment to make.

Paris,
February 2013

I identify quotations and list references chapter by chapter in the order in which subjects appear.

In a work that covers so many areas, there isn't room to list all possible secondary sources. I have included references to the most important of these sources; I do list all the seventeenth-century works that first drew my attention to the issues I discuss in the various chapters.

Introduction: "Capital of the Universe"

Paris guides and maps

"Un volume commode et portatif": [Le Rouge/Saugrain] 1716, vi.

Brice 1684, "avertissement," iv.

Maps of Paris: Boutier et al.

Early French cartographers: Ballon 1991, 212–14; Konvitz.

Contemporary periodical on the de Fer map: *Mercure galant*, April 1692, 124, 128.

Brice 1698: "Le nom de toutes les rues, par ordre alphabétique" is added on, with separate pagination, at the end of vol. 2. In 1698, the supplement was also published separately.

Persistent urban images: Lehrer, 189. (I am aware that some of Lehrer's sources have been questioned.)

Tourists' interests: Brice 1684, iii–iv.

Publication history of guidebooks from 1660 to 1680: Chabeau, 326, 341.

Lister walking, 2.

Liger on using Brice, 5; Liger on walking in Paris, 225.

Blégny 1691, 27–28, 24.

Literature of Paris

Milne, introduction.

Paris in 1597

Michel Félibien, 1:7, 9; 4:34.

Wolves in the streets

Babelon 1969, 50.

Paris as a world unto itself

On the history of this idea: Babelon 1986, 28–29.

"Une ville qui n'a pas sa pareille": Brice 1684, ii.

"L'abrégé du monde": Michel Félibien, "prospectus," i.

"Elle-même un monde": Le Maire, 1:5. See also *Triomphe royal*, 7; d'Ouville 1647, 3:3.

"Le pays de tout le monde": Richelet, 1:77.

Bernier 1699, 2:72. See also Colletet 1664, 1–2.

Marivaux, *La Méprise*, 1:xiii.

Caraccioli 1777, 137; Caraccioli 1802, 1.

Henri IV and Paris

"Faire un monde entier de cette ville": *Registres des déliberations du bureau de la ville de Paris*, 12:386.

Le Mercure françois 1612, 475–76.

Cardinal de Joyeuse: May 3, 1607, Henri IV, 7:220.

Delamare, 1:81–82.

Vacant land in Paris: Delamare, 1:81.

"Une ville nouvelle": *Le Mercure françois* 1612, 475–76.

Louis XIII and Paris

Lough (xvi, 124) has pointed out that much less information is available about urban planning in this period in the seventeenth century than about those that precede and follow it.

Louis XIV and Paris

Colbert: *Lettres, instructions . . . de Colbert*, 7:290; 3:163.

His achievements greater than Henri IV's: Lavedan 1975, 177; Lavedan 1926, 333.

"I want to know everything": Colbert, 5:326.

Plans for London: Rykwert, 49.

Paris' influence in Europe: Caraccioli 1777, 122.

Paris' influence in the United States: Field, 136.

English visitor in 1698: Lister, 111.

Paris' fortifications: Delamare, 1:87–90.

Funding for the rampart: Brice 1725, 1:299.

On La Reynie's role: Delamare, 4:230–33.

On land speculation: Babelon, 9; Bernard, 6–7.

Size of Paris in the seventeenth century

"Full of people": Petit, 15; Loret, December 1, 1663, 4:131.

Paris' population: Descimon, 401; Dethan, 178–79; Dupâquier et al., 94; Pillorget, 114–19, 336–37; Le Comte, 1:119–25; Le Maire, 1:6; Brice 1713, 1:24; Liger, 5.

London's population: de Vries, 270; Harding, 112.

Multilevel homes: Petit, 12–13, 15; Brice 1684, 1:10; Brice 1725, 1:24.

Siamese ambassadors: Donneau de Visé, 286.

Bernier, 2:71–72.

Population Delhi, Beijing: Chandler, 483, 529.

Statistics on baptisms and deaths: Le Maire, 1:6; Bardet, 202–03; Dethan, 178–79.

État général des baptêmes, mariages, et mortuaires . . . de Paris, 1–3.

Parisian architecture

Evelyn, 108.

Procès-verbaux de l'Académie Royale d'Architecture, January 8, 1674, 1:56–57. See also November 22, 1694, 2:292–93.

Michel Félibien, 1:1.

Street lighting

Marana, 39.

Aristocrats walk in Paris

Nemeitz, 1:402, 154.

Marana, 13.

In London even as late as the first half of the eighteenth century, upper-class women were rarely seen walking: Corfield, 161 n.4; Hunt, 121; McNeil and Riello, 179. Shoemaker claims a more visible role for women in London's public life, but even he stresses "the suspicion that every woman in public could be a whore" (147, 165).

Women walked in mules: Nemeitz 1712, 13.

Caraccioli 1777, 229. Still in the 1770s, Caraccioli claimed, Spanish and Italian nobles rarely got out of their carriages to walk. Caraccioli 1772, 65, 119.

River views

Lister, 8.

Henri IV as first monarch to consider their potential for the city: Babelon 1969, 60.

Fashion on display in Paris

Neimitz, 1:154; Le Maire, 3:196–97.

Nemeitz, 1:79.

Shops and shopping

Shops of Paris: Nemeitz, 2:587–88, 592; Marana, 17; Liger, 357.

"Quintessence of the shop": Nemeitz, 2:594.

Lister, 242; see also *Vitrines d'architecture*, 28.

Lights in windows: Nemeitz, 1:119.

Cafés light up the street: Liger, 335–36.

Critique of luxury

Marana, 36, 17; Lister, 166; Louis XIV in Saint-Simon, 4:307.

City comedies

Two sixteenth-century comedies were nominally set in Paris: Jacques Grévin's 1560 *Les Esbahis* and Adrien Odet de Turnebe's 1584 *Les Contens*. In only one scene (*Les Contens* v:1) is anything more than lip sevice paid to Paris.

Son rushes his father around: Corneille, *Le Menteur*, 2:5:549–50.

Characters run right by their friends: Corneille, *La Galerie du Palais*, 2:2:387; 4:2:1081–83.

Parisians move quickly

"[Les Parisiens] sont toujours actifs": Du Fresny, 61–62.

"Fast-paced": Nemeitz 1712, 13.

"Day and night": Marana, 8.

Brice 1684, "avertissement," iv.

Course: Furetière 1690, Académie Française 1694 dictionaries, entry *course*.

Social scientists and the pace of walking: Lehrer, 189–90; Jacobs, 150.

Haussmann followed seventeenth-century urban planning

Pillorget, 273; Ballon 1991, 250–52; Babelon, 9; Lavedan 1926, 333; Bernard, 7–8; Sutcliffe, 47.

"Cet étourdissant Paris"

Monet, June 3, 1859, in Cahen, 24.

Dreaming of Paris

Pöllnitz, 2:189.

Flaubert 1930, 79; Flaubert 2004, 49.

Freud, 4:195.

Chapter One: The Bridge Where Paris Became Modern: The Pont Neuf

Getting to the Louvre from the Left Bank

Boucher 1925, preface by Lavedan, 8–10.

Mercier, 1:156.

Pont Neuf as quintessential Parisian street: Marivaux, *Le Paysan parvenu*, 128.

The Pont Neuf's history

Official documents: Michel Félibien, 5:7, 12; 4:17–18; Lasteyrie, 20, 45.

No houses on the bridge: Du Breul, 247; Delamare, 1:81.

Its importance in urban history: Lavedan 1926, 2:148–50; Ballon 1991, 3: 114–65; Sauval, 1:232.

Henri IV crosses it: L'Estoile, 8:83–84.

Documents concerning the bridge's technology: Lasteyrie, 23–24; 26–27.

The rue Dauphine: L'Estoile, 8:359–60.

Henri IV's vision for the city and his plans to improve city-wide circulation: Babelon 1969, 47, 52–53.

Order in which parts of bridge project were completed: Ballon 1991, 121.

Publications devoted to the statue of Henri IV
Le Conte, 8, 26.
Savoy, 2.
Conférence du crocheteur du Pont-neuf, 1.

Snowball fights
L'Estoile, 10:136.

Bathing and sunbathing
Colletet, *Le Journal*, 30, 32.
Affiches de Paris, July 7, 1716, 149–51.
Satyre nouvelle sur les promenades, 28–29.

Chestnuts on the bridge
Nicolas Peiresc, 5:161.

Diverse crowds on the bridge
Berthod, i–ii.
Brice 1684, 178.

What the French knew about sidewalks in the late
seventeenth century
Sidewalks on Roman roads: *Procès-verbaux de l'Académie Royale d'Architecture*, 3:96.
Sidewalks in seventheenth-century China: Le Comte, 2:118.

Sidewalks reserved for pedestrians
Varennes, 178–79; Nemeitz, 1:116–17.

Words for "sidewalks"
Banquette: Furetière 1690, entry *banquette*; Delamare, 1:81.
Levée: Brice 1684, 177.
Allée: Charron, 62; Varennes, 178; Limnaeus, 1:582.
Trottoir: Michel Félibien, 4:423–24; Académie Française dictionary 1762, entry *trottoir*.

Words for "pedestrians"
Gens de pied: Lasteyrie, 20; Charron, 64; Varennes, 179; Limnaeus, 1:582.
Piéton: Furetière 1690, entry *piéton*.
Piéton's first appearances: Avity, 2:333; Fremin, 169; Bordelon, 13.

Traffic jams
Lasteyrie, 20, 22.
Evelyn, *The State of France*, 109.
James Howell, cited in Lough, 54.
Sévigné, 2:749.
Marana, 8, 14.
Le Comte, 121, 184.

The word *embarras*

Académie Française dictionary 1694; Richelet 1680.

Trévoux 1771, entry *embarras.*

"Hubbub" in Paris

"Day and night": Marana, 8.

"La ville qui remue": Benjamin, 516.

Danger for pedestrians: Nemeitz, 116; *Mémoires d'un soldat,* 365.

Pont Neuf "most bustling place": Marana, 14.

Carriages in Paris

The first carriage: Sauval, 1:191.

Carriages during Henri IV's reign: Sauval, 1:188, 194; Roche 1989, 10; Pillorget, 163.

Brice 1698, 1:12.

Steps removed

Hurtaut and Magny, 4:100–101.

News and the bridge

Mercure françois: vol. 1, which begins its coverage with 1604, was published in 1613; coverage of 1637 appeared in 1646.

The sale of images: Retz, 2:72.

People reading posters to each other: Loret, 1:140.

Professional readers: Colletet, 88.

Literacy in Paris: in particular: Roche 1987, 197–207 and Roche 1985, 158–60; also Chartier 1989, 113 and Chartier 1981, 276; Milliot, 33; Van Damme, 13.

The Fronde

Retz, 1:305–27.

Public rejoicing: *À Monsieur de Broussel,* 4.

"Entire city": *Arrest de la cour,* 3.

Frondeurs du Pont Neuf: Aubignac, 111.

Assembling mobs: Serres, 3:998.

Political songs

Pont Neuf singers: Académie Française dictionary 1694, entry *chanteur;* Furetière 1690, entry *chantre.*

Pont Neuf songs: Furetière 1690, entry *chanson;* Le Roux, entry *chronique.*

Pont Neufs: Panard, 3:378–82.

Vaudevilles: Saint-Simon, 16:237–38; Furetière 1690, Académie Française 1694, entry *vaudeville.*

Sévigné, 2:401.

Dupuy-Demportes, 1–2.

Street theater
Turlupin, 7, 18–20.
Tabarin 1623, 7, 10.
Charlatans and *opérateurs*: Loret, 2:398.
The charlatans' claims: Marana, 43.
Philippot, 125, 8.

Shops on the bridge
Bookshops: Saugrain, 110.
Sauval, 217.
Brice, 4:185.
Nemeitz, 2:599.
Hurtaut and Magny, 4:100.

Clothing theft
Value of men's clothing: Sévigné, 1:471.
Showing off new clothes: Colletet, 61; Loret, 1:18.
Handkerchief theft: Loret, 1:437; 1:503.

The *filou*
Definitions: Richelet 1680, entry *cheval*; Furetière 1690, entry *bronze*; Académie Française 1694, entry *tireur*.
Filou is attested once before the seventeenth century (Gaufreteau, 1:125) but with a different meaning.
Synonyms for *filou*: Oudin, entry *pont*, 335–36.
Cloak theft: Heylyn, 86–87; Retz, 1:216; Nemeitz, 1:410–20; L'Estoile, 11:17; Loret, 1:335; Berthod, 3–4; Villers, 228; Poisson, scene 7.
Outlawing the *filou*: Michel Félibien, 5:68, 73, 33.
L'Estoile, *L'Intrigue des filous*: 1:1: p.1; 2:3: p.28; 3:7: p.71; 4:1: p.73; 5:1: p.93; 5:2: p.103; 5:3: p.105.

Used-clothing shops and stolen cloaks
Blégny 1691, 25; Blégny 1878, 1:60n.2.
Altering stolen cloaks: Berthod, 67.
An article in the contemporary press: *Mercure galant*, September 1710, 166.
Nobles stealing cloaks: Courtilz de Sandras, 152–53.
Stealing cloaks during the day: Nemeitz, 1:116–17.

Viewing from the bridge
Accoudoir, cul de lampe: Du Breul, 247.
Tablette: André Félibien, 487.
Praise for the view: Lister, 7; Sauval, 237; Brice, 4:176; Bernier 1699, 2:78–80.

Urban landscape

The word *paysage* ("landscape"), first came into wide use in the course of the seventeenth century, as definitions in Nicot's (1606), Furetière's (1690), and the Académie Française's (1694) dictionaries show.

Perrault saw the Pont Neuf and "the landscape the bridge makes visible" as essential to the concept's spread: Perrault 1696, 1:26.

Peter the Great

Saint-Simon, 31:381.

Fans

Sévigné, 1:469–74.

The earliest Pont Neuf fans: fan from c. 1680 depicting a Pont Neuf scene, Musée Carnavalet D8388; fan from c. 1670 showing the Pont Neuf in the background, Musée Carnavalet 8448. Numerous other Pont Neuf fans are also in the museum's collections.

Pont Neuf expressions

"Crier sur le Pont Neuf": Guez de Balzac, February 2, 1633, 1:4.

"Chanter sur le Pont Neuf": Tallemant des Réaux, 2:112.

"Amuser le Pont Neuf": Bordelon, 2:143.

"Faire le Pont Neuf": Sévigné, 1:494; 3:1033.

"Je me porte comme le Pont Neuf": Laurens, 226.

"Le Pont Neuf dans mille ans": Montreuil, 349.

Chapter Two: *"Light of the City of Light": The Place des Vosges*

Gaspar de Vega: Babelon 1922, 47–50; Lavedan 1993, 173; Girouard, 171.

The word *place*

Nicot 1606

Richelet 1680

Furetière 1690

Académie Française 1694 dictionaries, entry *place*.

The original documents on the building of the square

Deville and Hochereau, 1:1 and 3:2; Félibien, 5:40.

Industry in an urban setting

Sixtus V: Giedion, 226.

Kind of silk manufactory: Babelon 1969, 51.

The history of the Place Royale

Ballon 1991, 57–113; Ballon 1996, 39–49; Babelon 1975, 695–713; Pillorget, 276–78.

Henri IV, *Lettres missives*, 6:385.

The 1605 decree: Babelon 1969, 47–50.

Terraced housing
    Evelyn, 111.
    Barbon: Summerson, 44–49.

The king visited the site
    Babelon 1966, 100.

Demolition of the workshops
    Babelon 1975, 711–12.

The first residents
    Barbiche, 50–58; Dumolin 1926.
    Camus: Tallemant des Réaux 2: 21–22; Barbiche, 55; Bayard, 416.
    Moisset: Mouton, 72–104.
    Moisset's investment: Ballon 1991, 62.
    Chastillon: Ballon 1991, 245–47.

The new conception of public space
    Ballon 1991: 29–47; Dennis, 44–51; Lavedan 1926, 2:281–84 and 295–98; Lavedan 1975,
        202 and 231.

Henri IV bought land
    Babelon 1975, 696.

The April 1612 inauguration as inherently Parisian
    Stegmann, 3:373n.2, 377.

The crowd assembled for the Place's inauguration
    Mercure français, 353; Rosset, 67; Wilson de La Colombière, 432; Malingre, 606.
    Place intended for sixty thousand: Chastillon, 1.

Contemporary accounts of the 1612 celebration
    Previous festival books: Long, 1–2; Stegmann, 372–73.
    Triomphe royal, 9.
    Cardinal Bentivoglio, 163–65.
    Rosset, 65.
    Laugier de Porchères, 26, 154–55, 322, 104.
    Malingre, 606, 612, 618.
    Carrousel des pompes et magnificences, 8–18.
    Chastillon, 1.
    Wilson (or Vulson) de La Colombière, 432–33.
    Bassompierre, 1:322–28.

The pleasure of walking in the *place*
> La Rochemaillet, 22; Hauteroche, 5:4:p.149.

Homes changed hands
> Dumolin 1926 records all sales until the Revolution of 1789.

The square during the civil war
> Military parade ground: Dubuisson-Aubenay, 1:112, 118, 125.
> Frondeurs camped there: Motteville, 3:182.

The evolution of its central space
> Fence, sand, and "grass carpets": Montpensier, 3:256.
> Poëte, 42; Dérens, 74–77; Lambeau, 65–78.
> Decorous walking: Newman, 60–75; Poëte, 93–108; Turcot, 25–90.
> Benches: Montpensier, 3:256.

State visits
> Sainctot, 13.
> *La Gazette*, no. 116, 1656, 995.
> "The most beautiful spot": *La Gazette*, no. 116, 1656, 995.

Montbrun and his party
> Loret, 3:35; Dumolin 1926, 295–96, 300–301; Gady, 249–50, 256.
> Other private parties in the square: Dubuisson-Aubenay, 2:280; Loret, 2:88.

Balconies
> Gallet-Guerne and Bimbenet-Prival, 19.

Marais as administrative district
> It was originally known as "le Temple ou le Marais." The ARTFL database indicates
> a growing acceptance of the name "le Marais" beginning in the 1630s, in particular
> with Corneille's 1633 comedy, *La Galerie du Palais*.

Place chronicled by seventeenth-century inhabitants
> Viau, 2:39.
> Scarron, 282–88.
> Sévigné: 2:506, 517, 564, 865–66; 3:366, 952, 1087.

1633 *Place Royale* plays
> One play, by Claveret, was never printed. It is described in Mahelot, 94–95, 110.
> Corneille: 1:1:178; 1:1:76; 1:4:275; 1:4:449–50 and 445; 5:8:1506–7; 4:4:985–98.

Place royale as setting in later plays
> Corneille, *Le Menteur*, 2:4:198.
> Ouville, 1:4: p.8; 4:1: p.105; 4:4: p.119; 5:4: p.148.

Hauteroche, 1:1: pp.1–2; 4:7: p.128.
The Marais as a "fun" place: Furetière 1690, entry *canton*.

Marais as a place no one wants to leave

Alquié, 2:339.
Liger, 41–65. (Liger's work has been attributed, with no justification, to publisher Pierre Ribou.)
Other *places royales*: Cleary, especially 108–33.

Historians and travel writers

Doubdan, 388.
Le Nain de Tillemont, 2:420, note.
Sauval, 1:626, 186.
Sauval's biography: Fleury, 305–24.
Place Royale's influence on European urban architecture: Blunt, 165; Babelon 1975, 712–13.
Peter the Great in Paris: Saint-Simon, 31:370–71.

Chapter Three: "Enchanted Island": The Île Saint-Louis

A commentator on the speed of the island's construction: Israël Silvestre, "Vue de l'Île Notre-Dame," Eau forte, c. 1650, caption.
The island's development: Dumolin 1931, 3:7–271; Lavedan 1926, 2:340–46; Andia and Courtin, 10–44.
Edicts and contracts: Deville and Hochereau, 3:4–8; Michel Félibien, 5:11–14.
Marie's title: Dumolin 1931, 3:6.
Henri IV bought the islands: Dumolin 1931, 3:10–11.
Lugles, an odd name no one can explain: Dumolin 1931, 3:9.
The island's streets: Brice 1725, 2: 335–47.

Sales of land

Dumolin 1931, 3:21–24.
Bretonvilliers sale: Dumolin 1931, 3:37.

Rumors about the richest men on the island

Bretonvilliers: Tallemant des Réaux, 2:654.
Lambert: Tallemant des Réaux, 1:249

Enchanted island

Corneille, *Le Menteur*, 2:5:552–56.
Ouville, *L'Esprit folet*, 1:1:1–5.

The island's architecture, architects who worked there, construction techniques used

Babelon 1965, 25–33, 50–66, 74, 230; Blunt, 222–28.
First dining rooms and bathrooms: DeJean 2009, 67–79.

Stone construction in sixteenth-century Paris: Sutcliffe, 17.

Pierre de taille: the expression does not appear in Nicot's 1606 dictionary but is found in Furetière's 1690 and the Académie Française's 1694 dictionaries.

Pierre de taille first appeared as an established expression in the 1630s: Peiresc, 7:95.

Foreign visitors on Parisian architecture

Evelyn 1955, 2:131; Locatelli 1905, 138; Lister, 7–8; Lady Mary Wortley Montagu, 1:442; Madrisio, 1:173.

See also: La Roche, 102.

Parisians admire the view

Le Petit, 2:265.

Pamphlet from 1649: *Le Cours de la reine*, 6–7.

See also: *Entretiens galants*, 24.

Cost of Bretonvilliers' construction and value of his view

Brice 1706, 1:482; Piganiol de La Force, 1:287.

Dumolin questions this figure, 3:73.

Gallery of the Hôtel de Bretonvilliers: Wilhelm, 137–50.

Contemporaries admired Bretonvilliers' view: Bernini: Chantelou, 46; Tallemant des Réaux, 2:654.

Seventeenth- and eighteenth-century guides to the city on Bretonvilliers' view: Piganiol de La Force, 1:278–88; Le Roux, 295–301; Sauval, 1:90–94; Brice 1706, 1:481.

The word *palais*

Nicot and Académie Française 1694, entry *palais*.

Corneille, *Le Menteur*, 2:552–56.

Brice 1725, 2:336.

Called "*the* Island"

Sauval, 1:93.

Became an administrative unit

Le Moël, 63.

L'École des bourgeois

Allainval, 2:9: p. 60.

Haussmann prefigured by seventeenth-century architecture

Sutcliffe, 47.

Chapter Four: City of Revolution: The Fronde

For a general history of the Fronde, see the works by Jouhaud, Bellanger, Descimon, Feuillet, and Ranum.

Changes brought about by the Fronde

Officials insulted, dragged from their carriages: Motteville, 3:15.

"Demolish the Bastille": Retz, 1:497.

"Hardened to the sight of the dead": Montpensier, 1:179.

Aristocrats walking and eating in public: Montpensier, 1:297–98, 320, 325; 2:55, 87, 146.

Duchesse de Longueville

Dubuisson-Aubenay, 1:111, 136.

"An uprising in Paris"

Motteville, 3:28.

Collectors of civil war material; amount of such material published

Pallier, 52, 45. Ongoing research indicates that Pallier's estimate of Fronde publication is quite low.

Charles I

News of his execution: Motteville, 3:204; Retz, 1:413.

"Under a bad star": Motteville, 2:414.

Participants describe the specific route they took

Montpensier, 1:325; 2:97–99.

How it began

On tax issues in 1648 and poverty in France: Motteville, 2:381–407.

"Vive le roi": Motteville, 2:437.

"Humiliating" the Parlement: Motteville, 3:4–5.

The mass at Notre-Dame and Broussel's arrest: Retz, 1:301–20; Montpensier, 1:176–77; Motteville, 3:4–9.

"Earthly delights": Motteville, 3:13.

Barricades

The *journées des barricades*: Pillorget, 218–35.

The use of chains: Montpensier, 1:177.

What they were made of: Dubuisson-Aubenay, 1:54.

Considered solid work: Le Fèvre d'Ormesson, 1:565.

Fifty thousand to one hundred thousand armed bourgeois: for an estimate from February 1659, see d'Ormesson, 1:655; for various other contemporary estimates, Descimon, 401–4.

Chains down, shops open: Retz, 1:321.

The months that followed

"The city" or "Paris": Dubuisson-Aubenay, 1:112; Patin 1921, 57.

Île Saint-Louis: Descimon, 415.

Paris unified: Le Fèvre d'Ormesson, 1:568–69; Patin 1921, 57. See also Descimon, 411–12, nn.46–47.

Guy Patin 1907, 1:646.

"Against the king": Montpensier, 1:195.

"Point de Mazarin": Montpensier, 1:362–63.

The word *fronder*

Montpensier, 1:180–81; Retz, 1:505.

Anne d'Autriche retaliates

The flight from Paris: Montpensier, 3:132–42; Motteville, 1:193–99; Retz, 1:341.

Parisians' fear of "losing their king": Motteville, 3:307.

She orders the siege: Motteville, 3:144–47; Retz, 1:377.

The opposition takes shape

Aristocrats' pact: Vallier, 1:168.

Noirmoutier: Retz, 1:415.

Broussel and the Bastille: Dubuisson-Aubenay, 1:112; Patin 1921, 45.

The city under siege

Prices of staples: Dubuisson-Aubenay, 1:124, 129, 181.

The weather: Dubuisson-Aubenay, 1:118, 141, 160.

Individuals paid to infiltrate crowds: Dubuisson-Aubenay, 1:182.

Sévigné, 1:10, 13.

Attempt to flee Paris: Motteville, 3:151–54.

Royal soldiers defect: Dubuisson-Aubenay, 1:112.

"Within 8 to 10 days": Vallier, 1:158.

The end of the siege: Dubuisson-Aubenay, 1:184.

The royal family returns: Motteville, 3:324.

Print and the Fronde

Images awaken pity: Retz, 2:72.

"Blanket the city" and in front of Notre-Dame: Dubuisson-Aubenay, 1:298.

Mazarin a "scoundrel": Vallier, 1:124.

Distributed door-to-door: Dubuisson-Aubenay, 1:219.

Group readings: Loret, July 30, 1651, 1:140; Dubuisson-Aubenay, 1:298.

Debating placards' messages: Loret, December 24, 1651, 1:190.

Billets used to warn Parisians: Motteville, 3:30; Dubuisson-Aubenay, 1:61.

Billets used to assemble a crowd: Vallier, 4:68n.

Vaudevilles

Definitions: Richelet, Furetière, Académie Française 1694; see also Furetière, entries *chanson* and *chanter*; Académie Française, entry *chanteur*.

Produced quickly: Retz, 2:97.

"Réveillez-vous, belle endormie": Retz: 2:570n.

Coureurs and *coureuses*: Motteville, 4:293.

Selling songs: Panard, 3:378–82.

Compilations of the greatest hits: *Receuil général de toutes les chansons mazarinistes*, 8–9.

Newspapers of the Fronde

La Gazette: August 29, 1648, 1160.

Parlement requires permission to publish: Patin 1921, 50, 74.

Speed of printing: Dubuisson-Aubenay, 1:81; Retz, 2:149.

Sacks of flour: Dubuisson-Aubenay, 1:154–59.

Courrier français: 1:1–4; 7:7.

Mazarinades

"*Affamée de nouvelles*": Patin 1921, 48.

Peddlers selling pamphlets: Le Dru, 5–6.

Thirty-five hundred had appeared: *L'Adieu et le désespoir des autheurs*, 7.

Multiple printings: the 1649 *Catéchisme des courtisans*, for example, was reedited in Cologne (Elzevir) in 1680.

"Remerciement des imprimeurs": Moreau, 1:289–93.

Mazarinades as political treatises: *Le Raisonable plaintif*, 3–4.

Exact moment of publication: *Lettre du vrai soldat français*, 8.

Bronze statues come to life: *Lettre de Henry IV*, 7–8; *Réponse du roi Louis XIII*, 3.

Dialogue entre le roi de bronze et la Samaritaine sur les affaires du temps présent, 3, 8.

Contrat de mariage: Moreau, 1:39, 46–47.

"I was not Paris": *Remerciement de Paris*, 3, 8.

The war's toll and its end

"100,000 begging": Loret, May 12, 1652, 2:241–42. Loret gives the price of everything from bread to eggs.

"The cemeteries are too small": *Relation extraordinaire*, 3.

"Le pain des pauvres": cited by Feuillet, 344–45.

Parisians write their king: "Requête présentée au roi en son château du Louvre," 4.

"The kingdom is going up in flames": Loret, May 12, 1652, 2:242.

Chains in the streets and the end of unity: Michel Félibien, 5:134–35; Loret, June 23, 1652, 3:257.

"Massacre at the Hôtel de Ville": Loret, July 7, 1652, 3:261; Retz, 2:365; Montpensier, 2:120–22.

Parisians turn against the Fronde: Vallier, 4:69; Retz, 2:382.

"Royal lanterns": Montpensier, 2:195.

The Fronde's effects: Evelyn 1652, 108–11; Berthod, 62.

Patin 1846, 3:254.

Billets advertising oysters

Loret, 2:313–14.

Paris as philosophical, revolutionary capital:

Van Damme, 11–12, 101, 171, 231–38.

Mailly, 1:v, 65.

Chapter Five: The Open City: The Boulevards, Parks, and Streets of Paris

The best histories of urban planning during Louis XIV's reign are Lavedan's; the clearest discussion of the Bullet-Blondel map is Bardet's. On the history of boulevards in Paris, see also Turcot 2005.

All the decrees cited in this chapter were originally published as individual placards with one or two pages of unpaginated text. Almost all were republished in collections, some from the seventeenth century, some modern. Whenever possible, I will give references to the easily available modern collected volumes. Otherwise, I quote from the earliest collected volumes and abbreviate their titles. Thus, for example, *Ordonnance de Louis XIV roy de France et de Navarre donnée à Paris au mois de mars 1669 concernant la jurisdiction des Prévosts des marchands et des eschevins de la ville de Paris* is abbreviated as *Ordonnance de Louis XIV . . . au mois de mars 1669.* Some decrees are now available online.

France's borders
Paris' place in the kingdom: Delamare, 1:87.
Cost of Vauban's fortifications: Wolfe, 148.

The new rampart
"Un rempart d'arbres": October 28, 1704, Michel Félibien, 4:414.
The rampart's dimensions: Blondel 1675, 604.

"*Un lieu de délices*"
Delamare, 1:87.

Louis XIV's first festivities
Place Royale "*advenues*": Deville and Hochereau, 3:6.
The king "took possession of the city": Loret, August 28, 1669, 3:245, 248.

Colbert defined a great reign
September 28, 1665, Colbert, 2:CCX-CCXI.

Blondel's biography
Blondel 1683, 1–2; *Mercure galant*, September 1677, 244–45.

Documents related to the history of the rampart and street widening
Definitions of *rue*: Nicot 1606, Furetière 1690, Académie Française 1694, entry *rue*.
Sixteenth-century street dimensions: Lavedan 1975, 143–44.
Académie royale d'architecture: April 14, 1700, 3:94.
Delamare: 4:10.
A list of the key documents is found in Colbert, 5:555–57; most are reproduced in Michel Félibien, vols. 3, 4, and 5, and in the three volumes of Deville and Hochereau.
Decrees on street widening from the early 1670s are cited in Deville and Hochereau, 1:6–7; 3:7–11.

"Vehicles transporting merchandise and provisions": *Arrest du Conseil qui ordonne l'élargissement de la rue des Arcis*, December 31, 1670, in *Ordonnance de Louis XIV . . . au mois de mars 1669*, 619–20.

Saint-Antoine gate: Blondel 1675, 604–8.

"Most successful city gate": Piganiol de La Force, 4:423.

Homeowners object: Michel Félibien 4:425–28 gives the fullest overview of the different ways of dealing with homeowners who tried to resist the city's plans. See also *Arrest du Conseil pour l'élargissement . . . et la contribution à faire par les propriétaires des maisons opposés à celles retranchées*, July 23, 1673, in *Ordonnance de Louis XIV . . . au mois de mars 1669*, 629–30.

"Rendre Paris la plus belle . . . ville de France": Michel Félibien, 4:228.

Improving streets for pedestrians

Dimensions of paving stones: Delamare, 4:179; Lister, 10.

Subligny: November 29, 1665, in *Continuateurs de Loret*, 1:439.

A "paved street": "Arrêt du conseil qui ordonne la construction du nouveau rempart," in *Ordonnance de Louis XIV . . . au mois de mars 1669*, 617.

"Our paving stones are now gleaming": Robinet, November 28, 1666, in *Continuateurs de Loret*, 2:514.

Louis XIV walking in the streets: September 12, 1666, in *Continuateurs de Loret*, 2:271; December 24, 1667, in *Continuateurs de Loret*, 2:1125–26.

"Chacun pourra marcher tout à son aise": Robinet, October 31, 1666, in *Continuateurs de Loret*, 2: 431.

Sidewalks and *quais*

"Trotoy ou quay des Célestins": Michel Félibien, 4:120.

Meanings *quay/quai*: Jean Nicot 1606, Académie Française 1694.

Quai de La Grenouillère: October 18, 1704, Michel Félibien, 4:423.

Lister, 8.

Quais with *banquettes/marche-pied*: *Plan levé par les ordres du roy*, 3–4.

Quai d'Orsay: August 23, 1707, Michel Félibien, 4:424.

The Bullet-Blondel map

Bullet's involvement began: Langenskiöld, 9.

Bullet and the Ritz Hotel: DeJean 2009, 30–31.

Bullet as city inspector and his early work on the map: Archives Nationales H2 2012. Other documents in this series, including one dated September 24, 1672, are by Bullet.

Difficulty of the mapmaker's task: Bullet, *Pantomètre*, 65.

Writings of those involved with the project: Bullet, *Pantomètre*, "avant-propos"; Blondel 1675, 604; the king, see *Plan levé par les ordres du roy*, 1, as well as the privilege printed at the end of all copies of the map, and Clément 5:555.

Beltway: Bullet, *Pantomètre*, 48.

"Promenade publique": July 15, 1673, in *Ordonnance de Louis XIV . . . au mois de mars 1669*, 639–40.

The map taken seriously

Statute of November 4, 1684: Michel Félibien, 4:271.
Statute of October 18, 1704: Michel Félibien, 4:414–15.
Statute of December 1, 1715: Michel Félibien, 4:445–47.

Buttes and garbage

"Flatten several mounds of earth": April 7, 1685; Michel Félibien, 4:301 and 2:1517.
"An unpleasant sight": April 7, 1685; Michel Félibien, 4:272–73.
Garbage inspectors: *Ordonnance de Louis XIV . . . en 1685*, 288.
Fines for dumping garbage: *Interdiction de mettre des immondices*, n.p.
Chef's salary: Audiger, 20.
Damaging the trees: December 9, 1684, *Ordonnance . . . défendant d'endommager*, 1; August 24, 1667, Delamare, 4:396.

Access to the rampart

From the Place Royale: June 7, 1670, in *Ordonnance de Louis XIV . . . au mois de mars 1669*, 618–19; March 17, 1671, in Michel Félibien, 4:608–9.
From the rue Saint-Denis: April 1, 1672, in Deville and Hochereau, 3:9.
From the Place Vendôme: June 5, 1670, in Deville and Hochereau, 3:17.

Streets deleted from the map

June 21, 1704: Deville and Hochereau, 3:18.
Louis Dumesnil: October 12, 1679, Archives Nationales H2 2012.
Lister, 27.

Siamese ambassadors

Donneau de Visé, 289.

Avenues and boulevards

Boulevard and avenue interchangeable: Darin, 143 and ff.
Boullevers: 1597, in Michel Félibien, 5:34.
History of *boulevard*: Rey, 1:470.
Advenue or *avenue*: Dictionaries of Furetière 1690, Académie Française 1694.
The avenues near the Invalides: Michel Félibien, 4:414–15.
"Avenues des Thuilleries": 1667–68, Guiffrey, 1:187.
"Avenues du Roulle et des Thuilleries": August 6, 1672, Guiffrey, 1:653.
"Avenue des Tuileries": see Jouvin de Rochefort's 1676 *Plan de Paris*.
"Champs-Élysées": December 28, 1709, Guiffrey, 5:307, 392.
A passage in Sauval suggests that "Champs-Élysées" had emerged before Sauval's death in 1676, 1:771–72.
Early description of Champs-Élysées: Liger, 261.
Champs-Élysées as city park: [Le Rouge/Saugrain] 1716, 47.
Boulevards in the seventeenth century: Dumolin 1931, 2:110.
"Sans aucune interruption": Brice 1725, 1:299.
The phrase *sur le boulevard*: *Histoire du père La Chaize*, 1:17–18; Liger, 41; Challes, "preface."

Walking good for one's health: Caraccioli 1784, 77.

"Grands boulevards": 1776, Rétif de la Bretonne, 1:148.

Cours-la-Reine

Turcot, 73–75; Alphand, 46.

Traffic jams: Villers, 426, 450.

Number of carriages: low estimate, Lister, 178; high estimate, Nemeitz, 1:163.

Selling sweets and carrying billets doux: Nemeitz, 1:163.

Louis XIV in the Cours: Loret, April 29, 1662, 3:496.

"Paris où tout abonde": *Le Cours de la reine*, 16.

"Pour en faire montre": *La Promenade du Cours*, 1.

Tuileries

"Le pays des Promenades": DuFresny, 327.

Caraccioli 1772, 229, 246.

Vauxhall: Coke and Borg, 1–33. McNeil and Riello suggest that public promenade places really developed in London only from the mid-eighteenth century on, 179.

Men and women walking together: Nemeitz, 1:154; Marana, 4–5.

Women didn't walk in other countries: Hunt, 121.

Privacy in the afternoon: Nemeitz, 1:156.

Sévigné, April 8, 1671, 1:213; May 1, 1671, 1:242.

Cafés: Liger, 122.

"Viennent y promener leurs loisirs": Mercier 1788, 10.

The place where "on apprend les modes": Le Maire, 3:196–97; Nemeitz, 1:154; Caraccioli, 231.

The Parisian corporation or guild of master fanmakers was established in 1676. On fans in Paris, see Cowen, "introduction."

Wooden benches: October 4, 1678, Guiffrey, 1:1022; May 26, 1686, Guiffrey, 2:982. NB: Marble benches show up in the account books at about the same moment for use at châteaux such as Fontainebleau. On March 18, 1677, Barbier was paid for thirty-four wooden benches "to be placed in different places," Guiffrey, 1:945.

Price of meat: Audiger, 10.

Courtin 1671, 87, 86; 1702, 144–48.

Henry, 19–20.

Liger, 260–61.

Mercure galant: July 1677, 14–16, 119–20; July 1678, 170–73, 179–80.

Lister, 180–81.

Lady Mary Wortley Montagu, 1:442.

Praise for boulevards

Mercure galant: December 1678, 10–11.

Entretiens galants ou conversations sur la solitude, 1:26.

Delamare, 1:87.

Balzac, 40:610.

Boulevard and *boulevards* used interchangeably: Caraccioli 1777, 248; Caraccioli 1802, 221.

An early instance in which *boulevards* is used for boulevard: *Théâtre des boulevards, ou Recueil des pièces*. Paris: Gilles Langlois, 1756.

Chapter Six: City of Speed and Light: City Services That Transformed Urban Life

Corneille, *La Galerie du Palais*, 2:2:387.
"The age in which we live": Loret, May 1664, 4:176.

The postal system

On Villayer: Tallemant des Réaux, 2:1299. ("Villayer" is the more common spelling, but "Vélayer" appears regularly.)

Lettres patentes, May 1653: Archives Nationales X/1/A/8658, fol. 239–41.

Instruction générale: pièce 27, receuil 8-H-7840, in Paris' Arsenal Library.

Contemporary newspaper: Loret, 1:399.

Scudéry-Pellisson correspondence: *Chroniques*, ms. 15.156 in Paris' Arsenal Library.

On the postal system: Scudéry, 72, 75, 86, 248, 251.

The greeting card: Scudéry, 101.

Public transportation

The history of the collaboration between Pascal and Roannez: "Convention relative," in Pascal 1914, 10:147.

The contracts for their company: Pascal 1914, 10:147–48.

Carriages in 1658: Hurtaut and Magny, 2:78.

Carriages in 1698: Brice 1698, 1:12; Piganiol de La Force, 1:32.

Carriages in the mid-eighteenth century: Hurtaut and Magny, 2:78; Pardailhé-Galabrun, 224.

Big growth in second half of seventeenth century: Roche 2000, 10.

Some examples from Sévigné: December 4, 1673, 1:632; January 26, 1674, 1:683; February 5, 1674, 1:692.

Rental began in Paris: Delamare, 4:437; Roche 2000, 93.

Montbrun: Gady, 249–51.

Vehicles for rent: Sauval, 1:193–94; Pillorget, 164; Bernard, 61.

Cost of rentals: Delamare, 4:438.

Nemeitz: 1, 402–5.

All quotes from contemporary documents are from either Pascal 1914, 10:271–75 or Pascal 1992, 4:1397–1417.

The decrees: Pascal 1992, 4:1397–1401.

Test run: Pascal 1914, 10:275.

Loret, 3:481.

Glass windows: Pillorget, 163.

A broken carriage window: *Mercure galant*, October 1684, 113.

Gilberte Pascal: Pascal 1992, 4:1404–6.

The posters: Arsenal library, 4-J-1183.

Crimes against the carriages: Pascal 1992, 4:1418–19.

One writer described the experience: La Bruyère, "De la société et de la conversation," 233.

Sauval on the public for carriages: 1:192–93.

Huygens: Pascal 1992, 4:1439.

Chevalier

His career: Lancaster, 1:312–36.

The play's *privilège* was issued on December 7, 1662.

Intrigue des carrosses: 2:2: p.27; 2:6: pp.46–47; 1:1: pp.4–5; 2:4: p.31; 3:9: p.69; 2:1: p.24; 1:1: pp.2–3; 1:2: p.7; 2:2: p.25; 3:10: p.72.

Lauder, 159.

Other performances of the play: Lancaster, 1:323n.1.

Accounts of riding in carriages

Browne, 21; Skippon, 6:730.

Roannez sold his stake

Delamare, 4:441.

Omnibuses in the nineteenth century

Lavedan 1926, 3:101.

Laudati de Caraffe

The publicity flier for Laudati's *porte-flambeaux* is pièce 65 in collection 4-J-1183 in Paris' Arsenal Library.

Documents concerning his system: Monmerqué, 57–65.

Lettres patentes: Michel Félibien, 5:188, 191.

Street lighting prior to Louis XIV's reign

Herlaut, 129–33; Defrance, 28–30.

La Reynie

His mandate: Colbert, 10:393.

La Reynie and street lighting: Saint-Germain, 76–78.

Street lighting

The account in a newsletter from 1666: Subligny, December 24, 1666, *Continuateurs de Loret*, 2:584.

Edict on street lighting: Delamare, 4:230; Defrance, 36–37.

Robinet: *Continuateurs de Loret*, 2:1067.

Glass in lanterns: Lister, 25.

Schedule for lighting: Michel Félibien, 5:213–14.

For more on the different schedules: Herlaut, 165.

Citizens offered to pay more: Michel Félibien, 5:214.

Tax raised three hundred thousand *livres*: Delamare, 4:237.

Cost of candles: Brice 1698, 1:12.

Edicts concerning the financing of street lighting: Bibliothèque Historique de la Ville de Paris, 117945.

Safety before street lighting: Subligny, *Continuateurs de Loret*, 2:583.

Safety after street lighting: Robinet, *Continuateurs de Loret*, 2:1068.

Edicts regulating used clothing dealers: Bibliothèque Historique de la Ville de Paris, 27046.

"Exactitude" of the police: *Mercure Galant*, June 1677, 264–65.

"Pocket pistols": Michel Félibien, 4:286.

Colletet: *La Ville de Paris*, 159; see also Delamare, 4:230; Nemeitz, 1:118.

Marana, 40.

Poisson, 159.

Académie Française dictionary 1694: entry *filou*.

Improved the lives of Parisians: Michel Félibien, 4:214.

Sévigné, 1:632.

Nemeitz, 1:118–19.

Marana, 50–51.

Lady Mary Wortley Montagu, 1:442; see also Lister, 25.

Favre: *Machines et inventions*, 2:53–55.

Numbers of lanterns in Paris: Herlaut, 163.

Liger, 261.

Chapter Seven: Capitale de la Mode

Making Europe French
"Européens en 1600"; "rendre l'Europe française": Caraccioli, 8, 52.
"Frenchifying": Veryard, 108.
Shadwell, prologue.

English commentators
Veryard, 108–9. (He speaks of "toyish commodities," "trifles," and so forth.)
[J.B./Bethel], 2–6.

Shops carried *"au col ou sur le dos"*
Furetière 1690, entry *boutique*.

Galerie du Palais/Palace Gallery:
1577: Lippomano, 49.
London's Royal Exchange: Davis, 104; Howard, 35–37.
Account of the 1618 fire: Boutrage, 3–6.
Male and female merchants: Berthod, 9–13.
Gallery enlarged: in 1639–40, Michel Félibien, 5:105–6; in 1670–71, Michel Félibien, 4:220–25.
One hundred and eighty merchants: La Caille, "préface."
"D'une forme d'architecture la plus agréable": Michel Félibien, 4:222.

Arcades and the department store: Benjamin, 37.

Locatelli 1990, 107; Locatelli 1905, 122–23.

Notes in Colbert's hand

Colbert, 2:CCXVII; Louis XIV, 1:XXV.

Mercure galant

Terms of its permission: Klaits, 67.

First coverage of *la mode*: *Mercure galant* 1672, 275–85; 1673, 3:307–8 and 322–23.

Textiles and *la mode*: *Mercure galant* 1673, 3:305.

Food and *la mode*: *Mercure galant* 1673, 3:317.

Refers to Perdrigeon (Donneau de Visé writes "Périgon"): 1673, 3:286.

Information on Perdrigeon: Blégny 1878, 2:29; Franklin, 1:41–42; DeJean 2005, 42.

"C'est Perdrigeon tout pur": Molière, *Les Précieuses ridicules*, scene 9, 2:95.

Outfits illustrated in 1678's *Mercure galant*: "habit d'été" in the *extraordinaire* for April 1678. DeJean 2005, 47–52.

Engravings of fashion called *modes*: *Mercure galant*, September 1693, 210; *Dictionnaire universel français et latin* (*Dictionnaire de Trévoux*), entry *mode*. (This usage does not appear in Furetière 1690 but does figure in the 1732 edition of the Trévoux dictionary.)

Images of new Parisian shops

Engravings of shop interiors: Boucher, 123–25.

The evolution of the shop: Davis, 100–101.

Displaying goods: Walsh, 157, 164, 172.

"Greedy" customers: La Roche, 87.

Drawer-based storage, built-in storage: DeJean 2009, 131–33.

Large-paned windows: DeJean 2009, 156–57; DeJean 2005, 192.

Advertising in Paris

Enseignes: Savary des Bruslons, 2:323–24.

Lister, 22, 236–38.

Advertising as a "magic system": Williams 1980, 185, 189.

Advertising as "value enhancement": Sewell, 119.

Affiches de Paris: 1716, 4. (Jean Du Gone was the editor.)

The dream of changing status through dress:

French dictionaries: Furetière 1690 and 1727, entry *mode*.

"Parisians dress better": Le Maire, 3:196–97; Bernier 1699, 2:71, 73–74.

New way fashion functioned

Mode defined as changing often: Furetière 1690 (compare with Nicot 1606), entry *mode*.

Mercure galant: 1673, 3:283, 322–23.

"Le bel air": *Mercure galant* 1672, 324; 1673, 3:307; January 1678 *extraordinaire*, 522.

Bel air defined: Académie Française dictionary 1694, entry *beau*.

"Their whole Fortune upon their Backs": Nemeitz 1712, 16.

Guidebooks talk of fast change: Nemeitz 1712, 16.

"On peut s'y habiller à neuf": Liger, 364.

"On trouve [tout] sur le champ"; "d'une heure à l'autre": Marana, 35; Liger, 174.

Buying ready-made clothes: Blégny 1691, 25.

"À la mode du temps": Nemeitz, 1:79.

Mode and social mobility: Jones, 14.

"Choose your rank": Liger, 364.

Shopping

First used in English: 1764 (*Oxford English Dictionary*).

"Courant tous les magazins de Paris": Préchac, 20.

"Courir de boutique en boutique": Galland, 2:301.

Marana, 7, 12, 23.

Other warnings about the excessive cost of luxury in Paris: Lister, 166; Sauval, 1:626.

Nemeitz, 1:41, 44, 47; 2:581–82, 587, 592, 598–99.

Le juste prix: the earliest use of the phrase I have found is on a merchant's card from 1663.

La Frénai and fixed pricing: Nemeitz, 2:598. (Davis, 291, says fixed pricing began in England only in the early nineteenth century.)

Lister on fixed pricing, 181.

Information on La Frénai (also written "La Fresnaye" and "La Frainaye"): Blégny 1878, 1:236–37; Bordelon 1699, 32–33.

Jones, 14. In 1714, Bernard Mandeville had used a similar phrase in *The Fable of the Bees*.

Economics of French fashion

French shops throughout Europe: Nemeitz, 2:589.

Orders by foreigners: *Mercure galant*, March 1680, part 2, 61–65.

Veryard, 107–8, 110.

[J. B./Bethel], 10, 2–6.

Shift in English public opinion: Pincus, 336.

Zanon, 3:342.

"Empire de la mode": *Mercure galant* 1673, 3:317; April 1699, 274–75.

"Silks and fripperies"; "Wines and Brandy": [J. B./Bethel], 2.

1.5 million pounds: [J. B./Bethel], 6.

"Ribans, lace": Veryard, 109.

"The universal monarchy for Cloaths": Shadwell, prologue. Shadwell also refers to "the empire of fashion."

Louis XIV's role: Veryard, 108.

Colbert's role: [J. B./Bethel], 2–3.

Zanon on Colbert, 3:340–41. The words Zanon quoted, however, were not Colbert's but a pastiche produced in 1693 by novelist Courtilz de Sandras: Courtilz de Sandras, 492–94.

Caraccioli, 58,308.

Number of shops in Paris: Coquery, 340–41.

Mercier: Académie Française 1694, Furetière 1690, entry *mercier*.

Shops open at night: Nemeitz, 1:119.

History of the French involvement with luxury goods: Sewell, 82.

Chapter Eight: City of Finance and New Wealth

A culture "dominated by wealthy nobles": Soll, 34; for the opposite view, Dessert, 82.

"Une place séparée": Richelieu 1995, 177.

Guidebooks to Paris: Nemeitz, 2:411; Sauval, 3:50–51.

Financiers built homes of artistic significance: Dent, 183–85.

Descriptions of the wealth of Paris

"The Financiers give [Paris] its glow": *Partisans démasquez*, 1.

Paris "abounds with wealth": Sauval, 1:626.

"Paradise for the rich": Nemeitz, 2:582, 1:44.

One commentator in 1694: Henry, 25, 27.

The word *financier* in English

Its inaugural appearance: Evelyn, 33.

First appearance in a dictionary: Phillips (1678), entry *financier*.

Finances of the French monarchy in the seventeenth century:

The figures I cite in this section are based on these sources: Bayard, Bonney, Dent, Dessert, Martin and Bezançon. Many key financial documents from the period no longer survive; historians thus all stress that it is impossible to be absolutely certain of many figures. They all also agree, however, that figures taken from a variety of seventeenth-century sources nearly coincide and in addition that key overall trends are unmistakable; they all present almost identical figures and trends.

Henri IV's surplus: Martin and Bezançon, 6; Dent 58; Smith, 2:909.

Bankers in seventeenth-century Paris: Blégny 1691, 117–20.

Income in the sixteenth century: Dent, 9.

Income in the seventeenth century: Bayard, 28–29; Bonney, 306–13; Martin and Bezançon, 123.

A noted eighteenth-century economist: Forbonnais, 2: 290–97. (He says 2.8 times greater than that of the Dutch Republic.); see also Dent, 9.

Direct cost of war: Bonney, 306; Bayard, 33.

Size of French army: Bonney, 31, 173; Dessert, 156.

Size of French navy: Dessert, 157.

How radically Louis XIV changed the French navy: [J. B./Bethel], 1.

Smith, 2:909.

Extraordinary expenses: Bonney, 306–7.

The first financiers

Financier is first used to designate a man of finance in the late sixteenth century, notably by Montaigne, and first defined in Richelet's 1680 dictionary.

Extraordinary income: Bayard, 42–43.

Legal lending rates: Bonney, 19.

Rates on loan contracts: Marion, 537–38.

Amounts of contracts: Bayard, 197, 202.

Number of financiers: Bayard, 293; Dessert, 78–81.

Financier: Académie Française dictionary 1694.

Fermier, partisan, traitant: See the entries in Marion.

Parisian real-estate development:

Marchant: Ballon 1991, 299–301; Barbiche, 55.

Moisset: Mouton, 72–104; Bayard, 280, 439, 286; Ballon 1985, 21–22; Carsalade du Pont, 285–311.

Moisset's origins cannot be established with certainty, but it is clear that he was not born into the nobility and that his family was impoverished. It is also clear that the only connections on which he relied to break the cycle of poverty were contacts made while he worked as a tailor.

Moisset's will: Bibliothèque Nationale de France, Ms. fr. 17354, fol. 267.

Moisset's contemporaries: L'Estoile, 2:251–54; Carsalade du Pont, 285.

Moisset's lot on the Place Royale: Dumolin 1926, 12, 43.

Richelieu on Moisset: Richelieu 1823, 1:141; Richelieu 1856, 2:211n.

Moisset as adviser to Henri IV: Henri IV, 6:228, 243.

Le Barbier's importance: Dumolin 1931, 1:141.

Le Barbier's biography: Dumolin 1931, 1:139–40.

Le Barbier's Left Bank speculation: Dumolin 1931, 1:142–81.

Sale of property: Dumolin 1931, 1:162.

Financiers built in Paris: Dent, 184.

The homes of financiers: Bayard, 397.

Since the fourteenth century: Dumolin 1931, 2:111.

Le Barbier's Right Bank speculation: Dumolin 1931, 2:111–340.

Richelieu's urban planning: Dumolin 1931, 2:118–20.

Le Barbier and rental property: Dumolin 1931, 2:271–72.

Le Barbier's daughter's dowry: Dumolin 1931, 2:140.

Le Barbier's financial difficulties: Dumolin 1931, 2:135.

Moisset lost his fortune: Bayard, 286.

Wealthy Parisians

Sauval, 1:626.

Estimates by contemporary economic theorists: Martin and Bezançon, 130; Marion, 537–38.

Financiers' incomes: Dessert, 124–28.

The Place Vendôme

Crozat's home: Ziskin, 50–63.

First residents of the Place: Saint-Germain, 200–203.

Crozat and d'Evreux: DeJean 2009, 31; Ziskin, 50.

Brice 1706, 1:185–88; see also Sauval, 3:50–51.

The "quartier Louis-le-Grand": Delamare, 4:400, 406.

Manual laborer's wage: Baulant, 483.

A financier's annual income: Saint-Germain, 52.

Worker who maintained windows: Martin and Bezançon, 138.

Social status of financiers

Doubt still remains about the origins of many financiers. For example, though Moisset's family near Montauban has been described as "bourgeois," no documents have been produced to prove this. What is certain is that, like Moisset, a number of financiers move into the nobility only by royal decree, that this happened with extraordinary rapidity and because of their financial expertise. All this makes it easy to see why financiers were the object of intense scrutiny and resentment in the seventeenth century.

First half of the seventeenth century: Bayard, 438–39, 277; Dent, 117, 120–21, 123.

Second half of the seventeenth century: Dessert, 91–93.

Civil war and financiers

Borrowing in the 1640s: Bonney, 197, 317.

First awareness of financiers' fortunes: Talon, 6:299; Martin and Bezançon, 134.

Fiscal policy during the Fronde: Bayard: 340–41; Bonney, 193–201; Martin and Bezançon, 134.

Attacks on financiers' homes: Dubuisson-Aubenay, 1:35, 39, 41, 60, and so forth; Motteville, 38:4; Patin 1907, 1:664.

Parlement organized attacks: Dubuisson-Aubenay, 1:137, 139.

Rumors of wealth: Dubuisson-Aubenay, 1:157.

Image of the financier

Bayard, 297–301; Dessert, 83–86.

Financiers in political pamphlets:

Agréable et veritable récit de ce qui s'est passé, devant et depuis l'enlèvement du roi, 3.

Triolets sur le tombeau de la galanterie, 22,20.

Suite du catéchisme des partisans, 24.

Catalogue des partisans, 3–6,16,19.

Financiers in memoirs of those who lived through the Fronde

Lefèvre d'Ormesson, 1:238; Dubuisson-Aubenay, 1:269.

Financiers in French comedies

On English comedy: Howard, chapter 2.

Les Enfants de Paris: 1:7: p.17; 5:2: p.107; the play was staged in 1699, published in 1705.

Le Joueur: 5:6; 2:2; 5:4; 1:1.

Le Chevalier à la mode: 1:3: p.5; 1:7: p.14; 1:7: p.15; 3:2: p.42; 1:1: p.3; 1:1: p.8.

Turcaret: 1:1: p.39; 2:3: p.77; 1:9: p.67; 1:10: p.67–68; 4:11: p.152,154; 4:10: p.146,148; 1:1: p.30; 1:4: p.52; 3:7: p.112; 4:10: p.146; 5:13: p.174; 5:3: p.157; 5:14: p.172.

Libelous late-seventeenth-century attacks:

A contemporary periodical: Du Noyer, 1:301.

Unpublished attacks from early eighteenth century: Dessert, 82–85.

Partisans démasquez: 5–6, 10, 24, 42, 59, 179.

Pluton maltôtier: 6, 24, 39, 85–86, 177, 196, 40.

Anti-financier city guide: *Médailles sur la régence*, 9, 7, 10–11, 30, 20.

Vaudevilles: *Nouveau recueil de chansons*, 331–32.

The word *financier* in dictionaries

Richelet: entry *financier*.

Furetière 1690: entries *financier*, *partisan*, *traitant*.

Académie Française 1694: entries *traitant*, *financier*.

Financiers under investigation

Chambres de justice: Bayard, 318, 323; Bonney, 266; Dessert, 219–25; Martin and Bezançon, 139.

Investigations in 1700: Martin and Bezançon, 141–42.

Poisson de Bourvallais: Dessert, 671–72.

The term *nouveau riche*

The term was first used just after the Fronde to translate Aristotle's concept of undeserved fortune and the newly rich who attain office. Aristotle, 272–74.

Patru, 686–87.

Le Prestre, 326–27, 828. The passages are not found in the 1643 and 1665 editions of the work.

Le Noble, 44–45.

The word *parvenu*

Furetière, Académie Française 1694, entry *parvenir*.

Earliest appearance: "l'extravagance d'un nouveau parvenu et . . . d'un maltôtier." Dralsé de Grand-Pierre, 48.

A play called *Le Parvenu* was staged on February 13, 1721, but never published. Beauchamps, 3:141.

Marivaux, *Le Paysan parvenu*, 109.

The word *millionnaire*

Early usage: *Courrier politique et galant*, June 3, 1720; *Lettres historiques, contenant tout se qui se passe en Europe*, 562–63; Bordelon, *Lettres familières . . . à un nouveau millionnaire*, 1:2; Piossens, 5:239.

Lesage: *Histoire d'Estevanille Gonzalez*, 200; *Le Bachelier de Salamanque*, 211; *La Valise trouvée*, 172.

La Belle et la Bête: Villeneuve, 72.

Ill-gotten gains of millionaires: Grimoard, 1.

Financial vocabulary in English

Nouveaux riches: Edgeworth, 38.

Parvenu: Edgeworth, 43.

Millionaire: London *Times*, October 19, 1795; Byron, June 23, 1816, 5:80; Thompson, 1:225.

Financial vocabulary in other European languages

Parvenu first appeared in Dutch only in 1840; *millionaire* was first used in 1798.

Nouveau riche and *parvenu* appeared in French in eighteenth-century German works; their German equivalents began to be used in the nineteenth century.

Parvenu first appeared in Italian in 1721; *nuovi richi* began to be used in the 1730s.

How the financiers are viewed

They made possible France's new prominence: Bayard, 451.

Inequities of the French tax system: Bonney, 272–73; Vauban, 2–4.

Proof of the openness of French society: Bayard, 301.

Evolution in French society: Bayard, 453.

"Une place séparée": Richelieu 1995, 177. Arsenal ms. 3561, f.196R.

"Une partie séparée": Richelieu 1947, 251. Arsenal ms. 3853, f.306.

"Une classe séparée": Richelieu 1688, 158. Arsenal ms. 3739, f.72V. All early Dutch editions use *classe*.

Hume, 56–57.

History of "class": Williams 1985, 60–69.

Chapter Nine: City of Romance

"Love in Paris": Balzac 1992, 202–3; Balzac 1976, 3:236.

Women's freedom in Paris

"Elles vont par la ville": Marana, 16.

Masking in London used to disguise identity: Heyl, 119–20.

Women in the Palace Gallery

Corneille, *La Galerie du Palais*, I:vii–viii:105, 108, 128–30, 200, 211.

Berthod, 9–13.

Locatelli 1990, 107; Locatelli 1905, 122–23.

Lippomano, 49.

English comedies in the Royal Exchange: Howard, 38, 61–62.

The word *incognito* and masking

"The privilege of going maskt": Nemeitz 1712, 16.

In Italian: Battaglia, 7:702.

Taken over by French: Vaugelas, 464–65.

The first appearance of *incognito* in English, according to the *Oxford English Dictionary*, was in a 1652 translation from a French novel. On its spread in the second half of the seventeenth century: Heyl, 120.

Sévigné, 19 July, 1675, 2:11.

Peter the Great: Saint-Simon, 31:367.

Accounts of those visiting Paris *incognito*: Dubuisson-Aubenay, 1:27 (a cardinal); Donneau de Visé, June 1686, 23 (Siamese ambassadors); March 1679, 321–22 (many different ambassadors); Loret, 3:520, 589; Loret, 4:45, 219 (various ambassadors).

"Toutes les personnes qui ne veulent pas être reconnues": Académie Française dictionary 1694, entry *incognito*.

Masking in eighteenth-century Venice, where women did wear masks in public: Johnson, 9. Masking became popular in Venice in the 1680s and 1690s, slightly later than in Paris: Johnson, 126–28.

"Se cacher et se faire voir quand il leur plait": Marana, 16.

Mask called a *loup*: Furetière dictionary 1690, entry *loup*.

Chevalier, 1:4: p.16; 1:6: p.19.

Marana, 16.

Not noble: Furetière dictionary 1690, entry *dame*. In addition, the fact that the woman's dress is foreign, probably Dutch, indicates that she was unaccustomed to the French way of masking.

In England at the same period, women are always depicted wearing their masks: Heyl, 124–25.

Noblewomen and expensive clothing: Sauval, 82.

Gawking at celebrities: Loret, 3:496.

Corneille, *Le Menteur*, 1:5:257–58; 3:3:806.

The Parisienne

"Elles surpassent en agrément": Marana, 14.

The Parisienne and shopping: Préchac, *L'Illustre Parisienne*, part I (1679).

The Parisienne masked: *L'Illustre Parisienne*, part II (1690).

Dancourt 1694, 26–27, 32.

Marana, 17.

Sarasin, 2:172.

The coquette

The first coquettes: early examples in the *Oxford English Dictionary*; d'Aubignac, 8 and so forth.

Coquette as fashion victim: *Mercure galant* 1673, 3:309; Auneuil, 19; Caraccioli 1777, 307.

Dictionary definitions: Académie Française 1694, Furetière 1690, entry *coquet*.

Engraving: Nicolas Guérard, "La Coquette."

Baron, 1:2: p.9; 3:4: p.12; 2:4: p.17.

Dancourt 1690, scene 4.

Lesage 1709, 1:6: p.59; 1:9: p.66

Le Noble 1696, 4–5, 13; Le Noble 1698, sixth promenade, 17,19.

Le Noble 1698, sixth promenade, 17,19.

Coquettes pass for noble in the Tuileries: Liger, 260.

A contemporary satirist: *Satyre nouvelle sur les promenades*, 11.

Coquet: by the late seventeenth century, *coquette* became a noun, whereas *coquet* was still used only adjectivally. By 1700, the male *coquette* had virtually disappeared.

The *aventurier* and the *aventurière*

Aventurier's changing meaning: Académie Française 1694, entry *aventurier*; Furetière 1690, entry *adventurier*. NB: the word is also spelled *avanturier(e)*.

Le Chevalier à la mode: 1:3: p.5; 1:2: p.42; 3:6: p.50; 3:12: p.57.

Chevaliers aventuriers: Furetière 1690, entry *adventurier*.

"Fortune-hunters": Boyer, *Dictionnaire royal* 1702, entry *aventurier*. James Carlisle's 1689 comedy, *The Fortune-Hunters*.

Periodical: Le Noble 1698, 4–5.

Low-born *aventuriers*: Nemeitz, 2:411; Le Noble 1698, fourth promenade, 12.

Aventuriers in Le Noble 1697, 101, 147.

Aventurières in Le Noble's periodicals: Le Noble 1698, fourth promenade, 19.

Adventurier d'amour: Furetière 1690, entry *adventurier*.

Le Noble 1697, 193–94, 263, 301.

Tales in contemporary periodicals and gazettes

Mercure galant, February 1679, 68, 72–74, 82, 90–91.

Mailly, "avertissement," 4.

Contemporary rumors about the Loison sisters: Du Noyer, 1:12–13; 2:534; and *Les Soeurs rivales, histoire galante*.

L'École des filles

"Livre très méchant": Ravaisson, 1:8.

Pepys, 9:21–22, 58–59.

Foundlings (*enfants trouvés*)

In the fifteenth and sixteenth centuries: Pillorget, 521–26.

In the seventeenth century: Sauval, 1:589; Piganiol de La Force, 4:436–37; Hurtaut and Magny, 3:237–39.

Parlement's decrees from the 1660s: Michel Félibien, 5:205.

Hospital founded 1670: Michel Félibien, 5:212 and 217.

Louis XIV's decree: Sauval, 590.

Contemporary commentators: Piganiol de la Force, 1:486. In fact, Paris did not grow significantly between 1644 and 1669; the Fronde greatly reduced its population.

Child abandonment in seventeenth-century Paris: Lallemand, 741; Dupoux, 41 and ss., 80; in 1726, Brièle, 1:292.

In 1785, Paris was not much larger than in 1700, but six thousand babies were abandoned that year.

Visions of the Parisian coquette

Prévost, 64, 76, 88–89, 82–84, 100–102, 155–56.

Perrine: Le Noble 1696, 14.

Men want to be ruined: Le Noble 1696, 16–17.

"La liberté de Paris": Marana, 44.

Conclusion: Making the City Visible: Painting and Mapping the Transformation of Paris

The Étoile and the Bois de Boulogne first laid out: [Le Rouge/Saugrain] 1719, 1:123.

Contemporary reactions to Haussmann

Baudelaire, 90–92. At least one translator, Howard, omits "hélas."
Goncourt: Clark, 34–35.
Fear of change in the nineteenth century: Clark, 36–44; Terdiman, 119–27.
The destruction of Haussmann's maps: Clark, 41.

Portrait of Henri IV

Montgolfier 1970, 1,7.

Maps of Paris in the sixteenth and seventeenth centuries

Boutier, Sarazin, and Sibille.
The French become the greatest cartographers: Konvitz, 1–4.

The original urban views

The influence of cartography: Alpers, 139; Ballon 1991, 233–34, 244–45; Pollack, chapters 4 and 5.
London views: Galinou and Hayes; Hyde.
Dutch cityscapes: van Suchtelen and Wheelock.
Paris cityscapes: Montgolfier, de Maere and Sainte Fare.
Views of the Place Royale: Montgolfier 1970:1, 10–11.
Late-seventeenth and eighteenth-century painting that includes river views: Dubbini, 60–82.
Poultry and bread market: Delamare, 3:212.

Académie galante. Amsterdam: [Wetstein], 1682.

Adieu et le desespoir des autheurs et escrivains de libelles de la guerre civile, L'. Paris: Claude Morlot, 1649.

Affiches des jurés crieurs de Paris. Bibliothèque Nationale de France F49, no. 36.

Affiches de Paris, des provinces, et des pays étrangers, Les. Paris: C. L. Thiboust, 1716.

Agréable et véritable récit de ce qui s'est passé devant et depuis l'enlèvement du roi. Paris: Jacques Guillery, 1649.

Alembert, Jean Le Rond d'. "Éloge de Choisy." *Éloges lus dans les séances publiques de l'Académie Française*. Paris: Panckouke, 1779.

Allainval, Abbé Léonor Jean Soulas d'. *L'École des bourgeois*. Paris: Veuve Pierre Ribou, 1729.

Alpers, Svetlana. *The Art of Describing: Dutch Art of the 17th Century*. Chicago: University of Chicago Press, 1984.

Alphand, Adolphe. *Promenades de Paris*. Paris: Rothschild, 1868.

Alquié, François Savinien d'. *Les Délices de la France*. 2 vols. Paris: G. de Luyne, 1670.

À Monsieur de Broussel, conseiller du Roy au parlement de Paris. Paris: François Noel, 1649.

Andia, Béatrice de, and Nicolas Courtin. *L'Île Saint-Louis*. Paris: Action Artistique de la Ville de Paris, 1997.

Aristotle. *La Rhétorique d'Aristote en français*. Translated by F. Cassandre. Paris: L. Chamhoudry, 1654.

Arrest de la cour . . . portant deffenses à toutes personnes . . . de s'attrouper sur le Pont-neuf. Paris: Par les imprimeurs et libraires ordinaires du roy, 1652.

Aubignac, François Hédelin, Abbé de. *Conjectures académiques, ouvrage posthume, trouvé dans les recherches d'un savant*. 1715. Edited by G. Lambin. Paris: Champion, 2010.

———. *Histoire du temps, ou relation du royaume de la Coqueterie*. Paris: Charles de Sercy, 1654.

Audiger. *La Maison reglée*. Paris: Nicolas Le Gras, 1692.

Aulnoy, Marie Catherine Le Jumel de Barneville, Comtesse d'. *Relation du voyage d'Espagne.* 3 vols. Paris: Claude Barbin, 1691.

Auneuil, Louise de Bossigny, comtesse d'. *Les Colinettes, nouvelles du temps, mois de mars 1703.* Paris: Pierre Ribou, 1703.

Aviler, Augustin Charles d'. *Cours d'architecture.* Paris: Nicolas Langlois, 1691.

Avity, Pierre, and Jean-Baptiste de Rocoles. *Description générale de l'Europe: Nouvelle édition revue et augmentée.* 2 vols. Paris: Denis Bechet and Louis Billaine, 1660.

Babelon, Jean-Pierre. *Demeures parisiennes sous Henri IV et Louis XIII.* Paris: Le Temps, 1965.

————. "Henri IV, urbaniste au Marais." *Festival du Marais, programme.* Paris: Festival du Marais, 1966.

————. "Histoire de l'architecture au XVIIe siècle." *École pratique des hautes études, 4e section, Sciences historiques et philologiques, Annuaire 1975–1976.* Paris: École pratique des hautes études, 1976: 695–714.

————. *Jacopo da Trezzo et la construction de l'Escurial (1519–1589).* Bordeaux and Paris: Feret et Fils and E. de Boccard, 1922.

————. *Nouvelle histoire de Paris: Paris au XVIe siècle.* Paris: Hachette, 1986.

————. "L'Urbanisme d'Henri IV et de Sully à Paris." *L'Urbanisme de Paris et de l'Europe, 1600–1680.* Edited by Pierre Francastel. Paris: Klincksieck, 1969: 47–60.

Baillet, Adrien. *La Vie de Monsieur Descartes.* Paris: D. Horthelmels, 1691.

Ballon, Hilary. "La Création de la Place Royale," in Alexandre Gady, ed., *De la Place Royale à la Place des Vosges* (Paris: Action Artistique de la Ville de Paris, 1996): 39–49.

————. *The Paris of Henri IV: Architecture and Urbanism.* New York: The Architectural History Foundation, 1991.

Ballon, Hilary, and D. Helot-Lécroart. "Le Château et les jardins de Rueil du temps de Jean de Moisset et du Cardinal de Richelieu: 1606–1642," in *Mémoires de Paris et l'Île de France* 36 (1985): 21–94.

Balzac, Honoré de. *Histoire et physiologie des boulevards de Paris.* 1844. In *Oeuvres complètes.* 40 vols. Paris: Louis Conard, 1912–40.

————. *Le Père Goriot.* Edited by P. G. Castex. 3 vols. Paris: Gallimard, 1976.

————. *Père Goriot.* Translated by A. J. Krailsheimer. Oxford: Oxford University Press, 1992.

Balzac, Jean Louis Guez de. *Lettres de Mr de Balzac: seconde partie.* 2 vols. Paris: Pierre Rocolet, 1636.

Barbiche, Bernard. "Les Premiers propriétaires de la Place Royale," in Alexandre Gady, ed., De la Place Royale à la Place des Vosges (Paris: Action Artistique de la Ville de Paris, 1996), 50–58.

Bardet, Gaston. *Naissance et méconnaissance de l'urbanisme: Paris.* Paris: SABRI, 1951.

Baron, Michel. *La Coquette et la Fausse Prude.* Paris: Thomas Guillain, 1687.

Bassompierre, François de. *Mémoires du Maréchal de Bassompierre.* 2 vols. Amsterdam: Au Dépens de la Compagnie, 1723.

Battaglia, Salvatore. *Grande Dizionario della Lingua Italiana.* 21 vols. Turin: Unione Tipografico-Editrice Torinese, 1961–2002.

Baudelaire, Charles. *Les Fleurs du mal.* Translated by Richard Howard. Boston: David Godine, 1982.

Baulant, M. "Le Salaire des ouvriers du bâtiment à Paris de 1400 à 1762." *Annales*. March–April 1971: 463–83.

Bayard, Françoise. *Le Monde des financiers au XVIIe siècle*. Paris: Flammarion, 1988.

Beauchamps, Pierre de. *Recherches sur les théâtres de France*. 3 vols. Paris: Prault, 1735.

Bellanger, Claude, ed. *Histoire générale de la presse française*. Vol. 1. Paris: PUF, 1969.

Benjamin, Walter. *The Arcades Project*. Translated by H. Eiland and K. McLaughlin. Cambridge, MA: The Belknap Press, 1999.

Bentivoglio, Cardinal Guido. *Les Lettres du Cardinal Bentivoglio*. Paris: Étienne Loyson, 1680.

Bernard, Leon. *The Emerging City: Paris in the Age of Louis XIV*. Durham, NC: Duke University Press, 1970.

Bernier, François. *Événements particuliers, ou ce qui s'est passé de plus considérable . . . dans les états du grand Mogol*. Paris: Claude Barbin, 1670.

———. *Voyages de François Bernier . . . contenant la description des états du Grand Mogol, de l'Hindoustan*. 2 vols. Amsterdam: Paul Marret, 1699.

Berthod (later also written Berthaud), Claude Louis. *La Ville de Paris en vers burlesques*. 1652. Paris: Guillaume Loyson and Jean-Baptiste Loyson, 1654.

[Bethel, Slingsby.] J. B. *An Account of the French Usurpation upon the Trade of England, and What Great Damage the English Do Yearly Sustain by Their Commerce*. London, 1679.

Blégny, Nicolas de. (Abraham Du Pradel.) *Les Adresses de la ville de Paris*. Paris: Veuve de D. Nion, 1691.

———. *Le Livre commode contenant les addresses de la ville de Paris*. Paris: Veuve de D. Nion, 1692.

———. *Le Livre commode des addresses de Paris pour 1692*. Edited by E. Fournier. 2 vols. Paris: Paul Daffis, 1878.

Blondel, François. *Cours d'architecture*. Paris: Pierre Auboin et François Clouzier, 1675–83.

———. *Nouvelle manière de fortifier les places*. Paris: L'Auteur and Nicolas Langlois, 1683.

Blunt, Anthony. *Art and Architecture in France, 1500–1700*. London: Penguin Books, 1973.

Bonney, Richard. *The King's Debts: Finance and Politics in France, 1589–1661*. Oxford: Clarendon Press, 1981.

[Bordelon, Abbé Laurent.] *Lettres familières . . . à un nouveau millionnaire*. 2 vols. Paris: Cavelier, Saugrain, 1725.

———. *Le Livre à la mode*. 1695. *Diversités curieuses*. Dixième partie. Amsterdam: André de Hoogenhuysen, 1699.

———. *Le Voyage forcé de Becafort hypocondriaque*. Paris: Jean Musier, 1709.

Boucher, François. *Le Pont-Neuf*. 2 vols. Paris: Le Goupy, 1925–26. Preface by Pierre Lavedan: 5–60.

———. "Les Sources d'inspiration de l'enseigne de Gersaint." *Bulletin de la société de l'histoire de l'art français*. 1957. Paris: Armand Colin, 1958: 123–29.

Boutier, Jean, Jean-Yves Sarazin, and Marine Sibille. *Les Plans de Paris des origines (1493) à la fin du XVIIIe siècle*. Paris: BNF, 2007.

Boutrage, Raoul. *Histoire de l'incendie et embrazement du palais de Paris*. Paris: Abraham Saugrain, 1618.

Boyer, Abel. *Dictionnaire royal, François et Anglois*. 2 vols. La Haye: Chez Meyndert Uytwerf, 1702.

Brice, Germain. *Description nouvelle de ce qu'il y a de plus intéressant et de plus remarquable dans la ville de Paris*. Paris: Chez Veuve Audinet or Nicolas Le Gras, 1684 (identical first editions).

———. *Description nouvelle de la ville de Paris . . . à quoi on a joint un nouveau plan de Paris et le nom de toutes les rues, par ordre alphabétique*. 2 vols. Paris: Nicolas Le Gras, Nicolas Le Clerc, and Barthélemy Girin, 1698.

———. 2 vols. Paris: Chez Michel Brunet, 1706.

———. 2 vols. Paris: F. Fournier, 1713.

———. 4 vols. Paris: J. M. Gandouin et F. Fournier, 1725.

———. *Le Nom de toutes les rues de la ville de Paris par ordre alphabétique*. Paris: Nicolas Le Gras, Nicolas Le Clerc, and Barthélemy Girin, 1698.

Brièle, Léon. *Collection des documents pour servir à l'histoire des hôpitaux de Paris*. 4 vols. Paris: Imprimerie Nationale, 1881–87.

Browne, Edward. *Journal of a Visit to Paris in the Year 1664*. Edited by G. Keynes. London: Saint Bart's Hospital Reprints, 1923.

Bullet, Pierre. *Traité de l'usage du pantomètre, instrument géométrique*. Paris: André Pralard, 1675.

Byron, George Gordon, aka Lord. *"So Late into the Night: Byron's Letters and Journals*. Edited by L. Marchand. 6 vols. Cambridge, MA: Harvard University Press, 1976.

Cahen, Gustave. *Eugène Boudin: Sa Vie et son oeuvre*. Paris: H. Floury, 1900.

Caraccioli, Louis Antoine, Marquis de. *Paris en miniature*. Paris: Maredan, 1784.

———. *Paris, le métropole de l'univers*. Paris: Le Normant, 1802.

———. *Paris, le modèle des nations étrangères*. Paris: Veuve Duchesne, 1777.

———. *Voyage de la raison en Europe*. Paris: Saillant et Nyon, 1772.

Carrousel des pompes et magnificences faites en faveur du mariage du la Très Chrétien Roi Louis XIII avec Anne Infante d'Espagne. Paris: Louis Mignot, 1612.

Carsalade du Pont, Henri de. *La municipalité parisienne à l'époque d'Henri IV*. Paris: Éditions Cujas, 1971.

Catalogue des partisans, ensemble leur généologie, et extraction, vie, moeurs, et fortunes. Paris, 1651.

Chabeau, Gilles. "Images de la ville et pratique du livre: le genre des guides de Paris (XVIIe–XVIIIe siècles)." *Revue d'histoire moderne et contemporaine*. XLV-2 (April–June 1998): 323–45.

Challes, Robert. *Les Illustres françaises*. Edited by F. Deloffre. 1713. Paris: Les Belles Lettres, 1959.

Chandler, Tertius. *4,000 Years of Urban Growth*. Lewiston, N.Y. and Queenston: St. David's University Press, 1987.

Chandler, Tertius, and Gerald Fox. *3,000 Years of Urban Growth*. New York and London: Academic Press, 1974.

Chantelou, Paul Fréart de. *Journal du voyage du cavalier Bernin en France*. Edited by M. Stanic. Paris: Macula, 2004.

Charron, Jacques de. *Histoire universelle de toutes nations et spécialement des Gaulois ou François*. Paris: T. Blaise, 1621.

Chartier, Roger. "The Practical Impact of Writing." *A History of Private Life*. Vol. 3. *Passions of the Renaissance*. Edited by R. Chartier. Translated by A. Goldhammer. Cambridge, MA: Harvard University Press, 1989: 111–59.

Chartier, Roger, B. Quilliet, et al. *Histoire de la France urbaine*. Vol. 3. *La Ville classique: de la Renaissance aux Révolutions*. Paris: Seuil, 1981.

Chastillon, Claude. *Description succincte de la Place Royale, avec indice particulier tant pour icelle, que pour les pompes et magnificences qui y ont esté faites*. Paris: Gabriel Tavernier, 1612.

Chevalier. Jean Simonin, known as. *L'Intrigue des carosses à cinq sous, comédie*. Paris: Pierre Paudouyn le fils, 1663.

Choisy, François Timoléon, Abbé de. *Mémoires de l'abbé de Choisy, habillé en femme*. Edited by G. Mongrédien. Paris: Mercure de France, 1966.

Clark, T. J. *The Painting of Modern Life: Paris in the Art of Manet and His Followers*. New York: Knopf, 1985.

Cleary, Richard. *The Place Royale and Urban Design in the Ancien Régime*. Cambridge: Cambridge University Press, 1999.

Coke, David, and Alan Borg. *Vauxhall Gardens: A History*. New Haven, CT: Yale University Press, 2011.

Colbert, Jean-Baptiste. *Lettres, instructions, et memoires de Colbert*. Edited by P. Clément. 10 vols. Paris: Imprimerie Impériale, 1861–82.

Colletet, François. *Abrégé des Annales de la ville de Paris*. Paris: Jean Guignard, 1664.

———. *Journal des avis et des affaires de Paris*. 1676. Edited by A. Heulhard. Paris: Moniteur du Bibliophile, 1878.

———. *Tracas de Paris*. 1649. Paris: Veuve Nicolas Oudot, 1714.

———. *La Ville de Paris*. 1671. Paris: Antoine Raffe, 1689.

Conférence du crocheteur du Pont-neuf avec maître Pierre du Coignet. Paris, 1616.

Continuateurs de Loret, Les (1665–1689). Edited by J. de Rothschild. 2 vols. Paris: Damascène Morgand, 1882.

Coquery, Natacha. *Tenir boutique à Paris au XVIIIe siècle: Luxe et demi-luxe*. Paris: Éditions du Comité des travaux historiques et scientifiques, 2011.

Corneille, Pierre. *Oeuvres complètes*. Paris: Éditions du Seuil, 1989.

Cours de la reine, ou la grande promenade des Parisiens, Le. Paris: Denys Langlois, 1649.

Courses de bague, faites en la place Royale, en faveur des heureuses alliances de France et d'Espagne. Paris: Jean Millon et Jean de Bordeaux, 1612.

Courtilz de Sandras, Gatien de. *Mémoires de Mr L.C.D.R.* The Hague: Henry van Bulderen, 1688.

———. *Testament politique de Messieur Jean-Baptiste Colbert*. The Hague: Henry van Bulderen, 1693.

Courtin, Antoine. *Nouveau traité de la civilité qui se pratique en France parmi les honnêtes gens*. Paris: Hélie Josset, 1671.

———. Paris: Élie Josset, 1702.

Cowen, Pamela. *A Fanfare for the Sun King: Unfolding Fans for Louis XIV*. London: Third Millennium Publishing, 2003.

Dancourt, Florent Carton, known as. *Le Chevalier à la mode*. 1687. Edited by R. Crawshaw. Exeter: University of Exeter, 1980.

———. *Les Enfants de Paris*. Paris: Pierre Ribou, 1705.

———. *L'Été des coquettes*. Paris, 1690.

—————. *La Parisienne*. Paris: Thomas Guillain, 1694.

Dangeau, Philippe de Courcillon, Marquis de. *Journal*. Edited by M. Feuillet de Conches. 19 vols. Paris: Firmin Didot, 1854.

Darin, Michaël. "Designating Urban Forms: French *Boulevards* and *Avenues*." *Planning Perspectives* 19 (April 2004): 133–54.

Davis, Dorothy. *A History of Shopping*. London: Routledge and Kegan Paul, 1966.

Defrance, Eugène. *Histoire de l'éclairage des rues de Paris*. Paris: Imprimerie Nationale, 1904.

DeJean, Joan. *The Age of Comfort: When Paris Discovered Casual—and the Modern Home Began*. New York: Bloomsbury, 2009.

—————. *The Essence of Style: How the French Invented High Fashion, Fine Food, Chic Cafés, Style, Sophistication, and Glamour*. New York: The Free Press, 2005.

Delamare, Nicolas. *Traité de la police*. 1705–1719. 4 vols. Amsterdam: Aux Dépens de la Compagnie, 1729.

Dennis, Michael. *Court and Garden: From the French Hôtel to the City of Modern Architecture*. Cambridge, MA: MIT Press, 1988.

Dent, Julian. *Crisis in Finance: The Crown, Financiers, and Society in 17th-Century France*. London: David and Charles Newton Abbot, 1973.

Dérens, Isabelle. "La Grille de la Place Royale," in Alexandre Gady, ed., De la Place Royale à la Place des Vosges (Paris: Action Artistique de la Ville de Paris, 1996), 74–77.

Descimon, Robert. "Les Barricades de la Fronde parisienne: Une lecture sociologique." *Annales*. 45e Année, No. 2 (1990): 397–422.

Dessert, Daniel. *Argent, pouvoir et société au grand siècle*. Paris: Fayard, 1984.

Dethan, Georges. *Nouvelle histoire de Paris: Paris au temps de Louis XIV (1660–1715)*. Paris: Hachette, 1990.

Deville, Adrien, and Émile Hochereau. *Receuil des lettres patentes, ordonnances, décrets et arrétés préfectoraux concernant les voies publiques*. 3 vols. Paris: Imprimerie nouvelle, 1886–1902. (NB: The volumes were edited by A. Alphand and M. Bouvard under the direction of Deville and Hochereau; some libraries thus catalogue them under Alphand and Bouvard.)

Dialogue entre le roi de bronze et la Samaritaine sur les affaires du temps présent. Paris: Arnould Cotinet, 1649.

Donneau de Visé, Jean. *Voyage des ambassadeurs de Siam en France*. Paris: Au Palais, 1686.

Doubdan, Jean. *Le Voyage de la Terre-Sainte*. 1657. Paris: Chez Pierre Bien-Fait, 1666.

Dralsé de Grand-Pierre, Sieur de. *Relation de divers voyages*. Paris: C. Jombert, 1718.

Du Bail, Louis Moreau. *Les Filles enlevées*. 2 vols. Paris: Jonas de Briquegny, 1643.

Dubbini, Renzo. *Geography of the Gaze: Urban and Rural Vision in Early Modern Europe*. Translated by L. Cochrane. Chicago: University of Chicago Press, 2002.

Dubois, Marie. "Journal de la Fronde." *Revue des sociétés savantes*. 1865. Vol. 2: 324–38.

Du Breul, Father Jacques. *Le Théâtre des antiquités de Paris*. Paris: Claude de La Tour, 1612.

Dubuisson-Aubenay, François-Nicolas Baudot, seigneur. *Journal des guerres civiles: 1648–1652*. Edited by Gustave Saige. 2 vols. H. Champion, 1883–85.

DuFresny, Charles. *Amusements sérieux et comiques, seconde édition, . . . augmentée*. 1705. Paris: Veuve Barbin, 1707.

Dumolin, Maurice. *Études de topographie parisienne*. 3 vols. Paris: Daupeley-Gouverneur, 1931.

—————. *Les Propriétaires de la place Royale (1605–1789)*. Paris: Champion, 1926.

Du Noyer, Anne Marguerite Petit. *Lettres historiques et galantes.* 1713. 6 vols. London: Chez Jean Nourse, 1739.

———. 6 vols. Amsterdam: Pierre Brunel, 1720.

Dupâquier, Jacques, et al. *Histoire de la population française.* Vol. 2: *De la Renaissance à 1789.* Paris: PUF, 1988.

Dupoux, Albert. *Sur les pas de Monsieur Vincent: Trois cents ans d'histoire parisienne de l'enfance abandonée.* Paris: Revue de l'Assistance publique de Paris, 1958.

Dupuy-Demportes, Jean-Baptiste. *Histoire générale du Pont-Neuf.* London: 1750.

Edgeworth, Maria. *Maria Edgeworth in France and Switzerland.* Edited by C. Colvin. Oxford: Clarendon Press, 1979.

Entretiens galants ou conversations sur la solitude. 2 vols. Paris: Jean Ribou, 1681.

État général des baptêmes, mariages, et mortuaires des paroisses de la ville et fauxbourgs de Paris. Paris: F. Léonard, 1670.

Evelyn, John. *The Diary of John Evelyn.* Edited by E. S. de Beer. 5 vols. Oxford: Clarendon Press, 1955.

———. *The State of France.* London: G. Bedest and C. Collins, 1652.

Félibien, André. *Des Principes de l'architecture, de la sculpture, de la peinture.* Paris: Jean-Baptiste Coignard, 1676.

Félibien, Father Michel. *Histoire de la ville de Paris, depuis son commencement connu jusqu'à présent.* 5 vols. Paris: Guillaume Desprez and Jean Desessartz, 1725.

Feuillet, Alphonse. *La Misère au temps de la Fronde.* Paris: Librairie Académique, 1862.

Field, Cynthia R. "Interpreting the Influence of Paris on the Planning of Washington, D.C., 1870–1930." In *Paris on the Potomac: The French Influence on the Architecture and Art of Washington, D.C.* Edited by I. Gournay. Athens: Ohio University Press/The U.S. Capitol Historical Society, 2007: 117–38.

Flaubert, Gustave. *Madame Bovary.* Translated by E. Aveling and P. de Man. New York: W. W. Norton, 2004.

———. *Madame Bovary.* 1910. Paris: Louis Conard, 1930.

Fleury, Michel. "Notice sur la vie et l'oeuvre de Sauval." *"Si le roi m'avait donné sa grande ville."* Paris: Maison Neuve et Larose, 1974.

Forbonnais, François Véron de. *Recherches sur les finances de la France entre 1585 et 1721.* 2 vols. Basel: Frères Cramer, 1758.

Fougeret de Monbron, Louis Charles. *Le Cosmopolite, ou Le Citoyen du monde.* 1750. London, 1753.

Fournier, Edouard. *Histoire du Pont-Neuf.* 2 vols. Paris: E. Dentu, 1862.

———. *Les Lanternes.* Paris: E. Dentu, 1854.

Franklin, Alfred. *La Vie privée d'autrefois: Les Magasins de nouveautés.* 4 vols. Paris: Librairie Plon, 1894.

[Fremin, Michel de.] *Mémoires critiques d'architecture.* Paris: Charles Saugrain, 1702.

Freud, Sigmund. *The Interpretation of Dreams.* 1900. Volumes 4–5. *Standard Edition of the Complete Psychological Works of Sigmund Freud.* 24 vols. London: Hogarth Press and the Institute of Psycho-Analysis, 1953.

Gady, Alexandre, ed. *De la Place Royale à la Place des Vosges.* Paris: Action Artistique de la Ville de Paris, 1996.

Galinou, Mireille, and John Hayes. *London in Paint: Oil Paintings in the Collection at the Museum of London*. London: Museum of London, 1996.

Galland, Antoine. *Les Mille et une nuit*. 2 vols. Paris: Veuve Barbin, 1704.

Gallet-Guerne, Danielle, and Michèle Bimbenet-Prival. *Balcons et portes cochères à Paris*. Paris: Archives Nationales, 1992.

Gaufreteau, Jean de. *Chronique bordeloise*. Edited by J. Delpit. 2 vols. Bordeaux: Lefebvre, 1877.

Gazette, La. Paris: Bureau d'Adresse, 1657.

Giedion, Sigfried. "Sixtus V and the Planning of Baroque Rome." *Architectural Review*. No. 3. 1952: 217–26.

Girouard, Mark. *Cities and People: A Social and Architectural History*. New Haven, CT: Yale University Press, 1985.

[Grimoard, comte de.] *Lettre de M. le marquis de Carraccioli à M. d'Alembert*. N.p., c. 1781.

Guiffrey, Jules, ed. *Comptes des bâtiments du roi, sous le règne de Louis XIV*. 5 vols. Paris: Imprimerie Nationale, 1881–1901.

Harding, Vanessa. "The Population of London, 1550–1700." *London Journal*. 15: 2 (1990): 111–28.

Hautel, Charles Louis d'. *Dictionaire du bas-langage ou des manières de parler usités par le peuple*. Paris: d'Hautel, 1808.

Hauteroche, Noël Le Breton, Sieur de. *La Dame invisible, ou l'esprit folet*. 1684. Paris: Pierre Ribou, 1688.

Henri IV. *Recueil des lettres missives de Henri IV*. Edited by Berger de Xivrey. 8 vols. Paris: Librairie Impériale, 1853.

Henry, Pierre. *Pour et contre du mariage, Le*. Lille: F. Fievet, 1694.

Herlaut, Commandant. "L'Éclairage des rues à Paris." *Mémoires de la Société de l'Histoire de Paris et de L'Île-de-France*. Paris: H. Champion, 1916. Vol. XLIII, pp. 129–265.

Heyl, Christoph. "The Metamorphosis of the Mask in 17th- and 18th-Century London." In E. Tseëlon. *Masquerade and Identities: Essays in Gender, Sexuality, and Marginality*. London and New York: Routledge, 2001: 114–34.

Heylyn, Peter. *A Full Relation of Two Journeys: One into the Main-Land of France; the Other into Some of the Adjacent Islands*. London: E. Cotes, 1656.

Hillairet, Jacques. *La Rue Saint-Antoine*. Paris: Éditions de Minuit, 1970.

Histoire du père La Chaize. Cologne: Pierre Marteau, 1693.

Howard, Jean. *Theater of a City: The Places of London Comedy, 1598–1642*. Philadelphia: University of Pennsylvania Press, 2009.

Hume, David. *Political Essays*. Edited by K. Haakonssen. Cambridge: Cambridge University Press, 1994.

Hunt, Margaret. "The Walker Beset: Gender in the Early 18th-Century City." *Walking the Streets of 18th-Century London*. Edited by C. Brant and S. Whyman. Oxford: Oxford University Press, 2007: 120–30.

Hurtaut, Pierre Thomas Nicolas, and Magny. *Dictionnaire historique de la ville de Paris*. 4 vols. Paris: Moutard, 1779.

Hyde, Ralph. *Gilded Scenes and Shining Prospects: Panoramic Views of British Towns, 1575–1900*. New Haven, CT: Yale Center for British Art, 1985.

Interdiction de mettre des immondices. Registres du conseil d'état. Paris, January 21, 1679.

Jacobs, Jane. *The Death and Life of Great American Cities*. New York: Random House, 1961.

Johnson, James H. *Venice Incognito: Masks in the Serene Republic*. Berkeley and Los Angeles: University of California Press, 2011.

Jones, Colin. *Paris: Biography of a City*. London: Allen Lane, 2004.

[Jones, Erasmus.] *Luxury, Pride, and Vanity, the Bane of the British Nation*. London: E. Withers, 1736.

Jouhaud, Christian. *Mazarinades: La Fronde des mots*. Paris: Éditions Aubier Montaigne, 1985.

Klaits, Joseph. *Printed Propaganda under Louis XIV: Absolute Monarchy and Public Opinion*. Princeton, NJ: Princeton University Press, 1976.

Konvitz, Josef. *Cartography in France, 1660–1848*. Chicago: University of Chicago Press, 1987.

La Bruyère, Jean de. *Les Caractères*. Edited by E. Bury. Paris: Livre de Poche Classique, 1995.

La Caille, Jean de. *Description de Paris en vingt planches*. Paris: Jean de La Caille, 1714.

Lambeau, Louis. *La Place Royale*. Paris: H. Daragon, 1906.

Lancaster, Henry Carrington. *A History of French Dramatic Literature in the 17th Century*. 1936. New York: Gordian Press, 1966.

Langenskiöld, Eric. *Pierre Bullet, the Royal Architect*. Stockholm: Almquist and Wiksell, 1959.

La Roche, Sophie von. *Sophie in London, 1786*. 1788. Translated by C. Williams. London: Jonathan Cape, 1933.

La Rochemaillet, Gabriel Michel de. *Théâtre de la ville de Paris*. Written c. 1630. Edited by V. Dufour. Paris: A. Quantin, 1880.

Lasteyrie, R. de. *Documents inédits sur la construction du Pont-Neuf*. Paris, 1882.

Lauder, Sir John. *Journals of Sir John Lauder: 1665–1676*. Edinburgh: The Scottish History Society, 1900.

Laugier de Porchères, Honoré. *Le Camp de la place Royale*. Paris: Jean Micard, 1612.

Laurens, Abbé H. J. de. *Le Compère Matthieu, ou les Bigarrures de l'esprit humain*. London: Au Dépens de la Compagnie, 1732.

Lavedan, Pierre. *Histoire de l'urbanisme*, Vol. 2: *Renaissance et temps moderne*. 3 vols. Paris: H. Laurens, 1926–52.

———. *Histoire de l'urbanisme à Paris*. Vol. 16 of *Nouvelle histoire de Paris*. 20 vols. Paris: Hachette, 1975.

Le Clerc, Jean. *Bibliothèque ancienne et moderne*. Amsterdam: Frères Wetstein, 1721.

Le Comte, Louis. *Nouveaux mémoires sur l'état présent de la Chine*. 2 vols. Paris: J. Anisson, 1696.

Le Conte, Denis. *Métérologie ou l'excellence de la statue de Henri Le Grand soulevée sur le pont-neuf*. Paris: Joseph Guerreau, 1614.

Le Dru, Nicolas. *Lettre à Monsieur le Cardinal*. Paris: Arnould Cotinet, 1649.

Lefèvre d'Ormesson, Olivier. *Journal d'Olivier Le Fèvre d'Ormesson*. Edited by A. Chéruel. 2 vols. Paris: Imprimerie impériale, 1890.

Lehrer, Jonah. *Imagine How Creativity Works*. Boston and New York: Houghton Mifflin Harcourt, 2012.

Le Maire, Charles. *Paris, ancien et nouveau*. 3 vols. Paris: T. Girard, 1685.

Le Moël, Michel. "La Topographie des quartiers de Paris au XVIIe siècle." *Cahiers du CREPIF* 38 (March 1992): 63–73.

Le Nain de Tillemont, Sébastien. *Histoire ecclésiastique des six premiers siècles.* 15 vols. Paris: C. Robustel, 1694–1719.

Le Noble, Eustache. *L'École du monde.* "Premier entretien: De la Connaissance des hommes." 1694. Paris: M. Jouvenel, 1700.

———. *École du monde nouvelle, ou les promenades de Mr. Le Noble.* Paris: Guillaume de Luynes et Pierre Ribou, 1698.

———. *La Fausse comtesse d'Isamberg.* Paris: Martin et George Jouvenel, 1697.

———. *La Grotte des fables.* Paris: Martin Jouvenel, 1696.

Le Petit, Claude. "Paris ridicule." In *Oeuvres diverses du Sr. D. ***.* 1713. 2 vols. Amsterdam: Frisch and Bohm, 1714.

Le Prestre, Claude. *Questions notables de droit.* Paris: NP, 1679.

Le Rouge, Georges Louis / Claude Saugrain. *Les Curiositez de Paris.* Paris: Saugrain, 1716.

———. *Les Curiositez de Paris.* Paris: Saugrain, 1719.

Le Roux, Philibert Joseph. *Dictionnaire comique, satyrique, critique et proverbial.* Amsterdam: Michel Le Cene, 1718.

Lesage, Alain René. *Le Bachelier de Salamanque.* Paris: Valleyre, 1736.

———. *Histoire d'Estevanille Gonzalez.* Paris: Chez Prault Père, 1734.

———. *Turcaret.* 1709. Edited by P. Frantz. Paris: Gallimard, 2003.

———. *La Valise trouvée.* Paris: Prault, 1740.

L'Estoile, Claude de. *L'Intrigue des filous.* Paris: Antoine de Sommaville, 1648.

L'Estoile, Pierre de. *Mémoires-journaux.* Edited by G. Brunet et al. 11 vols. Paris: Librairie des bibliophiles, 1875–83.

Lettre du roi Henry IV, en bronze, du Pont Neuf, à son fils Louis XIII, de la Place Royale. Paris: Jean Paslé, 1649.

Lettre du vrai soldat français au cavalier Georges. Paris: Denys Langlois, 1649.

Lettres historiques, contenant ce qui se passe de plus important en Europe. May 1721. Amsterdam: Chez la Veuve de Jaques Desbordes, 1721.

Liger, Louis. *Le Voyageur fidèle, ou le Guide des étrangers dans la ville de Paris.* Paris: Pierre Ribou, 1715.

Limnaeus, Johannes. *Notitiae regni franciae.* 2 vols. Argentorati, Friderici Spoor, 1655.

Lippomano, Luigi. *A Description of Paris.* In *In Old Paris.* Translated by R. Berger. New York: Italica Press, 2002.

Lister, Martin. *A Journey to Paris in the Year 1698.* London: Jacob Tonson, 1699.

Locatelli, Sebastiano. *Viaggio di Francia (1664–1665).* Moncalieri: Centro Interversitario di Ricerche sul Viaggio in Italia, 1990.

———. *Voyage de France (1664–1665).* Translated by A. Vautier. Paris: Alphonse Picard, 1905.

Long, Yuri. *From the Library: The Fleeting Structures of Early Modern Europe.* Washington, D.C.: National Gallery of Art, 2012.

Loret, Jean. *La Muze historique.* Edited by J. Ravenel and V. De La Pelouze. 4 vols. Paris: P. Jannet, 1857.

Lough, John. *France Observed in the 17th Century by British Travelers.* Stocksfield: Northumberland, 1984.

Louis XIV. *Mémoires de Louis XIV pour l'instruction du Dauphin*. Edited by C. Dreyss. 2 vols. Paris: Didier, 1860.

Machines et inventions approuvées par l'Académie Royale des Sciences. 10 vols. Paris: Gabriel Martin, Jean-Baptiste Coignard, fils, Hippolyte-Louis Guérin, 1735.

Madrisio, Nicolò. *Viaggi per l'Italia, Francia, e Germania*. 2 vols. Venice, 1718.

Maere, Jan de, and Nicolas Sainte Fare Garnot. *Du Baroque au classicisme: Rubens, Poussin, et les peintres du XVIIe siècle*. Paris: Musée Jacquemart-André, 2010.

Mahelot, Laurent. *Le Mémoire de Mahelot*. Edited by H. C. Lancaster. Paris: Honoré Champion, 1920.

Mailly, Jean-Baptiste. *L'Esprit de la Fronde, ou histoire politique et militaire des troubles de la France pendant la minorité de Louis XIV*. 5 vols. Paris: Moutard, 1772.

Mailly, Louis de. *Avantures et lettres galantes, avec la promenade des Tuileries*. Paris: Guillaume de Luyne, 1697.

Malingre, Claude. *Annales générales de la ville de Paris*. Paris: Pierre Rocolet, 1640.

Marana, Giovanni Paolo. *Lettre d'un Sicilien à un de ses amis*. Chambery: P. Maubal, 1714.

Marion, Marcel. *Dictionnaire des institutions de la France aux XVIIe et XVIIIe siècles*. Paris: Auguste Picard, 1923.

Martin, Germain, and Marcel Bezançon. *Histoire du crédit en France sous le règne de Louis XIV*. Paris: Librairie de la Société du Receuil J.-B. Sirey et du Journal du Palais, 1913.

McNeil, Peter, and Giorgio Riello. "The Art and Science of Walking: Gender, Space, and the Fashionable Body in the Long 18th Century." *Fashion Theory*. 9, no. 2 (2005): 175–204.

Médailles sur la régence; avec les tableaux symboliques du Sieur Paul Poisson de Bourvalais. A Sipar [Paris]: Chez Pierre Le Musca, 1716.

Mémoires d'un soldat de l'ancien régime. 1719. In *Souvenirs et mémoire*. VI (January–June 1901). Paris: Lucien Gougy, 1901.

Mercier, Louis Sébastien. *Entretiens du jardin des Tuileries*. Paris: Buisson, 1788.

———. *Le Tableau de Paris*. 8 vols. Amsterdam [Neuchâtel: Jonas Fauche and Jérémie Witel], 1782.

Mercure françois, Le, ou la suite de l'histoire de la paix. Paris: Jean Richer, 1612.

———. Paris: Étienne Richer, 1625.

Milliot, Vincent. *Paris en bleu*. Paris: Parigramme, 1996.

Milne, Anna-Louise, ed. *The Cambridge Companion to the Literature of Paris*. Cambridge: Cambridge University Press, 2013.

Molière, Jean-Baptiste Poquelin de. *Oeuvres*. Edited by A. Regnier. 11 vols. Paris: Hachette/Grands Écrivains de la France, 1875.

Monmerqué, L. J. N. *Les Carrosses à cinq sols, ou les omnibus du 17e siècle*. Paris: Firmin Didot, 1828.

Montagu, Lady Mary Wortley. *The Complete Letters of Lady Mary Wortley Montagu*. Edited by R. Halsband. 3 vols. Oxford: Oxford at the Clarendon Press, 1965.

Montgolfier, Bernard de. "Galerie des vues de Paris." *Bulletin du Musée Carnavalet*. 1970:1 (6–17); 1970:2 (23–43).

———. "Trois vues de Paris." *Bulletin du Musée Carnavalet*. 11, no. 1 (June 1958): 8–15.

Montpensier, Anne Marie Louise d'Orléans, Duchesse de. *Mémoires*. Edited by A. Cheruel. 4 vols. Paris: G. Charpentier, 1858–59.

Montreuil, Mathieu de. *Les Oeuvres de Monsieur de Montreuil.* Paris: Thomas Jolly, 1666.

Moreau, Célestin. *Choix de mazarinades.* 2 vols. Paris: Renouard, 1853.

Motteville, Françoise Bertaut, Dame de. *Mémoires pour servir à l'histoire d'Anne d'Autriche, épouse de Louis XIII.* Edited by C. Petitot. 5 vols. Paris: Foucault, 1824–25.

Mouton, Léo. "Deux financiers au temps de Sully: Largentier et Moisset." *Bulletin de la société de l'histoire de Paris et de l'Île de France.* LXIV (1937): 65–104.

Nemeitz, J. C. *The Present State of the Court of France and City of Paris.* London: E. Curll, 1712.

———. *Séjour de Paris, c'est à dire, instructions fidèles pour les voyageurs de condition . . . durant leur séjour à Paris.* 1719. 2 vols. Leiden: Jean Van Abcoude, 1727.

Newman, Karen. *Cultural Capitals: Early Modern Paris and London.* Princeton, NJ: Princeton University Press, 2007.

Nouveau recueil de chansons. La Haye: J. Neaulm, 1723.

Ordonnance du bureau de la ville défendant d'endommager les arbres qui sont plantés sur les remparts. Paris: Frédéric Léonard, 1684.

Ordonnance de Louis XIV, roy de France et de Navarre, donnée à Paris au mois de mars 1669 concernant la jurisdiction des Prévosts des marchands et des eschevins de la ville de Paris. Paris: Frédéric Léonard, 1676.

Ordonnance de Louis XIV, roy de France et de Navarre, donné à Paris en 1685, concernant la jurisdiction des Prévosts des marchands et des eschevins de la ville de Paris. Paris: Frédéric Léonard, 1685.

Oudin, Antoine. *Curiosités françaises.* Paris: Antoine de Sommaville, 1640.

Ouville, Antoine Le Métel, Sieur d'. *La Coiffeuse à la mode.* Paris: Toussaint Quinet, 1647.

———. *La Dame suivante.* Paris: Toussaint Quinet, 1645.

———. *L'Esprit folet.* Paris: Toussaint Quinet, 1642.

Pallier, Denis. "Première flambée d'occasionels de la Ligue à la Fronde." In *Éphémères et curiosités.* Chambéry: Bibliothèque municipale de Chambéry, 2004: 44–55.

Panard, Charles François. *Théâtre et oeuvres diverses.* 4 vols. Paris: Duchesne, 1763.

Pardailhé-Galabrun, Annik. *The Birth of Intimacy: Privacy and Domestic Life in Early Modern Paris.* Translated by J. Phelps. Philadelphia: University of Pennsylvania Press, 1991.

Partisans démasquez, nouvelle plus que galante, Les. 1707. Cologne: Chez Adrien l'Enclume, Gendre de Pierre Marteau, 1709.

Pascal, Blaise. *Oeuvres de Blaise Pascal.* Edited by Léon Brunschvicg et al. 10 vols. Paris: Hachette, 1914.

———. *Oeuvres complètes.* Edited by Jean Mesnard. 4 vols. Paris: Desclée de Brouwer, 1992.

Patin, Guy. *Lettres.* Edited by J. H. Reveillé-Parise. 3 vols. Paris: J.-B. Baillière, 1846.

———. *Lettres de Guy Patin, 1630–1672.* 2 vols. Paris: Champion, 1907.

———. *Lettres du temps de la Fronde.* Edited by A. Thérive. Paris: Frédéric Paillart, 1921.

Patru, Olivier. *Plaidoyers et autres oeuvres d'Olivier Patru.* Paris: S. Mabre-Cramoisy, 1670.

Peiresc, Nicolas Claude Fabri de. *Lettres de Nicolas Peiresc.* 7 vols. Paris: Imprimerie Nationale, 1888–98.

Pepys, Samuel. *The Diary of Samuel Pepys.* Edited by R. Latham and W. Matthews. 9 vols. Los Angeles and Berkeley: University of California Press, 1976.

Perrault, Charles. *Courses de têtes et de bagues faites par le roy . . . en l'année 1662*. Paris: De l'Imprimerie Royale, 1670.

———. *Les Hommes illustres*. 2 vols. Paris: A. Dezallier, 1696–1700.

Petit, Pierre. "De l'Antiquité, grandeur, richesse, etc. de la ville de Paris." Preface to *Le plan de Paris de Jacques Gomboust*. 1652. Edited by Le Roux de Lincy. Paris: Techener, 1858.

Petitguillaume, Laurent, et al. *Les Coulisses du Pont-Neuf*. Paris: Chêne, 2010.

Philippot. *Recueil nouveau des chansons du Savoyard par lui même chantées dans Paris*. Paris: Veuve Jean Promé, 1665.

Phillips, E. *The New World of Words, or a General English Dictionary*. London: Obadiah Blagrave, 1678.

Piganiol de La Force, Jean-Aimar. *Description de Paris*. 10 vols. Paris: Guillaume Desprez, 1765.

Pillorget, René. *Nouvelle histoire de Paris sous les premiers Bourbons: 1594–1661*. Paris: Hachette, 1988.

Pincus, Steven C. A. "From Butterboxes to Wooden Shoes: The Shift in English Popular Sentiment from Anti-Dutch to Anti-French in the 1670s." *The Historical Journal* 38, no. 2 (1995): 333–61.

Piossens, Chevalier de. *Mémoires de la régence*. 1729. 5 vols.; Amsterdam, 1749.

Plan levé par les ordres du roy par le Sr. Bullet architecte du roy et de la ville sous la conduite de M. Blondel de l'Académie royale d'Architecture. Four-page text that is found with certain copies of the Bullet-Blondel map. Paris: Boissière, 1676.

Pluton maltôtier. Cologne: Chez Adrien l'Enclume, Gendre de Pierre Marteau, 1708.

Poëte, Marcel. *La Promenade à Paris au XVIIe siècle*. Paris: Colin, 1913.

Poisson, Raymond. *Les Faux Moscovites*. Paris: Quinet, 1669.

Pollack, Martha. *Cities at War in Early Modern Europe*. Cambridge: Cambridge University Press, 2010.

Pöllnitz, Karl Ludwig von. *The Memoirs of Charles Lewis, Baron de Pöllnitz*. 1734. 2 vols. London: D. Browne, 1737–39.

Pont-Neuf, Le: (1578–1978). Exhibit. Musée Carnavalet, Paris. 1978.

Pradel, Abraham Du. See Blégny, Nicolas de.

Préchac, Jean de. *L'Illustre Parisienne*. Lyon: F. Amaury, 1679. Part II. 1690.

Procès-verbaux de l'Académie Royale d'Architecture: 1671–1793. Edited by Henri Lemonnier. 10 vols. Paris: Edouard Champion, 1913.

Promenade du Cours, La. Paris, 1630.

Pure, Michel de. *La Prétieuse*. Paris: Chez Pierre Lamy, 1656.

Raisonable plaintif sur la declaration du roi . . . , Le. Paris: Jacques Belle, 1652.

Ranum, Orest. *The Fronde: A French Revolution, 1648–1652*. New York: Norton, 1953.

Ravaisson, François. *Archives de la Bastille: documents inédits*. 15 vols. Paris: Pedone-Lauriel, 1874.

Recueil général de toutes les chansons mazarinistes. Paris, 1649.

Registres des délibérations du bureau de la ville de Paris. Edited by P. Guérin, 12 vols. Paris: Imprimerie Nationale, 1909.

Regnard, Jean-François. *Le Joueur*. Paris: Thomas Guillain, 1697.

Relation extraordinaire concernant . . . la nécessité de donner un prompt secours aux malades (10 août 1652). N.p., 1652.

Remerciement de Paris à Monseigneur le Duc d'Orléans. Paris: Denys Langlois, 1649.

Réponse du roi Louis XIII , en bronze, de la Place Royale, à son père Henry IV, de dessus le Pont Neuf. Paris: Jean Paslé, 1649.

Requête présentée au roi en son château du Louvre. Paris: N. Poulletier, 1652.

Rétif de la Bretonne, Nicolas. *Le Paysan perverti*. 2 vols. Amsterdam [Paris]: [Veuve Duchesne], 1776.

Retz, Jean François de Gondi, Cardinal de. *Mémoires*. Edited by S. Berthière. 2 vols. Paris: Garnier, 1987.

Rey, Alain. *Dictionnaire historique de la langue française*. 3 vols. Paris: Le Robert, 1992.

Richelet, Pierre. *Les Plus belles lettres françaises, sur toutes sortes de sujets tirées des meilleurs auteurs*. 2 vols. Paris: M. Brunet, 1705.

Richelieu, Armand Du Plessis, Cardinal Duc de. *Lettres, instructions diplomatiques, et papiers d'état du Cardinal Richelieu*. Edited by M. Avenel. 8 vols. Paris: Imprimerie impériale, 1853–77.

———. *Mémoires du Cardinal de Richelieu sur le règne de Louis XIII, depuis 1610 jusqu'à 1638*. Edited by M. Petitot. Paris: Foucault, 1823.

———. *Testament politique*. Amsterdam: Henry Desbordes, 1688.

———. *Testament politique*. Edited by F. Hildesheimer. Paris: Société de l'Histoire de France, 1995.

Roche, Daniel. *People of Paris*. Translated by M. Evans and G. Lewis. Los Angeles: University of California Press, 1987.

———. "Les Pratiques de l'écrit dans les villes françaises du XVIII siècle." In *Pratiques de lecture*. Edited by Roger Chartier. Paris: Rivages, 1985: 158–80.

Roche, Daniel, et al. *Voitures, chevaux, et attelages: Du XVIe au XIXe siècle*. Paris: Art équestre de Versailles, 2000.

Rosset, François de. *Le Romant des chevaliers de la gloire*. Paris: Pierre Berthaud, 1612.

Rubinstein, G. M. G. "Artists from the Netherlands in 17th-Century Britain: An Overview of their Landscape Works." *The Exchange of Ideas: Religion, Scholarship, and Art in Anglo-Dutch Relations in the 17th Century*. Edited by S. Groenveld and M. Wintle. Zutphen: Walburg Instituut, 1994.

Rykwert, Joseph. *The Seduction of Place: The City in the Twenty-first Century*. New York: Pantheon Books, 2000.

Sainctot, Nicolas de. Unpublished memoirs. Cited by Bernard de Montgolfier. "Trois vues de Paris." *Bulletin du Musée Carnavalet*. 11, no. 1 (June 1958): 8–15.

Saint-Germain, Jacques. *Les Financiers sous Louis XIV*. Paris: Librairie Plon, 1950.

———. *La Reynie et la police du grand siècle*. Paris: Hachette, 1962.

Saint-Simon, Louis de Rouvroy, Duc de. *Mémoires*. Edited by A. de Boislisle. 44 vols. Paris: Hachette, 1879–1930.

Satyre nouvelle sur les promenades du cours de la Reine, des Thuilleries. Paris: Florentin et Pierre Delaune, 1699.

Saugrain, Claude-Marin. *Code de la librairie et imprimerie de Paris*. Paris: Aux dépens de la Communauté, 1744.

Sauval, Henri. *Histoire et recherches des antiquités de la ville de Paris*. 4 vols. Paris: Charles Moette and Jacques Chardon, 1724.

Savary des Bruslons, Jacques. *Dictionnaire universel du commerce.* 4 vols. Paris: J. Estienne, 1723–30.

Savoy, Louis. *Discours sur le sujet du colosse du grand roi Henry posé sur le milieu du Pont Neuf de Paris.* Paris: Nicolas de Montroeil, c. 1617.

Scarron, Paul. *Oeuvres de M. Scarron.* Paris: Guillaume de Luyne, 1654.

Scudéry, Madeleine de, and Paul Pellisson. *Chroniques du samedi suivies de pièces diverses.* Edited by A. Niderst, D. Denis, and M. Maître. Paris: Honoré Champion, 2002.

Serres, Jean de. *Inventaire général de l'histoire de France, depuis Henry IV jusques à Louis XIV.* 3 vols. Lyon: Claude La Rivière, 1652.

Sévigné, Marie de Rabutin Chantal, Marquise de. *Correspondance.* Edited by R. Duchêne. 3 vols. Paris: Gallimard, 1978.

Sewell, William H., Jr. "The Empire of Fashion and the Rise of Capitalism in 18th-Century France." *Past and Present.* No. 206 (February 2010): 81–120.

Shadwell, Thomas. *A Comedy Called The Miser.* London: Thomas Collins and John Ford, 1672.

Shoemaker, Robert. "Gendered Spaces: Patterns of Mobility and Perceptions of London's Geography, 1660–1750." In J. F. Merritt. *Imagining Early Modern London: Perceptions and Portrayals of the City from Stow to Strype, 1598–1720.* Cambridge: Cambridge University Press, 2001: 144–165.

Skippon, Sir Philip. *An Account of a Journey Through part of the Low Countries, Germany, Italy, and France.* In vol. 6 of Awnsham Churchill and John Churchill, eds. *A Collection of Voyages and Travels.* 6 vols. London: J. Walthoe, 1732.

Smith, Adam. *An Inquiry into the Nature and the Causes of the Wealth of Nations.* Edited by W. B. Todd. 2 vols. Oxford: Clarendon Press, 1976.

Soeurs rivales, histoire galante, Les. Paris: Michel Brunet, 1698.

Soll, Jacob. *The Information Master: Jean-Baptiste Colbert's Secret State Intelligence System.* Ann Arbor: University of Michigan Press, 2010.

Stegmann, André. "La Fête parisienne à la Place Royale en avril 1612." *Les Fêtes de la Renaissance.* Edited by J. Jacquot and E. Konigson. 3 vols. Paris: Études du CNRS, 1975: 3: 373–92.

Suite du catéchisme des partisans. Paris, 1649.

Summerson, John. *Georgian London.* New Haven, CT: Yale University Press, 2003.

Sutcliffe, Anthony. *Paris: An Architectural History.* New Haven, CT, and London: Yale University Press, 1996.

Szanto, Mickaël. "Les Peintres flamands à Paris dans la première moitié du XVIIe siècle." *Les Artistes étrangers à Paris: De la fin du Moyen Age aux années 1920.* Edited by M.-C. Chaudronneret. Paris: Peter Lang, 2007: 70–83.

Tabarin, Antoine Girard or Jean Salmon, known as. *Les Étrennes admirables du sieur Tabarin, présentées à Messieurs les Parisiens en cette présente année 1623.* Paris: Lucas Joufflu, 1623.

———. *Recueil général des oeuvres et fantaisies de Tabarin.* 1621. Rouen: David Geuffroy, 1627.

Tallemant des Réaux, Gédéon. *Historiettes.* Edited by Antoine Adam. 2 vols. Paris: Gallimard, 1967.

Talon, Omer. *Mémoires.* Edited by Michaud and Poujoulat. Paris: Chez l'Éditeur du commentaire analytique du code civil, 1839.

Terdiman, Richard. *Present Past: Modernity and the Memory Crisis.* Ithaca and London: Cornell University Press, 1993.

Thompson, T. Perronet. *Exercises, Political and Others.* London: E. Wilson, 1842.

Triolets sur le tombeau de la galanterie. Paris, 1649.

Triomphe royal, contenant un bref discours de ce qui s'est passé au Parc royal à Paris au mois d'avril 1612. Paris: Anthoine du Breuil, 1612.

Trout, Andrew. *City on the Seine: Paris in the Time of Richelieu and Louis XIV.* New York: St. Martin's Press, 1996.

Turcot, Laurent. "L'Émergence d'un espace plurifonctionnel: les boulevards parisiens au XVIIIe siècle." *Histoire urbaine* 1:12 (April 2005): 89–115.

———. *Le Promeneur à Paris au XVIIIe siècle.* Paris: Le Promeneur, 2007.

Turlupin, Henri Le Grand, known as Belleville or. *Harangue de Turlupin le souffreteux.* Paris, 1615.

Vaillancourt, Daniel. *Les Urbanités parisiennes au XVIIe siècle.* Québec: Les Presses de l'Université de Laval, 2009.

Vallier, Jean. *Journal de Jean Vallier, maître d'hôtel du roi.* Edited by Henri Courteault and Pierre de Vaissière. 4 vols. Paris: Librairie Renouard, 1902–16.

Van Damme, Stéphane. *Paris, capitale philosophique: De la Fronde à la Révolution.* Paris: Odile Jacob, 2005.

Van Suchtelen, Ariane, and Arthur K. Wheelock, Jr. *Dutch Cityscapes of the Golden Age.* The Hague and Washington: Waanders Publishers, 2008.

Varennes, Claude de. *Le Voyage de France dressé pour l'instruction et la commodité des François et des étrangers.* Paris: Olivier de Varennes, 1639.

Vauban, Sébastien Le Prestre de. *Projet d'une dîme royale.* N.p., 1707.

Vaugelas, Claude Favre de. *Remarques sur la langue françoise.* Paris: Veuve Jean Camusat, 1647.

Veryard, Ellis. *An Account of Divers Choice Remarks, Taken in a Journey Through the Low Countries, France, Italy.* London: S. Smith and B. Walford, 1701.

Viau, Théophile de. *Oeuvres poétiques.* Edited by Jeanne Streicher. 2 vols. Geneva: Droz, 1951–58.

Villeneuve, Gabrielle Barbot Gallon, dame de. *La Belle et la Bête.* 1740. Edited by E. Lemirre. Paris: Gallimard, 1996.

Villers, Philippe de Lacke, sieur de, and François de Lacke, sieur de Potshiak. *Journal d'un voyage à Paris en 1657–1658.* Edited by A. P. Faugère. Paris: Benjamin Duprat, 1862.

Vitrines d'architecture: Les Boutiques à Paris. Edited by F. Fauconnet. Paris: Éditions du Pavillon de l'Arsenal, 1997.

Vries, Jan de. *European Urbanization 1500–1800.* Cambridge, MA: Harvard University Press, 1984.

Wagner, Marie-France. "L'Éblouissement de Paris: promenades urbaines et urbanité dans les comédies de Corneille." *Papers on French 17th-Century Literature* 25, no. 48 (1998): 129–44.

Walsh, Claire. "Shop Design and the Display of Goods in 18th-Century London." *Journal of Design History.* 8, no. 3 (1995): 157–76.

Wilhelm, Jacques. "La Galerie de l'Hôtel de Bretonvilliers." *Bulletin de la Société de l'Histoire de l'Art Français.* 1956: 137–50.

Williams, Raymond. "Advertising: The Magic System." *Problems in Materialism and Culture*. London: Verso, 1980: 170–95.

———. *Keywords: A Vocabulary of Culture and Society*. 1983. New York: Oxford University Press, 1985.

Wilson (or Vulson) de La Colombière, Marc. *Le Vrai théâtre d'honneur et de chevalerie*. Paris: Augustin Courbé, 1648.

Wolfe, Michael. *Walled Towns and the Shaping of France: From the Medieval to the Early Modern Era*. New York: Palgrave Macmillan, 2008.

Zanon, Antonio. *Dell'Agricoltura, dell'arti, e del commercio il quanto unite contribuiscono alla felicitá degli stati*. 4 vols. Venice: Appresso Modesto Fenzo, 1763–64.

Ziskin, Rochelle. *The Place Vendôme*. New York: Cambridge University Press, 1999.

ILLUSTRATION CREDITS

41   "Le Pont Neuf vu de la Place Dauphine." Anonymous painting. c. 1635. Detail. Musée Carnavalet. Photo: Gérard Leyris.

42   Hendrick Mommers. "Le Pont Neuf." c. 1665. Musée du Louvre.

43   "Le Pont Neuf." Fan. Mid-eighteenth century. Musée Carnavalet. Author's photo.

47   Abbé Delagrive. Map of Paris. 1728. Detail. Author's collection.

51   Claude Chastillon. "Carrousel de la Place Royale, 1612." Engraving. 1612. Musée Carnavalet. Photo: Gérard Leyris.

53   Perelle family (Nicolas, Gabriel, Adam). "La Place Royale." Engraving. Seventeenth century. Private collection.

55   "La Place royale." Anonymous painting. 1655–60. Musée Carnavalet. Photo: Gérard Leyris.

56   "La Place royale." Anonymous painting. 1655–60. Detail. Musée Carnavalet. Photo: Gérard Leyris.

57   "La Place royale." Anonymous painting. 1655–60. Detail. Musée Carnavalet. Photo: Gérard Leyris.

63   Vassalieu. Map of Paris. 1609. Detail. Adolphe Alphand. *Atlas des anciens plans de Paris reproduits en fac-simile*. University of Pennsylvania. Van Pelt Library.

65   Mathieu Mérian. Map of Paris. 1614. Detail. Adolphe Alphand. *Atlas des anciens plans de Paris reproduits en fac-simile*. University of Pennsylvania. Van Pelt Library.

66   Jean Messager. "Le Plan de l'île et le pourtrait du Pont." 1614 or 1615. Adolphe Alphand. *Atlas des anciens plans de Paris reproduits en fac-simile*. University of Pennsylvania. Van Pelt Library.

67   Abbé Delagrive. Map of Paris. 1728. Detail. Author's collection.

69   Bretez-Turgot. Map of Paris. 1734–39. Detail. University of Pennsylvania. Van Pelt Library.

70   "Vue cavalière de Paris avec le portrait de Pépin des Essarts." Anonymous painting. c. 1640. Detail. Musée Carnavalet. Photo: Gérard Leyris.

74   Bretez-Turgot. Map of Paris. 1734–39. Detail. University of Kansas. Spencer Libraries.

81   "Barricades à la Porte Saint-Antoine." Anonymous engraving. 1648. Private collection.

84   "Avis que donne un frondeur aux Parisiens qu'il exhorte de se révolter contre la tyrannie du Cardinal Mazarin." Anonymous engraving. 1649. Private collection.

85   Print shop of Pierre Bertrand. "La Marche de Louis XIV, roi de France et de Navarre." Engraving. 1649. Private collection.

86   "Salut de la France dans les armes de la ville de Paris." Anonymous placard. 1649. Private collection.

87   Hendrick Mommers. "Le Pont Neuf." c. 1665. Detail. Musée du Louvre.

91   "Dialogue entre le roi de bronze et la Samaritaine." Anonymous pamphlet. 1649. University of Pennsylvania. Van Pelt Library. Rare Books and Special Collections.

94   Nicolas de Larmessin. "L'Entrée du roi et de la reine dans la bonne ville de Paris le 26 août, 1660." Almanach pour 1661. Private collection.

100 Georg Braun. Map of Paris. 1572. Detail. Collection of Jack and Barbara Sosiak.

104–5 Pierre Bullet and François Blondel. Map of Paris. 1676. Detail. Adolphe Alphand. *Atlas des anciens plans de Paris reproduits en fac-simile.* University of Pennsylvania. Van Pelt Library.

106 Pierre Bullet and François Blondel. Map of Paris. 1676. Adolphe Alphand. *Atlas des anciens plans de Paris reproduits en fac-simile.* University of Pennsylvania. Van Pelt Library.

108 Abbé Delagrive. Map of Paris. 1728. Detail. Author's collection.

110 Abbé Delagrive. Map of Paris. 1728. Detail. Author's collection.

111 Abbé Delagrive. Map of Paris. 1728. Detail. Author's collection.

114 Perelle family (Nicolas, Gabriel, Adam). "View of the Tuileries Gardens as They Are Now." Engraving. c. 1670. Private collection.

117 Nicolas Arnoult. "Noblewoman in the Tuileries." Engraving. 1687. Author's collection.

119 Nicolas Bonnart. "Ladies in Conversation in the Tuileries." Engraving. c. 1690. Musée Carnavalet. Photo: Gérard Leyris.

126   "Le Pont Neuf." Anonymous painting. c. 1665. Detail. Musée Carnavalet. Photo: Gérard Leyris.

129   Poster advertising the inauguration of the third public carriage route. Paris. Bibliothèque de l'Arsenal.

136   Nicolas Guérard fils. "La Sonnette a sonné, abaisse la lanterne." Engraving. Late seventeenth century. Musée Carnavalet. Photo: Gérard Leyris.

138   Nicolas Guérard fils. "Voleur de nuit est pris au trebuchet quand à ses trousses il a le guet." Engraving. Late seventeenth century. Musée Carnavalet. Photo: Gérard Leyris.

140   Frontispiece. Louis de Mailly. *Entretiens des cafés de Paris*. Trévoux: E. Ganeau. 1702. Anonymous engraving. Bibliothèque de l'histoire de la ville de Paris. Photo: Gérard Leyris.

141   Hérisset. "Lampe pour éclairer une ville." Engraving. 1703. Private collection.

146   Nicolas Guérard fils. "Street Peddlers in Paris." Engraving. Late seventeenth century. Musée Carnavalet. Photo: Gérard Leyris.

147   "Le Pont Neuf." Anonymous painting. c. 1665. Detail. Musée Carnavalet. Photo: Gérard Leyris.

149   "La Galerie du Palais." Anonymous engraving. c. 1640. Musée Carnavalet. Photo: Gérard Leyris.

154   Jean Berain (drawing). Jean Le Pautre (engraving). "Habit d'hiver." *Le Mercure galant*. January 1678. Photograph by Patrick Lorette for Joan DeJean.

155   Jean Berain (drawing). Jean Le Pautre (engraving). *Le Mercure galant*. January 1678. Photograph by Patrick Lorette for Joan DeJean.

157   Alexandre Le Roux. "Le Cordonnier." Engraving. c. 1685. Musée Carnavalet. Photo: Gérard Leyris.

158   Nicolas de Larmessin. "La Coifeuse." Engraving. c. 1685. Photograph by Patrick Lorette for Joan DeJean.

159   Enseigne for Jean Magoulet. Etching and engraving. c. 1690. Waddesdon Manor, The Rothschild Collection (The National Trust). Photograph: University of Central England.

160   "Agneau couronné." Trade card for Beguet and Serire, furriers. Late seventeenth century. Author's collection.

162   Nicolas Guérard fils. "Puisqu'on affiche tout dans le temps où nous sommes." Engraving. Late seventeenth century. Musée Carnavalet. Photo: Gérard Leyris.

179   Jean Marot. "Hôtel La Vrillière by François Mansart." Engraving. Late seventeenth century. Musée Carnavalet. Photo: Gérard Leyris.

181   Perelle family (Nicolas, Gabriel, Adam). "La Place Louis-le-Grand." Engraving. Late seventeenth century. Private collection.

182   V. Antier. "La Place Louis-le-Grand en 1705." Gouache. Musée Carnavalet. Photo: Gérard Leyris.

183   Alexandre Le Roux. "Distribution du pain." Engraving. 1693. Private collection.

185   Henri Bonnart. "Le Financier." Engraving. 1678. Author's collection.

192   Hendrick Mommers. "Le Pont Neuf." c. 1665. Detail. Musée du Louvre.

193   "La Galerie du Palais." Anonymous engraving. c. 1640. Musée Carnavalet. Photo: Gérard Leyris.

196   Jean Dieu de Saint-Jean and Frantz Ertinger. "Homme de qualité allant incognito par la ville." Engraving. 1689. Private collection.

197   Jean Dieu de Saint-Jean and Frantz Ertinger. "Femme de qualité allant incognito par la ville." Engraving. 1689. Musée Carnavalet. Photo: Gérard Leyris.

198   Jean Dieu de Saint-Jean. "Dame allant par la ville." Detail. Private collection.

201   Nicolas de Larmessin. "Les Amants dupés par la malice des filles." Engraving. c. 1685. Author's collection.

204   Henri Bonnart. "Medemoiselles Loison Walking in the Tuileries." Engraving. c. 1690. Photograph by Patrick Lorette for Joan DeJean.

212   Georg Braun. Map of Paris. 1572. Collection of Jack and Barbara Sosiak.

213   Georg Braun. Map of Paris. 1572. Detail. Collection of Jack and Barbara Sosiak.

214   "Henri IV devant Paris." Anonymous painting. c. 1600. Musée Carnavalet. Photo: Gérard Leyris.

216   Pierre Bullet and François Blondel. Map of Paris. 1676. Detail. Adolphe Alphand. *Atlas des anciens plans de Paris reproduits en fac-simile.* University of Pennsylvania. Van Pelt Library.

220   "Marché à la volaille et au pain, Quai des Augustins." Fan. c. 1680. Musée Carnavalet. Author's photograph.

222   Jean Dieu de Saint-Jean. "Homme de qualité sur le théâtre de l'Opéra." Engraving. 1687. Author's collection.

COLOR PLATES

"Henri IV devant Paris." Anonymous painting. c. 1600. Musée Carnavalet. Photo: Gérard Leyris.

"Vue cavalière de Paris avec le portrait de Pépin des Essarts." Anonymous painting. c. 1640. Detail. Musée Carnavalet. Photo: Gérard Leyris.

"Place royale en 1612." Anonymous painting. Musée Carnavalet. Photo: Gérard Leyris.

"La Place royale." Anonymous painting. 1655–60. Musée Carnavalet. Photo: Gérard Leyris.

"Le Pont Neuf." Anonymous painting. c. 1665. Musée Carnavalet. Photo: Gérard Leyris.

Hendrick Mommers. "Le Pont Neuf." c. 1665. Musée Carnavalet.

"Marché à la volaille et au pain, Quai des Augustins." Fan. c. 1680. Musée Carnavalet. Author's photograph.

Hendrick Mommers. "Le Pont Neuf." c. 1665. Detail. Musée du Louvre.

Abraham de Verwer. "La Grande Galerie du Louvre avec le Pont Neuf et la Cité." c. 1640. Musée Carnavalet.

"Le Pont Neuf vu de la Place Dauphine." Anonymous painting. c. 1635. Musée Carnavalet. Photo: Gérard Leyris.

"Le Pont Neuf." Anonymous painting. c. 1665. Detail. Musée Carnavalet. Photo: Gérard Leyris.

"La Place Royale." Anonymous painting. 1655–60. Detail. Musée Carnavalet. Photo: Gérard Leyris.

"Le Pont Neuf." Anonymous painting. c. 1665. Detail. Musée Carnavalet. Photo: Gérard Leyris.

V. Antier. "La Place Louis-le-Grand en 1705." Gouache. Musée Carnavalet. Photo: Gérard Leyris.

"La Place Royale." Anonymous painting. 1655–60. Detail. Musée Carnavalet. Photo: Gérard Leyris.

Pierre-Denis Martin. "Visite de Louis XIV à l'Église de l'hôtel royal des Invalides nouvellement achevée, le 14 juillet 1701." Musée Carnavalet.

INDEX

Illustrations are indicated by references in italics.